A Perfec

'Heartwarming, emotional and full of community spirit. I couldn't put it down' **Amanda Prowse**

READERS LOVE DEBBIE MORRISON!

'An absolute delight to read – a beautiful story of family, loyalty, and self discovery'

'This gripping novel will take you on an emotional rollercoaster'

'Perfect for fans of compelling women's fiction'

'A must-read for anyone seeking an engaging story with relatable characters and unexpected twists'

'Incredibly refreshing . . . I found it hard to put the book down'

'An entertaining fiction novel that raises so many important, real-life issues'

'Packed with suspense and drama that will keep you hooked until the very end'

Also by Debbie Morrison

The 'Perfectly Imperfect' Duet:

A Perfect Algarve Villa
A Perfect Chelsea Townhouse

The Brambleton Series:

A Perfect Devon Farmhouse
A Perfect Devon Pub
A Perfect Devon Christmas
A Perfect Devon Manor

A Perfect Devon Pub

Debbie Morrison

PROSPERINA PRESS

First published in the UK in 2025 by Prosperina Press
This edition first published in the UK in 2025 by Prosperina Press

9 7 5 3 1 2 4 6 8

A catalogue record for this book is available from the British Library.

ISBN (E): 978-1-0686884-5-4
ISBN (PB): 978-1-0686884-8-5

Cover design: Hannah George (illustration) / Cherie Chapman (design)
Text design by Ellipsis, Glasgow

PROSPERINA
PRESS

Prosperina Press,
Grenville House, 9 Boutport Street,
Barnstaple, Devon, EX31 1TZ

This book is for everyone in North Devon's hospitality sector – thank you. Here's to bustling kitchens, full tables, and wonderful reviews.

"Wine, because no great story ever started with a salad"
– Anon

One

Amid the vibrant bustle of London's Portobello Road Market, an unassuming restaurant lay ensconced between antique dealers and vintage clothing stalls. In perfect harmony with the market's spirit – equal parts tradition, innovation and authenticity – it beckoned with understated charm, a quiet presence amid the ever-shifting crowds.

The Fork & Cork, its name painted in crisp white letters on a modest green awning, was a place where the market's energy spilled over into every plate and every conversation. It had quickly become the neighbourhood's worst-kept secret. Seating just thirty, the intimate space had drawn a steady stream of devotees over the past eighteen months, lured by TikTok clips showcasing the fluid grace of the open-plan kitchen and reviews exalting the aromas that swirled through the air: rosemary's earthiness mingled with bright zesty lemon and the rich warmth of melting butter.

On this August evening, passers-by could glimpse the choreographed dance of the four junior chefs through the windows, hands flying between chopping boards and pans, knives scattering light into the steam that spiralled up from copper pots. In the centre of it all, conducting this symphony of flavours, stood London's latest culinary sensation: the head chef, Ruben Nkosi. His broad-shouldered frame pivoted between stations, each movement precise and purposeful as he tasted sauces, adjusted seasoning and issued commands with quiet authority. The stark white of his chef's jacket emphasized his athletic build, while the kitchen's warm lighting caught the waves in his dark, closely cropped hair. When he turned to inspect a dish, his high cheekbones caught the light, and his square jaw tensed in concentration before relaxing into an easy, confident smile that seemed to energize his team.

At one end of the gleaming kitchen counter was the Chef's Table. Here, four privileged diners were perched on leather topped barstools, leaning forward as if tethered by an unseen string, following each flick of Ruben's wrist, each subtle nod of approval. The occasional sizzle or burst of flame drew soft gasps, and when an aromatic haze billowed up from a pan, they inhaled deeply, running their tongues across their lips in anticipation of the feast to come.

Behind them in the restaurant, a short, curvaceous woman named Fiona weaved between the cramped tables, pouring wine, uncorking bottles, recommending pairings for the food. She was the kind of woman who radiated an infectious energy that could light up a room. Her dark blonde hair, cut to frame her round, freckled face, accentuated her usually bright blue eyes. Today, though, those eyes were clouded. When the restaurant had opened its doors at 6.30 p.m., Fiona had painted a bright smile on her face. Now, nearly two hours later, she wasn't sure how much longer she could keep up the cheerful façade.

As she explained the differences between Champagne and Crémant to a couple celebrating their wedding anniversary, the ghastliness of the last three days kept intruding on her thoughts. No, not the last three days. The first two had been invigorating. Even most of the third had been stimulating. But the sixty seconds between 4.30 p.m. and 4.31 p.m. yesterday had lodged in her mind like a splinter buried too deep to remove. Tonight, her head throbbed painfully with the memory of something she could neither forget nor face.

Fiona's eyes flicked towards the Chef's Table, where Ruben was laughing and posing for selfies. Further along the polished stainless steel bar, two middle-aged women, wide-eyed with excitement, were eagerly trying to catch his eye.

'Chef! We've seen your videos!' called out one, waving her phone in the air.

He turned, grinning and walked over with the poise of someone well used to being the centre of attention.

The women swooned as the celebrity chef started talking them through the evening's specials, his deep voice describing the lemon sole with thyme and brown butter sauce with enthusiasm. Fiona felt her mouth water and her irritation at his showboating melt away.

She helped one of her team clear and re-lay a table, then, spotting empty glasses, fetched the correct wine from the central chilling bucket, wiped off the moisture with a cloth and poured it out precisely, up to the widest part of the glass. When she replaced the bottle in its bucket, the satisfying clink of glass against ice felt oddly final, like locking away a secret in an impregnable vault. But no matter how deeply she tried to bury the memory, those sixty seconds kept floating back up.

Fiona shook her head to clear her mind, pulled out her notepad and manoeuvred through the cramped space towards the Chef's Table, her movements graceful, but her shoulders tense. The stainless steel counter – Ruben's culinary stage – gleamed beneath the spotlights.

'Ah, Fiona,' Ruben said as she arrived. 'Perfect timing.' He gestured at the two women, both still wearing the eager expression of the dedicated fan. 'We need some advice on the ideal wine to match with tonight's scallop dish. What about a New Zealand Sauvignon Blanc?'

A flicker crossed Fiona's face. Her eyes narrowed briefly. Tonight, she wanted to forget all about New World wines. 'Ruben knows what goes with each of his creations,' she said, then chewed at her lip, sensing the resignation in her voice. Telling herself to be professional, she managed a weak smile, and added, 'Sauvignon Blanc is an excellent choice – bright, crisp, with a mineral finish that will really lift the seafood.'

She looked at Ruben, hoping to catch a glimpse of recognition for her skills, but he was already diverted – another customer was calling his name. Fiona wondered if he'd caught the flash of frustration in her expression before she refocused on the guests in front of her, advising them of the price of their wine choice.

'Service!' cried a junior chef. Plates clattered onto the serving counter and Fiona swivelled to collect them. The hiss of a hot pan rang out, as Ruben seared a fillet of fish, the herby aroma filling the room. The diners at the counter hunched forward, captivated by Ruben's hands, hanging on his every word as he explained the dish.

'You're amazing, Chef! Can we take a photo?' a young woman asked eagerly, phone already in hand.

Ruben flashed his trademark smile and obliged, leaning in for the snap. Fiona turned her back on the flurry of activity. She approached a table of regulars who had been coming here for months, knowing the service they would receive from Fiona and her team would always be personal, attentive and full of expertise.

'Your usual bottle of white Burgundy?' she asked with a knowing smile. On the cusp of engaging them in conversation, another burst of laughter erupted from Ruben's station, drowning out her words. Fiona glanced over to see the chef with a group of men, signing autographs on napkins as if he were a rock star. The chef was basking in the attention, his focus seemingly more on the camera flashes than on their shared passion for creating something special together. Fiona bit back her irritation, knowing it was unfair of her to blame Ruben for enjoying his newfound celebrity. He was a wonderful chef and a brilliant promoter of their restaurant. It was churlish of her to begrudge him his moment in the sun, when he had worked so hard for it.

As the night wore on, the energy in the restaurant swelled. Plates arrived at tables with bursts of colour – grilled sea bass with bright green herbs freshly picked that morning; warm, crusty bread with golden extra-virgin olive oil; and vibrant salads topped with orange and purple edible flowers. The smells of roasted vegetables, caramelized onions and grilling meat intermingled, making the space almost alive with flavour. Ruben, still centre stage, seemed animated by the buzzing atmosphere, chatting with customers between cooking, throwing in witty remarks that drew chuckles and applause.

At the Chef's Table, Fiona poured another glass of wine for a couple. 'You're so lucky to work with him,' commented the man.

Fiona's smile was polite, her tone light, but there was a knowing look in her eyes. 'Yes, he's very talented. But it's not all glitz and glamour. There's a lot more to running a restaurant than what you see on social media.'

As the door shut behind the last diners, Ruben took off his apron, mopped his brow and approached Fiona, his usually loose-limbed gait a little stiff, likely still fizzing from the evening's adrenaline. 'Busy night. The team did well,' he said with a grin.

Fiona gave him a small smile and kept her voice soft. She didn't want to hurt him, but she had to say something. 'Yes, they did do well. But what about you? You're not just cooking anymore, Ru. You're performing. I wonder how long you can keep that up.'

'Hey, come here.' He pulled her into his arms. Being a foot shorter enabled her head to rest on his chest and she breathed in the comforting smell of him. Her nose, fine-tuned to detect the subtle aromas of different wines, picked up top notes of lemon, rosemary, thyme and mint over the smoky base notes of cooked oil and fried fish. She inhaled deeply and felt a small lump form in her throat. 'Sorry, Ru. I shouldn't deny your success just because I'm a failure.'

'Forget it, Fi,' he whispered.

'I can't,' she muttered, her voice thick with emotion.

He spoke firmly. 'You *must*. You can't be like this tomorrow morning. Come on. Let's go home and leave the team to do the final clear-up for once. Their future depends on us. We need to prepare for some very important Morning Prayers.'

Morning Prayers. The name they used for business meetings, mostly with the team, occasionally with suppliers, all invariably scheduled for early mornings to dovetail with their restaurant commitments. Fiona suspected Ru's preparation plans wouldn't address their glaring blind spot. 'Ru, face it! Things have changed. They won't back us now.'

He smiled; it was the sort of cunning, assured smile that made her feel that he knew something she didn't but, this time, she suspected his confidence was misplaced. If only she hadn't persuaded Ru to change the concept of their second restaurant, to differentiate it by leading on wine expertise. If she'd messed up his future, she'd never forgive herself.

Using a finger, he tipped her head gently off his chest. 'Don't dwell on it, Fi,' he whispered. 'You'll get another chance and the investors will understand.' Then he kissed her, temporarily quenching all her thoughts of failure.

A voice called out from the stoves. 'Good luck tomorrow, Chef!'

Ru turned to wave at his team. 'Thanks! And guys . . . thanks for everything tonight. You all did brilliantly. See you tomorrow.'

They slipped outside and walked hand in hand through the empty market, a warm summer breeze brushing against their skin. The low hum of trucks collecting the day's discarded rubbish and the clatter of bottles being emptied into metal bins replaced the usual noise of vendors and tourists.

'I spoke to your aunt Ivy today,' said Ru. 'I thought we should get away this weekend, to celebrate.'

'Don't tempt fate,' she scolded. Sometimes Fiona thought his confidence bordered on cocky. Nevertheless, she wanted to see Ivy, who had hung up her clerical collar a few months earlier and for once would have time to spend with her favourite niece. Her aunt had recently moved out of the rectory into a cottage, and it would be fun to see Ivy's new home. The two women shared the same diminutive height and round freckled face, but that's where the similarities ended. Unlike Fiona, Ivy didn't give a fig for the trappings of success, and rarely worried about the future. She had been Fiona's sanctuary when her parents' cold silence echoed through her childhood home, her steady lighthouse through the stormy waters of adolescence, and a fount of wisdom through the maze of early adulthood. Perhaps Ivy's presence would be the balm Fiona needed.

Ru squeezed her hand. 'Hear me out. We both need a break. We haven't had a holiday for over a year. The team can manage without us for a week. I've made a decision. We are going down to Devon to stay with Ivy for a week. I've hired a car, and we can drive down after Friday night's service. It will be fun – walks on the beach, dips in the sea . . .'

Listening to his enthusiasm, she warmed to his plans.

They walked in silence, the kind that settles between people who've known each other long enough to be comfortable with their own thoughts. The sounds of metal lids clanging shut and the rumble of engines faded behind them, leaving only the soft shuffling of their steps. A stray newspaper page tumbled across the ground, rustling against Fiona's bare ankles, before skittering away into the shadows carrying yesterday's headlines into tomorrow. Just being with Ru and Ivy for a week would recharge her batteries. Allow her to get yesterday in perspective.

She sighed. 'What are we going to say to them tomorrow? You know . . . about . . .'

He grasped her hand. 'Leave that one to me, *pardner*.'

His voice was so reassuringly firm that she felt the stirrings of hope. Maybe her failure wasn't such a big problem after all.

Two

With her sandals in one hand and Ru's warm fingers intertwined in the other, Fiona walked steadily along Brambleton Beach. The soft sand felt silky and warm between her toes, yielding gently beneath each step. Under the intense summer sun, the grains sparkled as if someone had scattered crushed glass along the shore, forming a glimmering path above the waterline.

It was Saturday, and the beach seemed to pulse with energy. Locals and tourists lounged in canvas beach chairs under colourful umbrellas, or sprawled on towels behind garishly striped windbreaks. Some read books while others slept. Near the water's edge, children were building sandcastles, wet sand slipping through their fingers as they shaped towers and moats, their giggles drifting up over the steady rhythm of waves breaking on the sand.

The air carried a medley of scents: the salt-laden sea breeze, coconut scented sunscreen and the earthy tang of damp seaweed. Fiona smiled to herself. At least today, no one would ask her which wines those scents might evoke. She looked around at the kaleidoscope of relaxation and contentment. Swimsuit styles might have changed over the years, but the scene was reminiscent of Fiona's childhood summer holiday walks on this very beach. She could almost hear the soft hum of Ivy's favourite hymn, the one she used to sing under her breath when they strolled toward the ice cream hut, their usual destination.

It felt fitting, somehow, that her aunt had been the first to learn that the investors had agreed to back the new restaurant. Earlier that morning, Ru had delivered the news while whipping up a fluffy soufflé omelette in Ivy's tiny cottage kitchen.

'Well done, love!' Ivy exclaimed, pulling Fiona into a warm embrace. Her arms were strong and reassuring, and Fiona couldn't help but melt into them. 'Hopefully that's the last exam you ever have to put yourself through.'

Fiona hesitated before mumbling, 'No. I didn't pass.'

The words hung in the air for a moment as she glanced at her aunt, whose face softened instantly with a gentle smile of understanding.

'Well, you tried your best, and that's all anyone can do,' Ivy said, her tone filled with quiet encouragement. 'Besides, didn't you tell me only 25 per cent of people pass that exam first time?'

Ivy said no more, and Fiona felt a rush of relief. Her aunt's unspoken acceptance was as comforting as the summer sun streaming through the window. It reminded Fiona why this village – and this person – always felt like home. Still, she was disappointed in herself to have messed up the exam. She really *had* tried her best, yet she'd still failed. Wasn't that the worst possible outcome? Was it any surprise that a little worm of doubt had now wriggled into her mind, whispering that she simply wasn't good enough? She shook the thought away and hitched her shoulder bag closer, drawing comfort from the sharp edges of the books inside. She would soon be studying again, and if she passed next time, life would get a whole lot better.

'And the good news is,' said Ru, sliding a perfect omelette onto a warm plate, 'it doesn't matter.' Giving Fiona a pointed look, he put down the frying pan and bounded across the room, scooping her into his arms, lifting her off her feet and kissing her.

He set her down, saying, 'The investors are still stumping up the money for the second restaurant.'

That was a careful choice of words, Fiona thought.

At the kitchen table, Ru sliced the omelette. 'Come on, let's eat. Ivy has a meeting to get to, and,' he said, excitement clear in his voice, 'you and I have a date with a beach. Ivy, do me a favour and pass me that shoulder bag. *That* is not going with us.'

Ivy chuckled, and Fiona managed a smile. One day off wouldn't matter. But she did need to knuckle down and retake that exam. She'd borrowed over £1000 from Ru to pay for her studies, and he'd paid for the exam fee too. She'd no idea how she was going to repay him for his poor investment, let alone fund the resit. Maybe Ivy would lend her the money? Once she was a member of the elite Court of Master Sommeliers with an equally lofty salary, repaying her debts would be simple.

Ru's voice pulled her away from her worries and back to the warmth of the beach. 'Happy?' he asked.

She told herself it felt good to be on holiday, with the sun on her back and the man she adored beside her, not toiling in the fuggy heat of the cramped London restaurant. But she dodged his question.

'Fancy an ice cream?' she suggested.

He wrinkled his nose. 'Real ice cream? Or hydrogenated trans fats?'

Fiona punched him playfully on the arm. 'Proper Devon dairy ice cream made with real milk from local cows, of course. They've been selling it here for nearly a hundred years.'

'Well, how can I turn down the chance of that!'

They reached the ice cream kiosk, a hut painted in mint green and pale pink. It had a weathered wooden exterior, and white slatted shutters pinned back to let the cooling sea breeze inside. Above the entrance, on a large board, someone had written the flavours and prices in pink chalk: classic varieties like vanilla, strawberry, rum 'n' raisin and caramel, alongside local specialties like Devon clotted cream and elderflower.

Inside, vintage glass jars stuffed with toppings lined the shelves. The staff wore striped aprons just like the ones Ru's team wore in London, and Fiona gave her head a tight shake to dislodge the association. She didn't want to ruin today by constantly thinking about work.

'Two scoops of caramel, please!' she called cheerfully to an attendant, forcing a smile that didn't quite reach her eyes. She wanted to enjoy this moment with Ru, to bask in the sun's warmth and the sweet innocence of ice cream. She glanced sideways at him, his face a mask of quiet determination, although she sensed an underlying anxiety.

When their ice creams arrived, they took them outside. Ru chose the table furthest from the kiosk and they slumped into deckchairs, digging their feet into the sand. Fiona took a tentative lick, the ice cream melting in her mouth, sweet and silky smooth. As she savoured the moment, she reached for his spare hand, feeling the warmth of his skin against hers. She sensed his unease. This was rare – he was usually so easy-going and confident – but she decided not to ask, certain he would tell her when he was ready.

'I spoke to Ben this morning,' said Ru.

Ah, thought Fiona, Ru's troubles must be work related. Ben, Ru's sous-chef and best friend, was running the Fork & Cork while the couple were in Brambleton. Fiona suspected that, despite Ru's bravado at breakfast, he was regretting this holiday already, leaving his team at such a critical time. He would probably rather be in London nurturing them. Trying to keep the tension out of her voice, she asked, 'everything OK?'

Ru squeezed her hand. 'Relax. Everything is under control.'

So, business was not the source of Ru's anxiety – neither the new venture nor the existing one. A family of four flopped down at the table next to them. The two children, both in bright swimsuits and flip-flops, swung their legs eagerly beneath the table, while their parents, dressed in light summer clothes and sunglasses, eyed the chalkboard menu.

Ru frowned and slipped his hand into his pocket as if checking for his wallet.

'We're not in London. No pickpockets in Brambleton!' Fiona joked reassuringly.

'Sorry,' Ru mumbled, withdrawing his hand, but his eyes darted around as if he was expecting someone to jump out from the shadows. He glanced down at the ground before casting a quick, wary look over his shoulder. Even as he forced a small smile, his fingers twitched at his sides, betraying a nervous energy.

Fiona wondered if Ru was finding it difficult to unwind with so much going on in London. 'It's lovely to be here with you,' she said, stroking his arm. His muscle was tense, but as she stroked, she felt it relax, and a smile creased his face.

'It's going to be a magical week. Let's just chill. We've earned it,' said Ru. 'What do you fancy doing tomorrow? How about a day trip to Lundy?' She screwed up her nose; Fiona loved the rugged, windswept beauty of Lundy Island out in the Bristol Channel, but she couldn't spare another whole day away from her books.

'I think I should be revising.'

'Nope. Forbidden! We are on holiday.'

'For you maybe.'

He laughed. It was a wonderful sound, throaty and self-assured, filling her with courage, and despite herself, the corners of her mouth started twitching upward. He never let her stay down for long. His confidence was unshakable. He believed he would always succeed; on the rare occasions someone said no, Ru didn't listen, interpreting the word as a challenge, convinced that with time and effort, he could persuade anyone to change their mind.

'Fi, this is a celebration.'

'Except it's your celebration, not mine.'

He spoke forcefully. 'This is *our* celebration – the investors are backing *our* business.'

Except they weren't. The message from the investors had been clear. The restaurant concept had shifted. Gone was Fiona's dream of a wine lover's destination with Master Sommelier pairings, replaced by a model mirroring the Fork & Cork. What was worse, the investors had only backed Ru, claiming Fiona lacked his industry weight. They attributed all the value built up in the Fork & Cork to Ru – as the leaseholder – counting that as his investment in the new venture. Without a formal arrangement between them, and acknowledging he had shouldered all the financial risk, Fiona couldn't argue with the logic. She, like Ben and the team, would be merely an employee, not a partner. That wouldn't have happened if she had passed her Advanced Sommelier exam.

But things could have been a lot worse. The investors had taken the news of her failure surprisingly well. After asking her to step outside while they spoke with Ru alone – ten uncomfortable minutes in the corridor imagining him being berated for wasting their time – she rejoined to learn that while the concept had changed, thankfully, the financing was secure. Eating a slice of humble pie seemed a small price to pay to protect Ru's career.

'Fi, please, don't dwell on that exam.' He pushed his sunglasses off his face and his eyes sparkled with enthusiasm. 'We're a team, and an amazing one. Anyway, now it's not a high-end wine restaurant you don't need to be an Advanced Sommelier.'

'The investors think I do.' Fiona had not been surprised. In fact, she agreed with them. Certificates were there to prove one's worth. To separate the successful from failures like her. Her mother and father had proved that with their own careers, gradually accumulating more letters after their names as they advanced in the field of neurogenetic research. They hadn't taken much notice of her as a child, finding discussions of amyloid plaques much more alluring than reading bedtime stories. But they'd always been proud when she came home from school waving a certificate.

Ru shook his head playfully, 'Are you really going to pour yourself into study? You'll never have time to enjoy life.'

Fiona sighed. Hadn't he realized she'd been doing that all her life? In fact, it was Ivy who'd suggested a teenage Fiona channel her efforts into academia. Whether she did so to keep her niece busy, or because Ivy knew it was the only way Fiona could earn the sporadic attention of her parents, Fiona wasn't sure. Either way, it had been addictive. Her parents applauded each exam passed, every qualification she achieved, but like brief rays of sunshine on a dreary day, they withdrew their attention once the triumph had been celebrated and buried themselves back in their own work.

When Fiona turned eighteen and left home to study for her first sommelier exams in London, her parents had emigrated to Australia to take up a research post at the Florey Institute, a global leader in neurodegenerative diseases. Fiona couldn't help but think they'd been waiting for the opportunity ever since she was born. Communication dwindled to a text on her birthday and a phone call to congratulate her on each academic milestone: sailing through Levels 1 to 4 of her wine and spirit exams, her introductory sommelier qualification and later her certified sommelier exam. With no more progress to report, Fiona realized she hadn't heard from them in nearly a year.

A football thudded in front of Fiona, startling her and bringing her back to Brambleton Beach. She watched fondly as a boy in faded knee-length swimming trunks traipsed through the sand towards his toy. The child looked about ten, with gangly limbs and a skinny chest. His mother followed behind in a pink bikini, wincing slightly as the hot sand stung her feet.

Ru bent and picked up the ball, handing it to the boy.

'What do you say, Mark?' instructed the mother. She looked from her child to Ru, then did a double take. 'Oh, my goodness! It's you, isn't it? From the Fork & Cork? Wow! Are you on holiday here too?' She smiled coyly. 'Wait until I tell my girlfriends. I only live in Shepherd's Bush.' She batted her eyes at him. 'Could I be frightfully rude and ask for your autograph?'

Ru stood, smiling at his admirer, who twirled a lock of hair between her fingers. Involuntarily, Fiona pressed her lips together, her fingers fidgeting with the edge of her sleeve. *Come on*, she wanted to say to the woman. *We're on holiday!* She hoped he'd refuse.

'It's flattering to be asked,' said Ru, giving a self-deprecating laugh. 'I'd be happy to, provided you've got the pen and paper.'

The woman ran off, her feet sinking into the sand with each step.

Fiona tutted. 'Did you have to say yes?'

'It will only take a second, and you heard her, she lives near us in London,' he said, flashing a smile at the returning fan. 'She and her friends are our next customers!'

Fiona told herself that Ru was right. It was vital to cultivate support, especially now they were setting up a second restaurant. Except *they* were not setting up a second restaurant, Ru was. If only she'd passed that wretched exam. She watched Ru sign with a flourish, saying, 'I hope to see you in my restaurant when we get back to London.'

The word 'my' tore into her soul like a jagged shard of glass.

Watching Ru's latest fan walk away, Fiona spoke wistfully. '*Your* restaurant?'

'Fi, stop this,' he said. He took her hand in his, stroking it gently. 'I'm sorry, I didn't think.' He smiled at her, and it was a playful smile that made her think he was holding onto a delicious secret, as if he had something exciting tucked up his sleeve. Had Ru figured out a way to keep her as his business partner?

He released her hand, gesturing toward the cliffs. 'Run with me to the end of the beach where we can be more private.'

Keen to get away before anyone else accosted him, she ran, letting the wind ripple through her hair and the salty air fill her lungs. They sprinted along the shoreline, Fiona's feet skimming across the damp sand. The waves broke beside them, and she let out a childlike whoop as cold water swept over her feet. Beside her, the soft thud of Ru's footsteps blended with her own, their laughter rising and falling with the roar of incoming waves.

At the far end of the beach, Ru steered her towards the cliffs, where, sheltered from the sun, the sand was empty of tourists. He stopped and removed his sunglasses. His chest was heaving. Exhilarated from the run, Fiona bent over panting. 'That . . . was such . . . good fun,' she said, gulping air into her lungs. She straightened, laughing. Feeling like she was beginning to look at her situation more objectively, she asked something which had been niggling at her since the investor meeting. 'Tell me, how did you convince the investors not to walk? You must have had to do some fast thinking and some hard selling. They agreed to back the new idea without a business plan.'

'It was never in doubt.'

Now that really was being cocky. 'It was, I saw that knowing look on the lead investor's face when I promised I'd work all hours and pass the exam next time . . . like he'd heard it all before, people over-promising and under-delivering. I don't think I could forgive myself if they'd walked.'

'OK, truth time.' he said, grinning, 'I had warned them that I didn't think you were ready for that exam. I've been working with them on the new idea for the last month. I knew I had to protect you.'

His confession settled over them like a toxic cloud. She felt the blood drain from her face as the full weight of his betrayal crashed over her. Everything crystallized in that moment – the patronizing looks from the investors, their lack of surprise at her failure, the too-smooth transition to Plan B. It had been a set-up. The man she trusted, who had claimed to support her dreams, had actively worked to undermine her, while smiling to her face. And he claimed his motive was to *protect* her? From what? Her fingers went numb while shock and humiliation battled for dominance in her chest. As she was processing her thoughts, Ru dropped onto one knee. Fiona felt her insides quiver. There was a passion shining in those dark eyes. 'Fi, I love you. Please, say you will marry me.' In his hands was a tiny blue box. He flipped it open. Nestling on a cream velvet cushion was an art-deco ring. A stunning elongated emerald set in platinum, the sparkling green gem surrounded by tiny glittering diamonds. Thoughts rushed through her mind. *Why now?* They had never discussed marriage before. *Was this really what he wanted? Was it just pity, or another attempt at protection?*

Grinning, he rose. He evidently hadn't detected her doubts. He passed her the small box, and her heart started fluttering. Despite the size, it felt leaden in her hands: this box represented his offer of marriage. How could she marry him after what he'd just admitted to? His proposal was like being offered a sip of La

Tâche, the iconic red Burgundy crafted by Domaine de la Romanée-Conti, only to discover it was a humble plonk. He had shown his true colours – he didn't listen to her dreams; they were drowned out by his own.

She slipped the box into the pocket of her shorts.

He was still grinning at her. 'Fi, I love you, and I want to look after you for ever. I've reserved a slot at Chelsea registry office for when we get home. And I've got a surprise for you.'

She stuttered into laughter. 'Your proposal is already a surprise.'

'I've booked the honeymoon too! You're going to love it. We're off to Melbourne, so you can visit your folks, and I finally get to meet them!'

Her head shot forwards. She never talked about her parents, not even with Ivy. Fiona had only told Ru where they lived and worked to stop his incessant questions. What had given him the crazy idea of visiting them? Didn't he understand that they didn't want to see her? This was typical of him – confident he always knew best, secretly drafting a Plan B with the investors, booking the wedding and honeymoon without consulting her, tuning out every mention of her fractured relationship with her parents, assuming a leadership role and expecting her to acquiesce. Why bother consulting her on momentous decisions like business ventures or marriage plans? In a flash, she realized that much as she loved him, she couldn't marry him. He was so much surer of himself, so much more capable. And he obviously thought he was better than her, saw himself as her protecter, which was not what she wanted from a husband.

She swallowed, hearing the quake in her voice. 'No. I'm very sorry . . . but I can't marry you, Ru.'

His face seemed frozen. The beautiful jaw she loved to kiss went taut. He took a step aside, slanting his body away from hers and stared at the ground.

'Why not?' he said, the words sharp and clipped.

She blinked, shaking her head slowly. If he didn't realize what he'd done wrong, how could she find the words to explain? She loved him and didn't want to lose him, but she couldn't ignore what he'd done.

'Tell me,' he insisted, his voice rising as though the sheer force of his personality could break her silence. Ru turned to face her fully, his glare cutting into her. His jaw worked furiously, the muscles straining in disbelief. His brows drew together in a confused expression and his hands trembled as though barely able to contain the storm of emotions bubbling inside.

The combination struck Fiona mute. She had no idea how to respond. If she raised her concerns, she didn't think he would listen, dismissing them as mere frustration over her failed exam. But that wasn't it at all. His casual mention of how he'd approached the investors without consulting her, his undermining of her career, followed by his unilateral decision about their marriage plans had confirmed her deepest fear: he didn't see her as an equal partner, either in business or in life.

'Why?' he demanded. There was a hint of despair in his voice now, which sent a chill through her. 'Why won't you marry me?'

Silence hung between them, a chasm too wide to breach.

Ru was the one to break it. 'If you can't even explain yourself to me, don't bother coming back to my restaurant.' His lip curled – distorting his lovely features – as he channelled his pain into anger. 'And yes, you heard right. It's *my* restaurant. As you keep reminding me, you're just the wine waiter.'

Fiona gasped. She tried to swallow, but her throat was too dry. She felt hot tears slithering down her cheeks. How could he be so cruel? Yes, she'd said she couldn't marry him, but she'd expected him to row back from the proposal, revert to their easy, relaxed relationship, perhaps make a joke of it all, allowing her time to digest everything she'd learned and find a way to talk it through. The taste of her tears was a salty reminder of her failure and her sorrow. Ru reached out for her, but she pushed him away, evading his encircling arms, like a wild animal desperate to break free of its captor. Fiona tore up the beach, still sobbing, her chest heaving with each step. She heard him calling out to stop, to come back, to talk to him, but she raced on, her eyes swollen with tears. The damage was done. He'd finally spoken the truth, and he couldn't take that back.

Above her, seagulls cried out as if in sympathy with the lonely figure below them. Her chest ached with the weight of her decision, her heart torn between love for him and the unbearable truth she couldn't escape. But she had said *no*. Their relationship was over.

Listening to the waves crash against the shore, she felt as though the sea itself was mourning her loss, the pull of the tide mirroring the emptiness inside her. She had given him up – given *them* up. Every footfall in the sand took her further away from a life she didn't want to lose.

Somewhere in the distance, a ship's horn sounded, deep and almost mournful, and she collapsed to her knees on the sand, sobbing into her hands. She would never again feel his arms around her, his lips on hers.

What had she done?

Three

With intermittent breaks to catch her breath, Fiona hurtled across the beach and up through the village, ignoring the startled looks from those she passed. She let herself into Ivy's cottage, closing the door stealthily behind her, and crept up the stairs to the bedroom, where she dropped her sandals with a clatter.

Ru's proposal had been a naive attempt to rally her spirits, but it felt like salt in the wound of his betrayal, a painful reminder that he saw her as someone to be managed and protected rather than consulted. '*My* restaurant'. Those words would haunt her. They proved that her instinct to reject him was correct. The way he'd approached the investors privately, stung – not even a heads-up about the alternative business plan. It confirmed what she'd suspected for some time: in his mind, she was an accessory to his success, not an architect of their shared future. When she'd failed that exam, she'd shattered all of her dreams – she wasn't a Master Sommelier, she wasn't the business partner of a celebrity chef. Fiona wasn't good enough to become the wife of one, and she was no longer the girlfriend of one either.

She hurled herself onto the bed, sniffing her tears to a stop, then rolled on to her side, thumping her head against the pillow. But the musky scent of Ru clung to the bed linen, and she moaned. Her eyes danced around the room. Traces of him lay everywhere – his jeans slung over a chair back, his bag unzipped but unpacked, the clothes rumpled from his post-breakfast hurried delve to extract his swimming trunks.

Fiona pushed herself upright, yanking Ru's belongings off hooks, plucking them from chair backs, and sweeping them off the chest of drawers. She tossed them all into his bag and tugged at the zip. It was unyielding, as if mocking her attempts to shut away her memories. Fiona kicked the bag under the bed, then picked up a wine book, opening it randomly and staring unseeing at the page. However, she couldn't concentrate, and her ears strained for footsteps. Was Ru going to come after her?

For an hour, Fiona idly flipped pages. She heard footsteps clomp up the stairs, then a firm knock. She drew in a calming breath. The door opened and Aunt Ivy's round face peeped in, her eyes radiating love like the warm glow of a sunrise spreading across a tranquil sea. 'Ruben called me. We need to talk.'

Fiona examined her aunt's face for clues. Ivy didn't do drama. She wouldn't approve of this mess.

Ivy knelt in front of Fiona. Despite being in her late fifties, her aunt was flexible for her age and after decades of worship, was used to being on her knees. 'I'm not going to ask why you did this. You will tell me when you are ready.'

Fiona spoke earnestly. 'I'll tell you now. I'm not good enough for him.'

Ivy clicked her tongue. 'Let's deal with the practical side of things first. I've offered to take him the car keys so he can drive back up to London.'

Good, thought Fiona. It would be easier if she didn't see him. 'I've packed his bag. It's not heavy, so you can take it with you.' She wanted nothing left behind to remind her of him.

Ivy sighed. 'If that's what you think is best. When the dust has settled you can catch a train home and chat everything through together.'

'No need,' Fiona responded bitterly, 'He can sort everything out.'

Her aunt frowned. 'Ruben isn't going to tidy this mess up Fiona. It's your mess too. You need to talk to him. You are in business together.'

'Wrong tense. We *were* in business together. He'll find another sommelier. Guests come for the food.' That's what the lead investor had told her in that meeting, with a sardonic curl to his lips, 'Ru can replace me. I couldn't replace him.' She would never replace him. Fiona bit down on her lip, relishing the pain.

'What about the flat?'

She thought about their home in Ladbroke Grove. Fiona had done all the legwork, but it was Ru who'd found it in her discarded pile. It was Ru who'd seen the potential, Ru who'd hired and briefed the architect, transforming the flat into a light and airy space with oblique views over Holland Park. All the good ideas had been Ru's. His creative mind was why he was such a successful chef. Although possibly a miserable one today.

Fiona shook her head. 'It's his. He can buy me out.' As an up-and-coming celebrity chef with wealthy backers, he could afford the mortgage by himself. Fiona longed to contribute more than just her mountain of debts. She pictured the day she finally passed that wretched exam and started earning a proper salary – enough to pay back what she owed and be financially independent.

Ivy tutted, put her hands on her thighs and levered herself upright, her knees cracking as she rose. 'You've got this all figured out, have you?'

Fiona sniffed.

'No, sorry that was flippant, unhelpful.' Ivy paused and took a breath. 'What do you want to do? Stay in Brambleton for the rest of the week while you think things through?'

'I know what to do. I need to pass my Advanced Sommelier exams.' She couldn't think any further ahead. That qualification would set her free financially and prove her worth.

'Fiona, my darling, life is a serious of tests God sets for us, but passing exams isn't the key to a happy, fulfilling life. You won't earn love through your achievements. Love is freely given.'

For once, Fiona knew that her aunt was wrong. Passing exams was crucial to a successful career – and successful careers delivered happy and fulfilling lives.

'Ivy, I can't face Ru . . . not yet. Can I stay here with you?' murmured Fiona, sounding like her teenage self, reluctant to catch the train back to a silent Exeter home after spending an afternoon in Brambleton.

Ivy spoke decisively. 'OK. But you can't run away from this, Fiona. You need to sort out the practicalities.'

Spotting her opportunity, Fiona chewed her lip. 'I need to retake my exam. Would you lend me the money so I can book it? I promise I'll pay you back.' She studied her aunt's face for clues.

Ivy tutted. 'Why not ask your parents?'

'No!' That would involve admitting to them she'd failed the first time, and she wasn't doing that.

'I'm sure they'd help.'

Fiona was sure they wouldn't. Neither of her parents had ever failed an exam. 'I don't want their help. And I don't want them to know I've failed. Please don't tell them. Please, please lend me the money.'

Ivy sighed. 'If it's that important to you . . .'

Fiona ran her eyes around the little bedroom. Her heart felt ragged, as if someone had twisted a corkscrew into it. By rejecting Ru, she had pulled apart the fabric of her life. She loved him, lived with him, worked with him. All that was gone. Had she made the right decision? Should she call Ru and talk through what he'd done wrong? No, that would be a false reprieve. After rejecting his proposal, it wouldn't take long for Ru to realize he'd dodged a bullet and replace her with someone more suitable. Although it was the right choice, she would have to deal with the implications of her decision, which were settling, sharp and bitter, like over-aged wine she didn't want to swallow.

'Can I stay with you for a month or so?'

'Moping here won't help. You must be practical.'

Her aunt was right. There were practical considerations; Fiona needed to get a job so she could contribute to her living costs and eventually pay off her debts. 'Maybe the pub could use a pair of hands for a few weeks? I need some headspace. I promise I won't mope.'

That was an easy promise to keep – Fiona would be too busy studying to mope.

Ivy offered to cook dinner, but Fiona declined, knowing she would be unable to face food. Alone in the bedroom, she unpacked her suitcase, then repacked most of it – she had no use for a silk negligée anymore, and she wouldn't have time to wear a bikini or holiday clothes. She kept out her toiletries, all her books, jeans and t-shirts.

That night Fiona lay awake for hours. Her mind replayed snatches of the horrendous day: Ru's grinning face when he'd admitted what he'd done with the investors, oblivious to how she felt; Ru's dazed expression, his slumped shoulders, then those vicious stinging words and the look in his eyes as he'd spat them. Had she made a dreadful mistake? Should she call, patch things up, promise to catch the first train to London in the morning? She loved him enough to try, but then she remembered how worried she'd been on his behalf that by failing her exam she had messed up his career, when in truth, he'd been secretly undermining hers to protect his own. They were destined to split up. She had just precipitated the demise.

Eventually, she fell into a fitful sleep, but it offered no release. She dreamed she was being chased along Brambleton Beach by her parents, her feet dragging in damp sand, each step almost overwhelming her energy, while her eyes scoured for some unseen lost treasure.

She woke early, with a heavy ache in her chest. Today marked the start of her new life. One without Ru. The faint sounds of singing drifted through the door. Ivy was up early; Sunday was a busy day for her. Fiona shrugged on a cotton dressing gown and went downstairs.

Her aunt was in the kitchen, a morning church service flickering on the TV screen behind her.

'Good morning, love. Toast and tea. Why don't you sit down. I'll make it.'

Fiona took a seat, listening to the choir singing, '*Dear Lord and Father of mankind, forgive our foolish ways . . .*' *Well, the hymn was appropriate*, Fiona thought.

The little kitchen table was set for two. The empty place where Ru had sat yesterday morning, his long legs pressed up against hers, reminded her poignantly of her loss. The space where twenty-four hours earlier he had served a perfect soufflé omelette now held a pat of butter still wearing the foil wrapping and a jar of branded marmalade. Ivy added mugs of tea and Fiona sat, trying to derive energy from the warmth of the mug. She peered at the marmalade, an image of Ru shredding Seville oranges in their London flat forming in her mind. Fiona hadn't eaten shop-bought marmalade for three years – she'd better get used to the taste.

'I spoke to Rose this morning.' said Ivy.

'Rose?'

'Rose and George run the Smuggler's Inn. She's front of house, he's the head chef. He's not Ruben, but the food is very good. Rose would be happy to take you on as a waitress. I mentioned you're staying at mine for a few weeks and that you've recently split up with your boyfriend, so if you're a bit teary she'll understand.'

Relief flooded through her, and she told herself she would get through this. 'Thanks, Ivy. Should I give her a call?'

'No need,' said Ivy, as she smiled and turned back to the counter. 'Rose said for you to turn up at noon tomorrow.'

Fiona smelled toast. A rack appeared in front of her, each slice perfectly symmetrical. She added 'getting used to supermarket bread' to the list of adjustments she would be making.

On days when the restaurant was closed, Ru always made brunch, filling the flat with tantalizing smells, including her favourite cinnamon bread. Sometimes she selected a boutique Champagne to chill, and they would eat together, cross-legged on the bed. Eventually, their eyes would meet, and they would forget their plates and glasses, and focus on each other.

Fiona snapped out of her memories, drawn to the choir's swaying figures as their voices soared. '*Let sense be dumb . . .*' Those words reverberated and she winced. Had she been too rash yesterday? No, she told herself firmly. Couples couldn't just return to their relationship and pretend something as momentous as this hadn't happened. It was like trying to patch a cracked mirror; no matter how careful the mend, the fracture was still there, splintering every reflection.

The music surged, the choir reaching a powerful crescendo. '*Speak through the earthquake, wind, and fire . . .*' The words coursed through Fiona like a jolt of energy, stirring something restless inside her. But then the music softened, the voices lingering over the line: '*O still small voice of calm*'.

That last phrase pierced through the noise in her mind, cutting through her doubts. She must be strong. For a moment, a quiet settled within her. The tension she'd been holding onto since her decision eased a little, and she let herself breathe.

Fiona plonked a slice of toast onto her plate and pulled the pack of butter towards her. Ru wouldn't find it difficult to replace her. Someone else would soon enjoy his musky smell. She must succeed too, by passing her exam and forging a new, financially independent life.

After breakfast, Ivy left for church and Fiona cleared up, made herself a pot of coffee, then dragged herself back upstairs. It wasn't her childhood bedroom in the rectory, but as she sprawled across the patchwork quilt she'd known all her life, she felt at home, staring as intently at her wine atlas as she suspected Aunt Ivy would be gazing at an altar.

The aroma of freshly brewed coffee filled the space, yet even after her second mug, her mind felt cluttered. She was missing her simple flashcards on wine regions, grape varieties and tasting notes. She focused on the page in front of her. She must study – that qualification would enable her to repay her debts – which would balloon once Ivy lent her the money for the next exam. Just as she had immersed herself in the subtle differences between Bordeaux wines and the New World Bordeaux blends, her phone buzzed.

Ru. Again.

His name taunted her. Every missive was a reminder of the emotional baggage she was trying to shed. Her eyes flitted to the screen, glimpsing his latest message.

Can we please talk? I need to understand.

It was the fifth message today. All with Ru's trademark sign-off for his messages to her – a beating heart emoji. Just as Ru's emoji pulsed with a rhythmic, almost desperate vitality, guilt pulsed within Fiona – a persistent, haunting beat that refused to be silenced. She ignored all the messages – responding would only pull her into a spiral of conversations she wasn't ready for. She turned the phone facedown, hoping the distractions would stop, but the soft hum of incoming texts made it impossible to concentrate on tannins, terroir and tasting techniques. Every ping was a tug-of-war between her future life and her past.

She sat up and gulped her coffee. Catching sight of one of his socks under the bed, she pushed herself upright, the mattress creaking as if in disapproval. Fiona kicked the sock closer to the wall, picked up her phone, scrolled through her contacts and brought up Ruben Nkosi. A thick sensation filled her throat, as if something was lodged there. To allow them both to move on, and for him to soar without her holding him back, she had to do this. Fiona squeezed her eyes shut, opened them and quickly blocked his number. It was over.

Four

On Monday morning Fiona woke early with a tightness in her chest. The sun shone brightly through her curtains, but she pulled the covers up to her chin. She reached over for her wine book and snuggled down, cuddling it close to her chest, like a hot-water bottle.

After forcing down a slice of toast and coffee, she swotted up on Australian winemakers for a couple of hours, then wearing jeans and a t-shirt, walked into Brambleton to her new workplace. It was another glorious summer's day, and families traipsed downhill towards the beach. Hassled-looking fathers carried sun umbrellas, shrimping nets and cool bags, while their partners followed with children, voluminous bags and forced smiles. Today, she and Ru should have been enjoying their holiday. She wondered how he was spending his Monday. She imagined he would concentrate his efforts on setting up the new restaurant. *His* restaurant. It would take months to refurbish the premises, install the new kitchen, kit out the dining area and recruit the right staff to dovetail with opening night – including a new sommelier.

Ru would also sort out the practicalities of their split. He would pack up her clothes and books. He might even take that holiday to Australia – she doubted if holiday insurance covered one half of a couple dumping the other. A gust of wind blew tendrils of hair across her face, carrying with it a faint whiff of fish. Ru would go to Melbourne. He was an optimist and would make the best of this carnage.

She heard waves crashing against the shore, a constant, soothing roar punctuated by the sharp cry of seagulls. A few steps later and the harbour wall was in front of her. To her right, a group of wetsuit wearing youngsters surrounded a tall, bronzed man on the beach. The instructor, who had the physique of an athlete, looked to be in his late twenties, a few years younger than Fiona. As she watched, the man showed the children how to use their hands to paddle and then demonstrated clambering upright on a surfboard. He made it look so easy. But out of the water, it was. The pupils dropped to the sand, mimicking the instructor's actions, practising popping up and standing tall with their arms outright to balance, and then, with eager shouts, the group made their way into the waves, throwing themselves face-down on their boards, paddling furiously, before attempting to stand. Some wobbled and splashed, others managed a brief upright stance, their knees shaking before tumbling into the water. Listening to their laughter and cries of joy, Fiona felt invigorated. She, too, could learn a new skill – living without Ru.

On her left was a rustic painted wooden sign: *The Smuggler's Inn*. A flood of relief gushed through her like the waves lapping on the beach. This place could be her sanctuary, where no one knew her or about her past relationship with Ruben Nkosi.

Inside, low wooden beams created an intimate atmosphere, light spilled in from open windows and the scent of salt mingled with the comforting aroma of cooking onions and spilled beer. Black and white photographs of distant times decorated the walls alongside nautical trinkets – old fishing nets, brass ship lanterns and vintage maps.

Someone had already laid the tables, and a calmness swept

through Fiona. She could do this. These rustic tables and high-backed velvet chairs would be a busy haven for her to lose herself in other people's happiness. Beyond the dining room, the nooks and booths were pockets to hide in when she needed a moment to steel herself from her troubles. By working and studying, she could forget him, and then – only once she was part of the elite circle of master sommeliers – she would find a great job, repay her debts and start afresh.

'Hi there. I'm guessing you're Fiona,' said a south London accent. 'I'm Rose. Let me show you around.'

Her new boss looked like a woman used to getting things done, with practical length hair and an outfit to match. Fiona admired the quiet air of authority that she exuded. For a few months she wanted someone else to take charge. After a briefing from Rose, Fiona pulled on an apron. Within minutes, the pub was buzzing with activity. Every seat filled up, voices overlapping in boisterous conversation. Fiona jotted down orders from the short lunch menu and refilled glasses, offering a warm smile to each visitor, which hid her true feelings. She weaved her way through the maze of tables and chairs, whisking so many plates of fresh line-caught seafood and steaming bowls of moules marinière from the kitchen that she didn't have time to register the team working in there.

After a hectic service, Rose bolted the door on the last guest. Pulling out a chair and sinking down, the boss kicked off her shoes, picked up a menu and fanned herself. 'Phew! It's hot. Let's discuss tonight before Mum drops off the kids. I love them to bits, but it is tricky running your own business with a young family.' Rose blushed. 'Sorry. Ivy said you've recently split with your boyfriend. I wasn't thinking – how are you?'

Dazed, that was the only word to describe how Fiona felt. Yet, a wave of gratitude washed over her. Rose's question was far easier to answer than the relentless ones Ivy kept throwing her way. She forced a faint smile. 'Ghastly,' she admitted. It was like living in a parallel universe, a helpless spectator to the implosion of her own life. 'But keeping busy helps.'

Rose pointed a knowing finger at Fiona and said, 'You did well. You've done this before, haven't you? Ivy mentioned you had experience, but I wasn't expecting too much – everyone claims they've got experience these days.'

Fiona smiled, relieved to discover her facial muscles hadn't forgotten how that was done.

'Tonight is a more serious affair,' said Rose. 'Let me jot this all down for you.' She fumbled in her pockets. 'Blast! Where's my pen gone?'

'Don't worry, Rose, I've got a good memory.' Years of revising for exams had honed that to perfection.

Rose rewarded her with a smile. 'We set up at 6.30 p.m. and open at 7 p.m. Come to the back of the pub at six o'clock. That's where reception is for the B&B side of the business. The food's gastro pub fare – speak to George about the menu. The evening wine list is different too. George's uncle left him a fine wine collection, which we offer besides the more run-of-the-mill stuff we've just been serving. You'd be surprised how often the punters take us up. Lots of rich tourists come to Brambleton.' Rose reached down, massaging a foot. 'Do you know anything about wine?'

Fiona arched her eyes. 'I hope so. I'm a sommelier.' Just not a fully qualified one.

'Oh, what a treat for George. He's a bit of a wine buff. You two will get on well.'

'I'll speak to him about the food and the wine. Where's the cellar?'

Rose heaved herself up. 'For insurance we keep the key hidden. I'll show you.'

The pub's door burst open, and two whirlwinds ran towards the table. The girl was about six, her pigtails bobbing with each excited step. Her older brother followed more slowly, clutching a slightly scruffy stuffed bear. Their lively chatter filled the space and Fiona's face split into a smile.

'Hello, my lovelies,' cried Rose, scooping them into her arms. 'Have you had a wonderful morning?'

The children talked over each other, relaying adventures involving finger painting and helping Grandpa tidy his garden shed.

'We had such fun!' said Becky.

'Umm, yes, and I'm sure you made a lot of mess too,' said Rose.

Becky giggled. 'Grandma and Grandpa said it didn't matter. They just wanted to be with us,' she announced triumphantly.

Becky and Timmy introduced themselves and allowed Fiona to admire their morning's artwork.

'When I grow up, I'm going to be an artist like Daddy,' Timmy said solemnly.

Yes thought Fiona, *cooking was art*. Her heart clenched, picturing Ru in the kitchen of the Fork & Cork, inspecting food deliveries, his low, confident voice conjuring specials from the ingredients. In a high-pitched voice Becky jabbered, 'And I'm going to be an astronaut.'

'My, my,' said Fiona, 'you will have a lot of exams to pass. Make sure you study hard!'

Becky wrinkled her nose. 'Ugh! Tests! Nasty things!'

'But vital. You need qualifications to get on,' stated Fiona, smiling into the child's distorted face. 'I'll leave you alone,' she murmured to Rose. 'I'll be back early and have a word with George then.'

At six o'clock, Fiona turned left down a narrow alley. The road led her into a small car park sheltered behind a low stone wall, shielding vehicles from the sea's relentless spray. There was a stationary lorry, its engine idling. A man was unloading kegs of beer, rolling them towards an open hatchway, the metal containers rumbling and rattling on the tarmac. Hovering close by was a motorcyclist and next to him stood a man wearing a chef's apron over loose-fitting trousers. He wasn't as tall as Ru, and he didn't have his honed physique. This one was middle-aged, his slightly squat body and large tummy bearing the marks of two decades of thoroughly enjoying his profession. The man had muscly arms that wouldn't have looked out of place on a professional wrestler. She wondered if this was George, or one of his team. A thick plastic pouch disappeared into the rear top box of the motorcycle before it sped off. Fiona let the machine roar past her up the hill, then followed the chef up the steps.

Inside was an unmanned reception desk. She strode through the silent space feeling a stab of longing for Ru, imagining it was he she was about to consult about the evening specials. Would she ever get over loving him? It probably wasn't too late to have a serious chat. He wouldn't have made such an effort to get in touch yesterday if he had accepted their split as final. But then, he never accepted anyone's decisions, did he? His self-belief was so strong that he thought everything – and everyone – would eventually go his way.

She could unblock his number, arrange to meet up and talk things through. Then, she recalled his casual reference to undermining her with the investors and his undisguised pride in arranging a honeymoon which involved visiting her parents; he didn't think of her as his equal – and that was no basis for a marriage.

Fiona blew out a long sigh. She must stick to her guns. She pushed at the kitchen swing door, expecting to hear a symphony of clattering pots, sizzling pans and the sharp clang of knives on cutting boards. Silence met her. Only two individuals were present: the man she'd previously seen on the back steps and another near the sinks, washing dishes.

Compared to the Fork & Cork, the kitchen was larger, and the units were older, but the bright overhead lights illuminated similar gleaming stainless steel surfaces, and an array of familiar ingredients lined the shelves. She sniffed, identifying fennel and thyme and her wine brain kicked in, matching grapes to those smells.

'Hi,' she said. 'I'm Fiona, the new waitress. I was looking for George.'

'You've found him,' said the man in the chef's uniform. He had a low voice which reminded Fiona of a deep bell tolling.

'Rose suggested I have a word with you about tonight's specials . . . and the wine list.'

George glanced up. His forehead was shiny beneath his white hat and there was a grim, hassled expression on his face. 'No specials. I'm on my own.' Fiona's eyes drifted towards the other man. 'That's Josh, the KP,' explained George. *Right* thought Fiona, *this explained the short lunch offering.*

Her eyes switched to Josh. He spun around, and she recognized the bronzed face of the surf instructor she had seen on the beach earlier. Watching him scour pans, she thought he was fizzing with energy and liked his positivity. 'G'day. Welcome to the team,' said Josh, waving a silver scrubbing pad at her. He spoke with a slow Australian drawl and a surprisingly powerful voice, considering his age. The timbre of his voice strangely reminded Fiona of her father – what would he have to say about the mess his daughter was in? She shuddered.

Josh started whistling, bringing a cheerful atmosphere into the space.

Fiona tried to imagine Ru preparing for an evening service with just a kitchen porter to assist. No wonder George looked frazzled. But taking in the simmering saucepans, the bowls of chopped herbs, sliced lemons and filled sauce bottles, he appeared to have things under control.

'Rose says you've an interesting cellar. I'd love to hear about it. I'm a certified sommelier.'

The whistling stopped. 'What's that?' asked Josh.

'Not you,' barked George, laughing. 'You don't know anything about fine wine, whereas this woman,' he jabbed a thumb in Fiona's direction, 'can identify different grape varieties from a single mouthful.'

'Me too,' grinned Josh. 'Anyone can read a label.'

'We've not had a sommelier before. Josh, find the wine list and give it to someone who can appreciate its quality.' He wiped his hands on a cloth. 'We've one of the best cellars in Devon,' boasted George. 'Worth a fortune, so it deserves a sommelier!'

Josh rinsed a saucepan and jogged out. He returned, passing her a list which was surprisingly sophisticated. She hoped the evening would provide opportunities to delve into the nuances of these wines – she would be on solid ground while the fabric of her life unravelled.

An hour later, the dining room was bustling. With a deftness born of years of experience, Fiona glided through the unfamiliar labyrinth of tables and chairs, balancing laden trays. A welcoming smile never left her face. She seemed to anticipate guests' needs, from topping up a wine glass to fetching a bill before they asked for it. Fiona managed light-hearted banter with diners, all the while maintaining a keen awareness of her surroundings, excusing herself to deal with other customers beckoning her.

She spent an enjoyable ten minutes explaining to a couple that they shouldn't let their dislike of Beaujolais prevent them ordering a well-aged Burgundy, reassuring them that its earthy undertones and complexity were a sharp contrast to the young fruity Pinot Noir they didn't like. They took her advice. Fiona went to fetch their choice.

Descending the stone steps to the silent cellar, the familiar musty smell of damp stone enveloped her like a comfortable blanket. A dim, flickering light from a single hanging bulb cast a gentle, golden glow over the space. Exposed brick semicircular wine bins lined the walls, each holding bottles, some with peeling labels, reflecting their age. She shivered with contentment. And then a memory crashed over her like a wave.

She and Ru had celebrated their last anniversary in the cellar below the Fork & Cork. Fiona had spent an hour preparing the space, arranging wine crates bearing bowls of floating tealights, their soft flames casting dancing shadows on the exposed brick walls. She closed her eyes and pictured the scene as if it was unfolding in front of her. A white damask cloth draped the table, with a single red rose perched in a bud vase. Nearby, a bottle of Champagne from a small artisanal vineyard rested in a silver ice bucket.

She could practically smell the enticing aroma of basil and garlic that had drifted down from the kitchen, could almost hear Ru's footsteps on the stairs, followed by his powerful voice. 'Service,' he had called. Then, as Ru reached the bottom of the stairs, he dipped his head, urging, 'Sit, sit.' He waited while Fiona settled herself before lowering a plate in front of her with a flourish. 'For madam – Mersea Island oysters.'

She reached for the Champagne, expertly removing the foil and cage, then easing the cork free with practised hands. 'You're going to enjoy this one, Ru,' she said, pouring him a glass. 'Look at that mousse – it's almost dancing, pirouetting in the glass!'

The mousse's smooth, creamy texture told a story all its own. Delicate bubbles trembled and shimmered, catching and refracting the amber glow of candlelight– all hallmarks of a masterfully crafted Champagne. By contrast, larger bubbles that quickly dissipated betrayed the less refined nature of an ordinary sparkling wine.

Ru took the glass, lifting it to his nose, inhaling appreciatively before taking a sip. His eyes closed, a dreamy expression washing over his face as he swallowed. 'Wow, where did you find this mousse, Mousse?'

Mousse was his pet name for her, reserved for their most intimate moments. In French, *mousse* literally meant "foam," evoking the light, airy textures found in culinary creations and sparkling wines, like the frothy bubbles rising in a glass of Champagne or the delicate whipped sweetness of dessert. *Mousse* embodied luxury, indulgence, and delight – a perfect encapsulation of their shared worlds.

He gestured at her plate. 'Come on, try one.'

The oysters were nestled on a bed of crushed ice, exuding the scent of the ocean. Fiona lifted one to her lips, savouring the briny taste that melted into something almost buttery and fresh on her tongue. The flavours washed over her, and a warmth spread through her as a contented smile tugged at her lips.

'Take your time,' Ru whispered, his knee brushing against hers. 'Nothing's spoiling.'

Fiona looked around at the racks of dark glass bottles lining the walls, all bearing the silent history of their contents, like liquid time capsules. She reached across the table to take his hand, feeling its warmth in the cool air. His fingers rested gently on hers.

'Happy?' he asked, his voice soft.

'Happy,' she murmured.

The cellar at the Smuggler's Inn did not smell of garlic and basil, but of must and damp. Fiona blinked and wrenched herself back to the present. Her eyes were wet, and she wiped them with the back of her hand. The memory of Ru was just that – a memory. Firmly in the past as distant and foreign to her now as the lightness and joy she had experienced that night. The dull, empty ache in her chest reminded her why she had been trying so hard to forget him. It was too painful to remember everything they shared. She resolved to try and shut out the memories. Starting right now. She would focus on the matter at hand.

She engaged her brain back into wine-mode, assessing the chalk labels above each bin which listed the region the wines came from. After locating the wine, Fiona dashed into the kitchen to collect the order of extra chips for Table 5 she'd asked for earlier. The meticulous layout of pre-service had descended into organized chaos.

The kitchen was a cacophony of hissing pans and clattering utensils, full of the rich scent of roasting meat. His brow slick with sweat, a weary frown etched across it, George darted around the stove like a bird trapped in a greenhouse, flitting desperately from one end to the other, trying to juggle the orders. The methodical movements of his kitchen prep had morphed into a frantic two-handed muddle of stirring as if he were a sailor attempting to bail out a sinking boat.

Fiona leaned against the cool metal of the serving counter, her arms crossed, observing the mayhem.

'Josh! Get me the asparagus!' barked George.

Josh rinsed the tray he was washing, set it to drain, then ambled to the fridge, returning with a bag in his hand. 'Here ya go.'

Momentarily the chef took his eyes off the pans. He huffed, then shouted, 'No, not the frozen stuff.' George's voice sliced through the din. 'I want the fresh stuff.'

Josh grinned and strolled back to the fridge. Whistling, he rifled through the crates, examining then discarding produce like a museum curator examining ancient artifacts, each item worthy of careful consideration.

'Come on, come on!' George snapped, stirring a pot of sauce that bubbled furiously. The smell was intoxicating: a blend of tomatoes, herbs and something unidentifiable that lingered in the back of her throat. She could almost taste the acidity, the promise of a dish coming together. Her mind conjured wines to match the flavours.

'Sorry, Chef! There's no asparagus!' Josh's powerful voice echoed off the stainless steel surfaces, before being replaced by cheerful whistling. 'Hang on . . . got it' he announced, pulling out a limp bundle of herbs. George's face turned a shade darker. His low rumbling voice sounding like thunder, as he shouted. 'Not those! Asparagus, Josh! The ones I prepped earlier – you were here!'

Acutely aware of the brewing storm, Fiona stepped forwards. The heat from the stove smothered her, a comforting warmth compared to the tension crackling in the room. Once beside Josh, she elbowed him aside. 'Let me look,' she said, reaching into the fridge and quickly retrieving the asparagus.

'Hey, beauty! That'll sort out Mr Angry' joked Josh, strolling back to the sinks.

But George's voice rang out again, demanding and impatient. The kitchen felt like a ship caught in the middle of a violent storm, with George desperately spinning the wheel and shouting commands into the gale. Meanwhile, Josh lounged against the sinks like a man on Bondi Beach, watching his captain's panic with the mild amusement of someone who'd seen far worse swells back home. Thinking it safest to keep out of George's way, Fiona slunk back to the serving counter, where she remembered why she was in the kitchen.

'George,' said, 'I asked for extra chips for Table 5.'

'Shit sorry, coming up.' He charged to the deep-fat fryer.

Behind her, Fiona heard the swing door open, then Rose asking, 'George how long for Table 7's mains?'

He looked up, his face mutinous. 'Fifteen minutes?'

'Needs to be faster – they want pudding, and they've got a taxi booked for ten.'

'Delay it.'

'I didn't arrange it.'

'Well tell whoever did to delay it . . . I'm on my own back here,' the chef responded sarcastically.

'Chef,' said Fiona, sniffing, 'those chips . . .'

'Oh shit' said George, lunging for the deep-fat fryer. He rescued the chips, drained them and dumped the food on Fiona's tray. 'Rose I know we said we'd try and manage, but I need help!'

'The kids return to school soon, which will give Mum some time to help out, and at the end of September we'll start closing on Monday's too'

'No, get me some proper help' yelled George, stalking back to his saucepans.

'I'll advertise' promised Rose, mentioning the online recruitment firm Fiona always used when she was looking for staff. 'And I'll ask Mum to help as a stop-gap.' Rose turned to Fiona. 'Sorry you're not seeing us at our best. End of a long, busy season. We did have a sous chef and a junior. If he's overwhelmed his artistic side takes over, his temper flares and everyone suffers,' said Rose.

Fiona smiled. She didn't care how grumpy the chef was. Fiona wanted this job. She needed money to fund her studies, and the work was a diversion. Fiona picked up her tray and backed out of the kitchen.

'Hold that door!' shouted Rose. Fiona pressed herself backwards, allowing the other woman out, 'It's tough working with your other half,' huffed Rose.

Yes, thought Fiona, an image of the Chef's Table at the Fork & Cork forming in her mind, but that was in the past. And it would be a while before she was ready to revisit it.

Hearing someone whistling, Fiona cast a quick look around the kitchen. Josh was leaning against the sink, casually drying a plate, the tune light on his lips. When their eyes met, his smile deepened. Then he winked. Just once.

Fiona looked away, but not before the corner of her mouth betrayed her.

Five

Over the next few weeks, Fiona did her best to shut memories of Ru out of her mind. She threw herself into work, sometimes arriving early, though never as early as Josh, who was often taking a vape break on the pub's back steps. Occasionally she stopped to chat. He was cheerful company and mostly talked about his passion for surfing, which was a pleasant distraction for her. One day, as she stood beneath the weathered pub sign, swaying in the breeze, he asked her why she had become a sommelier.

She didn't have to think before answering: 'I love wine.'

'But you weren't born with a love of wine.'

She turned the questioning around. 'What made you start surfing?'

'I grew up with it. Australia is full of surfers. I used to do it professionally.' He gave a forced laugh, the first time she'd seen him look uncomfortable, then added, 'But that was my parents' dream, not mine. I just surf for fun now. Ever tried it?' He grinned, his joy clear.

'Never.'

'I could teach ya.'

She shook her head. She was too busy to frolic in the sea. 'Thanks, but no. I've got a lot of important stuff to do, and anyway, that water's freezing.'

'Aw go on. Live a little. What's more important than having fun?'

She didn't hesitate. 'Wine. It's my life really.'

'Wow, your life . . .' he said, his eyes widening. 'Did you grow up on a vineyard?'

She laughed. 'No, not many of those in Devon, but my parents loved fine wine. Every milestone was marked with a special bottle.'

Saying those words brought up an image of her parents and a dusty bottle of red wine. Fiona had been about twelve. She couldn't recall what was being celebrated, nor what they had eaten, but she remembered the dining room table covered with a linen tablecloth and her mother polishing crystal wine glasses. All day, that wine bottle had been the focus. Her parents urged her to shower and dress up for dinner, then the family gathered around the bottle with the same reverence as pilgrims before a sacred shrine. Her father carefully removed the cork, sniffed it, then poured a small amount; he swirled, inspected, tasted, sighed with pleasure and passed a glass to her mother, who repeated the exercise.

'Fi is old enough to try this,' her mother said. 'Give her a tiny glass.'

As her father poured, Fiona held her breath. She concentrated on the bottle, thrilled to be part of their celebration for the first time. He passed over the glass and she tossed it back like orange squash. Her tongue puckered and she fought to keep her face neutral. She had been expecting it to be sweet like the communion wine Aunt Ivy served at Brambleton Church on Sundays, but it was tangy and sharp. The flavours and their ability to please her parents intrigued Fiona, piquing her interest. Of course, she now knew the tanginess was from the tannins and had often wondered what that first wine she tasted had been, the one that had crystallized her journey into the wine world. Ru had never asked her that question. It was refreshing to meet someone less absorbed in their own passion. She smiled at Josh.

'My parents loved fine wine and when I expressed an interest in the subject, they encouraged me to study it.'

'I don't know anything about wine.' He sucked at his vape, letting out a sickly-sweet smelling mist; Fiona didn't want to ask what was in that cloud of nasties. Josh's vaping habit didn't square with his surfing hobby. She wondered why he didn't quit, maybe he lacked the will power? 'If you teach me about wine, I could teach you to surf.'

She flipped her hair back, a genuine smile spreading across her face. She didn't want to learn to surf, but it would be lovely to share her knowledge of wine with someone as enthusiastic as Josh. And it would take her mind off Ru. 'I don't mind teaching you about wine. But let's take a raincheck on the surf lesson.'

Fiona wiped the last remnants of lunch service from the polished bar top. The windows were open, letting in the warm summer air which carried the gentle sound of waves lapping against the harbour wall and the distant laughter of children playing on the beach. The restaurant had settled into a lazy hum of conversation, punctuated by clinking glasses and an occasional burst of laughter. Fiona glanced up to see Rose approaching, her hands cradling a brown envelope.

'You did a great job again this week, Fiona,' Rose said, her south London accent reminding Fiona of the life she had left behind. 'Here's your monthly pay packet. It's cash, but don't worry, there's a payslip in there. Everything is done properly through accountants.'

Accepting the envelope, Fiona felt a flutter of gratitude. It was more than just the money, although she needed that badly enough. It was acknowledgement of her hard work and the sense of belonging that Rose and the team offered her. She fumbled with the package, the crinkling texture rough against her fingertips, and took a deep breath. 'Thank you, Rose,' she replied, her voice steady but tinged with emotion. 'I really appreciate it.' The words felt inadequate.

As she opened the envelope carefully, the crisp notes inside felt foreign to her hands. She riffled through, counting the money. Far from the salary she had grown accustomed to in London, this would barely cover her direct debits. It would take her decades to pay off her debts at this rate. The realization settled over her like the shadow of a storm – the minimum wage was a harsh reality check. She needed to retake that exam as soon as the next date became available. She would register for email alerts from the CMS, the Court of Master Sommeliers, so she didn't miss the opportunity

As she tucked the pay packet safely into her pocket, she closed her eyes for a moment, sensing a glimmer of hope. This seaside pub, with its cranky chef, enthusiastic Aussie KP, and fine wine list, might be the place where she could rebuild her life, one service at a time. This job was a lifeline, a chance to breathe and to regroup so she could pass that wretched exam.

Back in Ivy's cottage, she counted out half her wages, folded the notes in half and tucked them under the kettle where her aunt would see them. She would pay the balance into her account. She bounded up the stairs and flopped onto the patchwork quilt with a wine book.

An hour later, the door opened. Ivy was waving the folded wad of notes.

'What's this?'

'You're lending me the money for my exam, so I want to pay my way,' mumbled Fiona.

Ivy came closer. 'Nonsense. It's lovely to have you. When are you going up to London?'

She wasn't. She couldn't. London was her old life, one she

tried every minute to forget – she was concentrating on building a new one. Her aunt sat on the edge of the bed, which squeaked as if it too was critical of Fiona's actions. Ivy clasped her hands together in prayer. 'I love you like a daughter, but I don't love what you are doing to a fine man. You're not being fair or kind, and you are both of those things. It's been nearly a month since you had your tiff, and you haven't spoken to him yet.'

Fiona screwed up her face. It was hardly just a lover's tiff! 'How do you know?'

Ivy pursed her lips. 'Because I *have* spoken to him.'

Six

Fiona puffed out her chest. Had Ru called Ivy or was her aunt interfering?

'You've blocked his number, haven't you?' said Ivy, 'You're behaving like a child. We're talking about a grown man who asked you to marry him, not a teenager with a crush. Doesn't he deserve an explanation? Rejection is painful, but it must be agony not knowing what you've done to deserve it.'

Briefly, Fiona closed her eyes, suppressing a memory of Ru's face, wishing she could trace a finger over his jawline one last time. 'Ru made a mistake. He chose someone who wasn't good enough for him.'

'What nonsense! Anyway, isn't that for him to decide? Fiona, my love, even if you don't talk to him as a lover, you must speak to him as a financial partner – you run a restaurant and own a flat together.'

Fiona cocked her head to one side. 'We *used* to run a restaurant together. We don't anymore. And we aren't financial partners.' Not after she'd failed her exams. To divert her aunt, she talked about the chaos in the pub kitchen. 'Poor Josh takes a pasting from George's temper, but he takes it in good spirit. Anyway, Rose's mum is going to help out and they're advertising for a junior so things should settle down.'

'Don't try and change the subject. When are you going to speak to Ru?'

'I don't need to. He'll sort it. He's good at everything. I must concentrate on getting into the CMS.'

'Why? You know more than anyone could ever ask of you – why do you want to be able to recognize a wine in a blind tasting?' Ivy stood, leaning over her niece, putting her arms either side of her on the pillow, and said, 'Let me know when you're up to talking this through sensibly.'

The door shut. As Fiona picked up her book, she rearranged the pillow behind her and, feeling something beneath the linen, pulled it out. It was the folded wad of money, left discreetly as if by an overly generous tooth fairy.

On the first Tuesday in September, Fiona woke to the sound of laughter. A car horn honked. She heard the high-pitched shrieks of excited children and sat up to yank back the curtain. Across the road youngsters were hurtling round the primary school playground, buzzing with energy like popcorn in a hot saucepan.

With a heavy heart, she watched. After she passed her exams, her next dream involved raising a family – two or three kids, not a single child, like she had been. She sighed. Now that she had split up with Ru, would that ever happen for her? He would have been such a good father; he was always so patient with his team. But how would those children have fared in a family where one parent was the star, and the other was just the also-ran? It wouldn't have been a good example to set and would probably have ended in divorce when Ru realized Fiona wasn't good enough and found someone who was.

Her eyes fell on the stack of study flashcards she'd ordered online. She reached for one and cuddled it against her chest. She was creating a rock-solid foundation for her future: a proper qualification which would command the sort of salary that enabled her to repay her debts and finance a stable life. By then, she should be over Ru and could start to look for love again.

As always, Fiona arrived early for lunch service. Another motorcycle courier was accelerating away, leaving George looking like he needed a decent night's sleep.

'Good afternoon, George,' she called.

He looked up, a startled expression on his face. 'Is it?' he muttered, scrambling up the steps looking like a man dodging deadlines that were in hot pursuit. *Poor man* thought Fiona. George clearly didn't deal with stress as well as Ru.

Rose was behind reception as George trudged past her.

'Cheer up, Grumpy. The cavalry is in sight!' Rose said breezily, 'Mum's coming in to help, and there are a few replies to the advert,' – her tone became resigned – 'though I've no idea when I'll get a chance to look at those with the kids' homework to supervise.'

Having overseen recruitment for the restaurant, Fiona knew how important a speedy response was to securing talent. And that was in London, let alone a rural position. She could spare an afternoon away from her studies to be with two children as endearing as Becky and Timmy. 'I could stay and supervise homework so you can crack on.'

'Really?' said Rose. 'That would be great. I don't know how I managed without you.'

Fiona felt the stirrings of pride, delighted to be needed again.

It was another busy lunch service and in the warm kitchen there was a powerful aroma of rosemary and seared lamb that mingled with a sharper scent. Fiona tracked that down to an oven tray George was deglazing, creating a sharp, vibrant smell from the acidity and alcohol of wine evaporating quickly in the hot pan. Next to him was a woman who introduced herself as Pat. She was the same size and shape as Rose and spoke with an equally strong south-London accent. Pat was chopping vegetables, the knife jerky and clumsy in her hands.

Fiona caught sight of Josh across the kitchen, his head down over a stack of dishes, whistling a cheery tune that cut through the noise.

'Fiona!' Josh's voice was bright. He glanced her way, eyes sparkling beneath the sweat beading on his forehead. 'Had any thoughts about wine lessons?' She couldn't ignore her studies, but something about Josh's enthusiasm – so fresh, so eager – nudged her to carve out time. She would plan each lesson – she didn't want to overwhelm him. Anyway, wasn't teaching one of the best ways to learn?

Through the clatter and steam, she realized thinking about teaching Josh was giving her a surprisingly warm sensation that had been distinctly lacking these last weeks. Although he was younger than her, there was a cockiness to his presence she found herself drawn to, something almost dangerous amid the humdrum of her life.

'Service!' boomed George. Two plates clinked against the metal serving counter. Fiona picked them up glancing at the order slip to check the table number. As she turned back to the dining room, her pulse quickened slightly. Maybe this would be more than just a lesson in wine.

Rose and George lived in a low-ceilinged flat tucked away in the pub's attic. Later that afternoon, in the flat's surprisingly spacious reception room, Becky and Timmy sat cross-legged on the floor with sketchpads in their laps. Fiona moved between them on all fours, dipping her face close to each child in turn. Becky's task was to draw a picture of her favourite animal, but she couldn't decide between an elephant and a dog. Knowing the child would have to write the name of the animal on the picture, Fiona was promoting the merits of the dog. Timmy's homework was to sketch a simple map of his neighbourhood and label important landmarks like the shops, the park or a friend's house. The top half of the boy's paper was hatched in blue crayon, the words 'Timmy's Sea' written in shaky misshapen letters.

In a corner, George sat at a desk scribbling, sighing and scratching his head. 'Daddy,' whined Timmy.

Fiona leaned across to the boy. 'Ask me, Timmy, your daddy's busy.'

'I want to ask Daddy.'

'Shush! I need to concentrate,' groaned George.

Rose dashed in waving a piece of paper and rushed over to her husband, 'George,' she whispered. And thrust the page at him.

'Not now,' he moaned.

The page rustled. 'George, look at this. Now.'

Sighing, he took the paper off her. Rose snatched up a pen from his desk. 'Mind if I borrow this? I've lost mine.'

Fiona removed the blue crayon from Timmy's grip and replaced it with a brown one. 'Why not draw the road up to the school? Then you could draw in where you live and maybe show where your grandparents live too?' she suggested.

Fiona switched her attention to Becky, who was drawing a stick dog, but this one had a trunk instead of a snout. 'What are you drawing there?'

'It's an *ele-dog*,' announced Becky. *Hmmm*, thought Fiona. How was she going to untangle this one without a tantrum?

George handed the paper back to his wife. 'Is this the best candidate?' moaned George, 'I'm grateful for Pat's help, but she takes five minutes to chop an onion.'

'Brambleton's a bit of a backwater for young chefs.' said Rose.

'We need someone who wants to surf like Josh don't we . . .' said George, closing and locking his desk.

Watching the ele-dog take shape, Fiona didn't interfere. There was no requirement for the subject to be a real animal. A long tail emerged, followed by multiple whiskers, each a similar length to the tail, making Fiona smile. 'Slow progress, Rose?'

Rose wandered over. 'Most of the applicants were straight out of school. Mum's doing her best, but' she dropped her tone to a conspiratorial whisper, 'I would like Mr Grumpy back to normal. Love may be accepting your partner's imperfections but there are moments . . .'

Fiona laughed. 'He is a bit stressed. Probably not sleeping well. How many years have you two been together?'

'If you asked me before Mum started helping him, I'd have answered too long,' quipped Rose. 'How's the homework going down there?'

'Fine, and I'm enjoying myself too.'

Rose crouched to inspect the drawings. 'They both look marvellous, darlings.' She raised her head, winked at Fiona and pointed at her daughter's picture mouthing, 'What is that?'

Fiona giggled. 'Don't you recognize an ele-dog when you see one?'

Not attempting to keep a straight face, Fiona explained what Becky was drawing,

'I see,' murmured Rose, stifling a laugh. 'How are you coping? Were you and your ex together long?'

Fiona suppressed a vision of Ru. She could almost feel his arms around her. She gulped away the memory. 'Three years.'

'That's a long time. George and I have been together about ten years. Not all plain sailing, I can tell you.'

'And your glue?'

Rose shrugged. 'Mutual respect?'

Fiona smiled inwardly. Mutual respect required equality between partners. Though painful, Fiona had made the right decision.

On her way to the pub for that evening's shift, Fiona noticed the sun beginning its leisurely descent over the village, washing the pavements in a soft amber shimmer. Passing her on their way back up from the beach, holidaymakers dawdled, their faces bronzed, a few tinged a painful-looking pink. She would treat herself to a holiday once she was qualified; the upside of having no social life was that studying had become second nature.

As the last of the evening diners finished their meals, Fiona stacked the empty wine bottles on the bar with practised precision, glancing up occasionally to see if anyone needed her attention. She caught sight of Josh hovering nearby, arms crossed, a knowing smirk playing on his lips. She suppressed an eye roll as he leaned casually against the counter, his apron slung low on his hips.

'Oi, Fiona!' he called out, loud enough to turn heads. His grin widened as he noticed Rose watching.

She turned toward him, one eyebrow raised. 'Yes, what is it?'

'That wine lesson you mentioned,' he drawled, running a hand through his messy, dark hair. 'Between you and me,' – he winked – 'the way you lot handle your wines here in Europe is a bit rough. No offence, but back home in the Barossa Valley, we've got standards.'

Fiona chuckled despite herself. She could begin with the basics – what wine was and the broad categories – then move on to grape varieties. That wouldn't take much planning.

'Let's meet in the staffroom tomorrow,' she suggested. 'Thirty minutes before work. We'll see if your knowledge matches your confidence.'

'Beauty!' Josh pushed off from the counter with a theatrical flourish. 'Fair warning though – I'm a quick study. Might end up giving you a run for your money.'

Later, as she strolled back up the hill through the quiet village, she breathed in the evening's stillness. The cool air brushed gently against her cheeks. Each window she passed seemed to hold a small, silent world. Fiona smiled; for the first time in ages, she was looking forward to tomorrow.

The following evening, already dressed for evening service, Fiona and Josh sat side by side in the staffroom, which was small, hot and stuffy from the sun streaming through the windows all day. Her pupil had brought a notepad and pen, and there was a sparkle in his eyes.

Fiona got up, fanning herself with a hand. 'Let's open a window before we both doze off in this heat.'

With a breeze circulating, she pulled out her notes, feeling the same ripple of nerves she always got before a blind tasting. Josh's face, shining with anticipation, was unnerving. She hoped she would live up to his expectations.

Josh sprawled in his chair, with a notepad balanced on one knee, twirling his pen between his fingers. His eyes never left her face.

'Wine is a world of endless flavours and styles, but at its heart, it's fermented grape juice. There are five main types of wine: red, white, rosé, sparkling and dessert, which some people refer to as pudding wine or sweet wine . . .'

As Fiona explained the basics, Josh leaned forward, the chair legs hitting the floor with a *thunk*.

'Fancy grabbing a glass sometime? For educational purposes, of course.' He winked.

Fiona felt herself blush. Were all Australians this forward? It was flattering to be flirted with, but she had no intention of reciprocating. She decided to change the subject.

'What part of Australia are you from? And how did you end up working in Brambleton?'

'Sydney. My gran used to live in Brambleton, before she came to live with us in Aus. She was a dinner lady at the local school. She told me a lot about the place, and I've always wanted to visit, try out the surf.'

'And does the surf live up to expectations?'

'I can see you're warming to the idea of a surf lesson.' He chuckled. 'It's not Snapper Rocks or Bells Beach, but it's fun. You can get good days, but it's no match for Australia's top spots. Easy place to learn.'

Though she couldn't help smiling, she steered the conversation back to wine. 'Let's focus on wine.'

'Right then, teach,' he said, but his grin suggested he'd caught her earlier blush. 'How do you decide what to recommend to a customer? Or do you just flog them the most expensive wine on the list? Some of the Barossa Valley wines cost more than a decent surfboard, don't they?'

She stiffened. 'And they're worth every penny, but no, that's the last thing a good sommelier does. It's kind of personal preference—'

'Like dating,' he interjected smoothly. 'Gotta know what suits, yeah?'

She pressed on, fighting to keep her voice steady. 'Pairing wine well with food can enhance both. I try to match the intensity: rich foods go well with full-bodied wines, whereas lighter dishes suit more delicate wines. For example, a classic claret . . .' She caught herself, glanced at him with an inquiring expression then asked if he was familiar with that term.

'George drinks claret,' Josh said. She noticed he was actually taking notes now, despite his flirting. 'Red wine from France. Though personally, I prefer Australian reds – bold, intense, not afraid to make a statement.' His eyes met hers meaningfully.

Through the open window Fiona heard a van screech to a halt, prompting her to wrap up the lesson. She glanced at her watch, then at Josh, who was watching her with undisguised interest.

'You really love this, don't you?' he said, his voice softer now, genuine. 'Is that what makes you such a good sommelier? Or is it just that you're passionate about everything you do?'

Laughing, Fiona brushed a lock of hair back, acutely aware of his gaze following the movement. 'Yes and no. I'm enthusiastic about wine, sure, but there's more to it.' She tapped her notes, trying to maintain a professional distance even as something warm and dangerous flickered in her chest. 'Being a good sommelier is about learning enough that I convince the Court of Master Sommeliers that I belong in their ranks.'

Their eyes met. His interest was obvious, and she felt her breath stolen. 'Well,' he said, standing and letting his hand brush hers, 'reckon you've got at least one person convinced already.'

'Thanks for that,' she replied, her smile widening. 'I have to convince them; prove I'm one of them. But I will if I study hard enough. I'm living with my aunt to save money and spending every spare minute studying.' She gathered up her notes, tucking them into her bag and stowing it beneath her raincoat. 'So do you think this sacrifice you're making to join this court of experts is worth it?' he drawled.

'Of course!'

'Just testing,' he said, jumping upright. 'But it seems to me you get enough joy out of your job already. Why not have some fun alongside it, instead of stuffing that pretty nose of yours in a book?'

Was he teasing her? She decided not to rise to the bait. 'Come on we need to clock on. I don't want George blaming me for making you late for work.'

'Don't remind me,' groaned Josh, thrusting his chair back under the table. 'Pat's a dear, but I can see her solid methodical approach to prep is driving George nuts . . . I gather they've finally found someone . . .'

'Someone experienced?'

'Supposedly' Josh smirked. 'George insisted on a Zoom interview – swore half their CV was pure fiction.'

Fiona laughed, familiar with her share of embellished résumés. 'Standard practice these days. A weekend washing dishes magically transforms into "culinary experience" at some trendy bistro.'

'Exactly. But at this point, anyone who can hold a knife without slicing their finger off will do. It's like waiting for the storm clouds to part when you know there's a rescue ship somewhere on the horizon.'

As they stepped into the quiet of the reception area, Fiona's mind lingered on a vision of joining the CMS. That was her own rescue ship, a vessel she'd tried to board once before, only to find her sea legs unsteady. But this time, she would study the charts more carefully. This time, she would prove herself seaworthy.

'And the great news is,' said Josh, 'this guy wants to be in Devon like me, Rose reckons it's 'cos of the quality of the local produce, but I reckon he's a surfing dude.'

Seven

On the Friday evening when George's new junior was set to arrive, Fiona set off for the pub, expecting the atmosphere in the kitchen to be more relaxed. She reached the harbour, where cottages with pastel coloured façades stood in cheerful contrast to the deep blue of the sea. Flower boxes overflowed with late-blooming geraniums, pansies and violas, a riot of purples and vibrant yellows. In one doorway stood a tub of lavender. It was her favourite flower and made her think of the pots growing on the balcony at the London flat. She hoped Ru was taking care of them.

Peeking through the kitchen window, she couldn't see the new assistant, but she heard a guffaw of laughter from Josh, and George's low rumbling voice sounding brighter than she'd recently heard it. 'I've never tried that. I'm open to all suggestions.'

Behind reception, with slightly blonder, newly styled hair, sat Rose, engulfed in the unmistakable acrylic smell of hairspray. She followed Fiona into the staffroom. 'He's awfully good looking,' she chirped, then winked and added, 'I'll have to keep an eye on you.'

Fiona wrapped herself in an apron and dipped her head to hide a smile. She wasn't anywhere near ready for a new romance, which is why she wasn't encouraging Josh's attentions. 'How many covers tonight, Rose?'

'Half full, but it's a Friday, so there'll be the chancers. Expect us to be busy.'

George bustled in, bringing with him a smell of frying onions. He was whistling a tune she recognized – one Josh often chose.

'How's it going?' asked Rose, an anxious expression distorting her face. 'Is he settling in?'

George grinned at his wife, then engulfed her in a bear hug and kissed her. It was five weeks since anyone other than Ivy had hugged Fiona, and she felt a pang of longing. Ru had been so tactile. She missed their intimacy.

'While I've got you both,' said George, 'we've come up with a special for tonight.'

'Long time since we've offered one of those,' quipped Rose, patting her pockets. 'Fiona, lend me a pen so I can scribble this lot down, would you, love,'

Fiona dug out a spare pen. 'Fire away,' said Rose.

'We're using up that partridge I ended up freezing. We're putting it into a pie. The base is spinach, cream, rich sherry vinegar and pine nuts, topped with the partridge mixture and a sauce that's been simmering for the last two hours.'

'Right,' said Rose, 'Sounds delicious. What's the pastry, and is it gluten-free?'

'No, it's filo – too thin for non-gluten flour. I've kept some of the mix aside and we can cook it in gluten-free puff pastry if someone asks. But it won't be as good.'

'Some of your red burgundies would go well with that combination. Any spices I need to know about?' asked Fiona, mentally scrolling through the wine cellar. 'I might nip down now and grab a few bottles to let them warm up a bit.'

George strode out, talking over his shoulder, 'Dash of this dash of that, nothing overpowering.'

'I think Chef is keen to return to his station,' said Rose laughing.

'I'll finish setting up. You know where the cellar key is, don't you, Fiona?'

Fiona padded down the stone steps, inhaling the musty smell and struggling to block out the memory of that anniversary with Ru, which occasionally still tormented her when she visited the cellar. She focused her attention instead on the wine labels, noting and assessing the quality both of the vintages and the growers. George's uncle had been a serious collector. The wines included famed growers from Bordeaux, Burgundy, Rhône, Tuscany, as well as New World stars from America, Australia, New Zealand and South America. There were even some from South Africa. Passing that bin, she swallowed down a lump in her throat – that was where Ru had been born. She wasn't doing very well at trying to forget him. Tears pricked at the corners of her eyes as more memories flooded in – still fresh, but now bittersweet. She remembered the way he would grin when he fed her a forkful of something he'd been working on, his eyes lighting up with pride, the heat from his kitchen always clinging to his skin. 'Try this, Mousse,' he would whisper, feeding her a confit tomato or a plump, newly sourced olive.

She shouldn't have pictured olives, because their walk through a bustling market in Provence hit her next. There had been an overwhelming rustic tang of olives. His fingers had brushed against hers as they strolled between rows of produce – tomatoes so red and shiny they looked polished, huge basil leaves, bright and fragrant, a hint of citrus zesting the warm breeze. Ru had pressed a finger to his lips thoughtfully, his eyes twinkling as he muttered some new recipe idea. She could almost hear his voice now, deep and confident, full of passion as he talked about flavours, textures, and the way a dish could change someone's mood.

She shook her head, trying to banish the thoughts. No. She had set him free so he could soar, and that meant she must forget him and keep moving forwards with her own life. Work hard in the pub. Pass that wretched exam. Repay her debts. Earn the right to fall in love again – but this time with someone who was a more equal match.

By 8.30 p.m., every table in the dining area was busy and laughter echoed throughout the pub. Fiona seated customers, took drinks orders and explained the menu. The special was popular, as were her wine recommendations. All evening, she jogged into the kitchen, ripping off order slips as she ran, tossing them onto the counter and dashing back out to fetch wines. At one point, she caught a glimpse of the new assistant – a figure hunched over, retrieving something from the walk-in fridge. Just a pair of legs and shoulders, but clearly the promised reinforcement hadn't done a runner. She made a mental note to introduce herself later, when things were less hectic. Rose coped with most of the plates while Fiona spent much of her evening below ground.

She was in the cellar for the eighth time that night, on her haunches scanning the chalk marks for Pomerol. The door was open, and the faint sound of whistling drifted down to her.

Tonight, the kitchen atmosphere seemed better, like a dense fog lifting at sunrise.

Spotting the correct region, Fiona switched her search to pink foil caps and removed a bottle labelled 'Vieux Château Certan'. She checked the year and frowned. Fiona was looking for the 2005 a glorious year for clarets. This was a bottle from 2017. She replaced it and crouched down for the next one. Finally, she located the correct vintage on the last rung of the rack, and clutching the precious bottle, cast a fond look around the room. In November, when the pub wasn't so busy, she'd spend some quality time down here, rearrange the layout and label the different vintages so it was simpler to locate things.

Back upstairs, the roar from the dining room hit her. Rose shot past, four plates of the special balanced in her arms, calling out, 'George says there's only two portions left! Can you hurry up with that wine please and help me. There's service piling up back there.'

The next thirty minutes evaporated as Fiona rushed in and out of the kitchen, responding to George's excited cries of 'service'. As she swept past the prep station, she glimpsed the new junior's hands – steady, confident and male – arranging garnishes. Just hands and a sliver of arms encased in a white chef's jacket, but enough to stir her curiosity. She felt a wave of gratitude that help had finally arrived and found herself hoping he was into surfing; if he was, he would stay, and Josh could use a mate in the water, stop him pestering her to join him. And perhaps the newcomer would enjoy her impromptu wine lessons? The thought of expanding their little educational circle made her smile as she grabbed another tray of starters. She circled the dining room, offering advice and topping up glasses, sprinting to and from the cellar, uncorking and decanting fine wines.

'That was unbelievably good food,' said a woman scraping her plate with a fork. 'Please send my compliments to the chef.'

Fiona felt a flush of pride, smiled at the customer, before collecting the dirty crockery and carrying it through to the kitchen.

'Another happy customer, George,' she said, stowing the plates for an absent Josh. 'The woman sends—' Her breath caught in her throat. She swallowed, staring wide-eyed at George's new assistant. The man smoothed his apron as he raised his eyes to hers.

He was smiling, but his dark eyes radiated sorrow.

'Hi,' said Ruben.

Eight

In front of her, the kitchen swam. Fiona staggered and clutched at the serving counter.

'Fi,' he whispered.

Her eyes darted round the room, checking for George. They were alone. 'What are you doing here?' she hissed.

'What do you think?'

She heard whistling, then Josh ambled in, grinning. 'Fiona, meet the hero of the night.'

'It's a team effort, Josh,' said Ru.

As Fiona turned and stumbled from the room, tears coursing over her face, she could hear Ru still talking. In the staffroom, she yanked her bag and jacket off the hook and fled up the cobbled main street. Halfway through Brambleton she flopped onto a bench and stared out to where lights from the night fishing boats twinkled and sparkled on the inky black sea. What was she going to do now? There was only one reason Ru was here – he hadn't listened to her. He was here to change Fiona's mind.

Succumbing to the hollow emptiness piercing her chest might have been tempting, but it would result in facing new, and worse, heartbreak when he inevitably found someone else who was a better match. How could she distance herself, give herself time to fall out of love with him? Should she tell Rose that Ru was her ex?

That wouldn't work. Asking Rose to choose between Ruben,

the celebrity chef, and Fiona, the nobody, was a sure route to her losing her own job. What if Fiona went back to London? But if she did that, Ru would come after her. Maybe she should go travelling, work her way round Europe from one restaurant to the other. Except now it was autumn, seasonal hires would be thin on the ground, and anyway, her precarious finances wouldn't stretch to buying tickets for travel.

With a heavy heart, she knew what she must do. Stay in Brambleton until her exam. With luck, there would be another sitting soon. All she had to do was keep her job in the pub, throw herself into her studies and smother her love for Ru.

On Saturday morning she awoke full of resolve. She forced herself out of bed and into the shower, then settled herself back on her bed, immersed in the wine world. She was researching a topic close to her heart – the shift towards more eco-friendly practices. She admired those wineries reducing their carbon footprint through organic and biodynamic farming. While organic farming simply avoided chemicals, biodynamic practices ventured into more peculiar territory – burying cow horns filled with manure during specific lunar phases, fermenting yarrow in stag bladders, and spraying vineyards with the burned ashes of the very pests they were trying to eliminate. These medieval sounding rituals followed astronomical calendars and cosmic rhythms. Amusing as these methods seemed, prestigious winemakers swore they produced more vibrant wines with superior terroir expression. Nestled cosily under one of Ivy's many crocheted blankets, she lost herself in her other world, blotting out all thoughts of who would be waiting for her at the pub.

Shortly before eleven, Fiona walked into Brambleton. From here the distant sea looked like a tranquil blue quilt, its surface sparkling with the sun's reflection. All around her, trees were turning colour: an array of soft fawns, yellows and reds, smudged with the occasional dark evergreen. Devon was in the throes of an Indian summer, and the warmth of the sun was a cruel reminder of the holiday she should have spent wrapped in Ru's arms. She understood why he'd followed her. It was a knee-jerk reaction from a supremely confident man focused on his goals – Ru never took no as the definitive answer from anyone.

For most people, having a marriage proposal rejected would extinguish the love flame like a bucket of cold water, but with Ru, it was more akin to pouring petrol on that fire. He would view this as a challenge. She must do everything to prove to him it was a hopeless case.

She passed Brambleton's café cum bookshop, Prosecco & Prose. Outside on the terrace were groups of tourists wearing T-shirts and shorts, many with dogs at their feet. A peal of laughter rang out, at odds with her own mood. Fiona had a sudden thought and retraced her steps. As she pushed open the door, a bell tinkled, and the warm smell of coffee and baking pastry enveloped her. Trish, the owner, stood behind the serving counter. Fiona and Trish had become friendly through Ivy. Trish was slim, with an athletic build and dark eyes that today were uncomfortably similar to those of the man Fiona was trying to forget.

'Hi, Fiona, what can I get you?' asked Trish.

'A job?'

'I thought you were helping Rose. Is that not working out? It's the end of the season, so I'm not sure I've anything to offer.'

'Forget it, it was a long shot. Please don't tell Rose I asked . . .' she took a breath, Trish would soon find out anyway, 'My ex, Ruben has started working in the pub.'

'Ruben?' laughed Trish, 'Cooking in Brambleton? Wow! Think I might book a table.'

Fiona dipped her head, feeling herself well up.

'Sorry, I was being flippant,' said Trish, her voice oozing sympathy. 'Poor you. You're not ready for this, are you?'

That was an understatement. She swallowed. 'I just . . . I needed to get away from him. Get some headspace.'

'It must be hard. I've no idea what you're going through, but if you want to talk, I'm here for you.'

'Thanks,' muttered Fiona, knowing she wouldn't take up the offer. Talking to anyone but Ru was pointless, and she wasn't ready for that conversation yet.

Before turning down the alleyway, she paused. Seagulls wheeled and called above the harbour wall, swooping to ferret among discarded lobster pots and fishing nets tangled on the walkway, no doubt tempted by the fishy smell. Ru, like those birds, was seeking something lost, but this was Fiona's doing. By blocking his number, she had pulled him to Devon like a ship drawn to a harbour's guiding lighthouse.

Fiona glanced one last time at the sunlit beach, gentle waves washing the sand. A couple stood hand in hand with the sea lapping over their feet. While she watched, they embraced, intertwining their arms, and kissed. Fiona let out a soft whimper and fled down the alleyway, tears pouring down her cheeks.

Rounding the corner, she heard laughter, stopped and sniffed her tears to a stop.

'Hey, Fiona,' hollered Josh, 'come join us!'

Beside Josh, looking achingly attractive in his white chef's jacket, Ru lounged against the back door. Fiona scrubbed at her eyes, hoping they weren't swollen and red.

'Josh, could you give me a moment with the sommelier? I'd like to see the cellar,' said Ru.

'No worries, mate.'

Keeping her face down, Fiona sidled past Josh, retrieved the key and led the way to the cellar, all the while conscious that Ru was mere inches behind her. If she stopped in her tracks, his chest would but up against her back. Would his arms snake around her waist? Would his face nuzzle into her neck and murmur 'Mousse' into her ear? She reached the cellar, unlocked it and stood aside to let him pass, then closed the door behind her – she didn't want anyone overhearing them. Fiona switched on the light and took a steadying breath, telling herself to be strong. She was determined she hadn't endured the last five weeks of sorrow in vain. She must not let him sweet talk her into changing her mind.

Fiona padded down the steps. Stopping at the bottom, she kept her head bowed. She couldn't look at him and risk seeing those eyes she loved. 'What are you doing here, Ru?'

'You blocked my calls. I had to see you; explain why I did what I did.'

She sighed; Fiona didn't want to listen to Ru claim his motive wasn't his own career. She would never match his talent or his success; but what hurt was realizing he never truly believed in her own abilities or her vision for that new restaurant, and instead of confronting her directly, he'd gone behind her back to the investors. His admission still burned. And if she stayed with Ru? He'd either find someone more talented eventually, or worse, she'd hold him back, becoming the compromise he silently resented. 'I'm not sure I want to hear your explanation.'

'Please. I agonised over this all the way driving back up to London without you. I get how this must look to you, that you think I went behind your back—'

Her head snapped up. 'Because that's exactly what you did.'

'But I did it for you . . .' he pleaded.

Her jaw fell slack. This was worse than she imagined. 'For me?'

'I knew you weren't ready for that exam; I was trying to protect you. I'm sorry, I was wrong, I should have talked it through with you.' Too dazed to reply, she listened as Ru rambled on. 'And I guessed that's why you turned me down and I get it, but I must put this right between us. I can't concentrate. Ben's even had to take over organizing my new kitchen . . .'

There it was again, that word: 'my'. A small word which punched above its weight. She knew right then that she'd made the right decision. 'I just know we aren't right for each other, Ru,' she spluttered, keeping her eyes away from his handsome face.

'Hey,' he whispered. 'Look at me.'

She couldn't look at him, not while the sight of him still sent an aching shudder of desire through her body. 'Mousse,' he said again, 'please look at me.'

She lifted her face.

He smiled at her and raised his voice. 'That's better.'

'Keep your voice down,' she hissed.

'You're wrong. I know we *are* right for each other, and I'm here to win you back. I still love you and I know you love me. Is this about your failed exam? Or your debts? Who cares about them?'

His words hit her like a punch in the stomach. She was a failure in his eyes and always would be. Somehow, she had to convince him to listen to her – she needed to set him free to meet the right woman, someone worthy of his love.

'Ru, you just don't get it. *I* care. The whole world cares. Without that qualification, I'm nothing.'

'Stop this nonsense. It's a piece of paper. Rose and George don't care that you're not a member of the CMS.'

'This is a pub in Brambleton, not a Michelin-starred London restaurant. When I am in the CMS I can command a proper salary in a proper restaurant.'

He rushed on, his voice thick with emotion. 'We don't need it. Let's just be together. I'll take care of you.'

She felt a hot spurt of frustration. He simply wasn't listening. 'I don't want to be taken care of!' With her heart pounding, she dredged her mind for a way to get him to back off. He wasn't listening to her real reasons, so she'd have to invent something he would believe. She swallowed and summoned all the grief and pain that had built up over the last five weeks. Then she leaned towards him and whispered, 'I was only staying with you for the money, so you could fund my exams.'

His face crumpled. She heard him inhale loudly, then his voice, gruff and tinged with anger, filled the room. 'And I was only with you because I felt sorry for you. You're right – you are a failure, and I want my money back. I can do so much better than a washed-up waitress.'

Finally. The truth. Even though he'd finally said the words she always dreaded, it hadn't made her hate him. His words were like a splinter pulled from flesh. Painful – oh, so painful – but with the promise of respite to come. There was relief in knowing she was right all along. Fiona exhaled, sensing her frustration subside.

'So will you go back to London, please?'

He hesitated. 'No. That's not fair on George and Rose. I've promised to work here as the sous chef. Anyway, Ben's in charge in London. We'll just have to find a way to work together.'

'Strictly professional?'

'Of course,' he said – too fast, too sharp.

'Right.'

'Right.' he echoed.

She didn't reply. Just turned and walked away.

Nine

While laying up for lunch, Fiona tackled Rose. 'Why didn't you tell me who the new sous chef was?'

Rose grinned. 'Thrilling, isn't it!' said Rose. 'We feared it was a prank. I mean, why would a celebrity chef want to work in a Devon country pub, and for the wages of a junior chef?' The phone rang and her boss rushed to answer it. Fiona laid a table and when the phone rang a second time, she prepared another, followed by a third. Her boss was clearly unaware of the history between Fiona and Ru. Should Fiona confess? Rose put down the phone and busied herself at the tables, fiddling with cutlery and glassware, seemingly unable to stop moving, all the time humming.

Fiona decided not to mention anything; she didn't want to make her employers nervous about staff interaction. She would warn Ru that no one knew about their history. They should behave professionally and treat each other as colleagues.

News that the London celebrity chef Ruben Nkosi was cooking at the Smuggler's Inn had spread quickly on social media, resulting in the pub being fully booked until October half-term week. When Rose promised to recruit another helper for front of house, Fiona became tangled in a web of overthinking. She didn't trust Ru to have listened to her when she claimed she had no interest in rekindling their relationship.

If she admitted their shared past, would her boss question why Fiona had concealed the information, jeopardizing her job? Should she have it out with Ru and get him to back out of her life pronto, head off to supervise setting up *his* new restaurant? Each thread she explored took her into dangerous territory. It was best to keep quiet – she needed this job.

One evening, about a week after Ru had shown up at the pub, Fiona arrived as Josh was firing up his vape, but she was so deep in thought that she didn't immediately notice him.

Josh's voice made her startle. 'When can we fix another lesson?'

She watched him take a long pull on his vape, not wanting to dampen his enthusiasm by pointing out the negative effects the habit would have on his palate.

'Unless you'd like a taste of surfing in exchange first? Go on! I dare ya!'

She blushed.

'What are you frightened of Fiona? That you might like it? That having fun might test that resolve to waste your life studying?' He chuckled.

'I'm too old to take up a new sport.'

'That's a crock of shit. Come on, dive in. Grab hold of what life has to offer.'

Fiona felt the breeze on her face and turned to admire the sea, sparkling in the autumn sunshine, the waves curling and rushing inwards before breaking on the beach. It did look inviting.

'Maybe.'

'That's better. Now what about that wine lesson?'

'Whenever you like! Tomorrow afternoon, thirty minutes before prep, like last time?'

Behind her, the back door creaked open, then a soft, powerful voice spoke, the one that still sent a shiver through her core. 'Hi, I need a break from gutting fish.'

She glanced over her shoulder and saw Ru step outside, his hands in his pockets, watching her with an unreadable expression.

'Am I interrupting something?' he asked, his voice deceptively light as he jogged down the steps towards them. 'Or are you just talking about *professional* matters?'

Josh straightened, his hands slipping into his pockets. 'We were talking about wine.'

Ru's mouth twitched into a half-smile, though his eyes held a hard gleam. 'Wine? With Fiona?' His voice had a faint edge. 'You might do better to find a professional.'

Fiona's jaw tightened. 'I've been helping Josh learn a bit about wine. He's interested.'

'Is he now?' Ru's eyes flicked over to Josh 'How *admirable*. Not everyone's got the palate for it, you know,' he added, his tone dripping with casual indifference. 'Especially not those who vape.'

Josh laughed, turning off his vape and pocketing it.

Fiona took a step closer to Josh, her tone firm as she spoke. 'Josh's doing fine. It's just finding the time for lessons.'

'Oh, I'm sure you'll find it,' Ru said, his gaze fixed on her now, his eyes cold. 'Between your shifts, that is.' There was something bitter in his voice, emphasizing she and Josh were junior employees doing shiftwork, and it made her heart twist.

She lifted her chin, meeting his stare with a challenge. 'I will make time.'

Josh shifted awkwardly, as if looking for an escape route from the tension. 'Uh . . . maybe I should just get back inside. I've got stuff to finish up in the kitchen.'

Ru stood his ground, his gaze fixed on Fiona. 'Why don't you? It seems we've all got things to do.'

Fiona smiled at Josh, touching his arm lightly. She noticed a shift in Ru's expression when she made contact with Josh, a flash of something almost vulnerable. 'Thanks, Josh. I'll see you inside, okay?' she said.

Ru's jaw tightened, his eyes darkening as they held her.

'I must get on,' she said, thrown by the coldness in Ru's eyes.

When Fiona arrived early the next evening for Josh's wine tutorial, he was waiting in the staffroom with his notepad and pen. 'What's on the curriculum tonight teacher?' he asked.

'I thought I'd explain the different geographical regions that grow wine – what type they specialize in and why. Sound interesting?'

'Very,' said Josh, his enthusiasm clear.

'Let's start with France. Most people think of it as the original home of wine. It isn't. Historians think the Ancient Greeks were among the first in Europe to cultivate grapevines and produce wine on any significant scale. The Greeks influenced the Romans, and the Romans significantly expanded winemaking in France.' She sat down opposite him, pulling out her *World Atlas of Wine* and opening it to a map of France. 'France is renowned for its diversity in wine production. Bordeaux,' she said, tapping at the area on the map with a fingernail, 'makes bold, tannic reds from grapes like Cabernet Sauvignon and Merlot, which grow well in its warm climate and mineral rich soils.' She shifted her nail, 'Burgundy . . .' She paused. 'Burgundy over here, this is where Pinot Noir and Chardonnay shine. It has a cooler climate and limestone rich soil, giving wines finesse and earthiness. Up here, is the Loire Valley where they make crisp whites, frequently using the Sauvignon Blanc grape, whereas Champagne over here has chalky soils, perfect for sparkling wines.'

Fiona flipped through the book until she found the section on

Italy, turning it toward Josh with a playful smile. 'Look here,' she said, her finger tracing the map. 'Tuscany is famous for Chianti. The deep ruby colour, aromas of cherry and dried herbs – it's like tasting the sun-soaked hills in every sip.'

Josh leaned closer, his warmth brushing against her arm, sending a delightful shiver through her.

'Like your shirt today – it's the same ruby colour as Chianti, right?' He gestured to her blouse with a knowing smirk.

Heat crept up her neck. She hadn't expected him to notice what she was wearing. 'I guess,' she managed, trying to stay professional.

'What about that glass of wine when we're both off duty?' He winked.

Fiona felt her pulse quicken. She'd forgotten what this felt like – the dangerous thrill of attraction, the way simple words could carry such weight. As if sensing her unease, he left the request dangling and reverted to *studious pupil* mode. 'And what about this place?' he asked, pointing to Piedmont.

'Ah, Piedmont! That's where Barolo comes from,' she explained, enjoying sharing her passion. 'It's a complex, age-worthy red – think rich flavours of tar and roses. You need to let it breathe, like letting a story unfold.'

'Sounds amazing,' he replied. 'What about Spain?'

Fiona grinned, spinning the pages to reveal the Iberian Peninsula. 'Spain has a rich history of winemaking. From Rioja's vibrant reds to elegant whites, there's so much diversity.' She paused, enjoying his interest. 'These countries have been crafting wines for centuries, laying the groundwork for what we now know as *New World* wines.'

'New World?' Josh echoed, leaning back in his chair with a cocky grin. 'Now you're talking my language.'

She glanced at her watch; the pub doors would open in ten

minutes. 'We've got just enough time to explore a few.' She turned to the Americas. 'California – big, ripe Cabernet Sauvignons thrive in its sunny climate. And Oregon is known for delicate Pinot Noirs, with its climate much like the cool, crisp air of Burgundy.'

'What about South America?' Josh asked, shifting closer. Despite the cleaning products clinging to his clothes, she caught a hint of something else – spice, maybe sandalwood. His cologne? She told herself her interest in his scent was strictly professional, testing her ability to detect scents. She stuck to their topic.

'Great question! Argentina and Chile are giants in the wine world.'

'And what about back home?' He flashed that disarming smile again. 'Barossa Valley's giving the French a run for their money these days.'

She chuckled, trying to ignore how his proximity made her pulse quicken. It must be his laid-back Aussie charm. He probably had this effect on all women. 'Actually, even here in the UK, we've come a long way. English wine used to be a bit of a joke, but not anymore. We produce some excellent sparkling wines now.'

'As sparkly as you?' He said and she smiled despite herself. She couldn't remember the last time someone had flirted so openly with her. Ru had saved his flirtation for the customers.

'But seriously,' he continued. 'Is it hard to compete with the big brands?'

Fiona nodded. 'It is. Wine has become a commodity, and many consumers prioritize price over quality. It's tough for artisanal wines that are made with care to break through.'

Josh watched her intently and she wondered what he was thinking about behind that bold stare. Suddenly her curiosity was piqued: what had made this supremely confident man quit professional surfing? Did he not have the willpower needed to make the sacrifices, like she did?

'So, what made you give up being a professional surfer? Is that why you're travelling? Did you just quit?' The moment the words were out of her mouth Fiona regretted them. Was she being too personal?

'No. I gave that dream up when I was seventeen. I was good enough to get to the top, but I was training six hours a day – I wasn't living.'

'That's a pretty grown-up realization for a seventeen year old.'

A wistful look came over him. 'Yeah, well . . . I had my reasons.'

There was a moment's silence which Josh broke, his voice husky, 'What's next in our . . . *exploration*?'

Fiona couldn't help the blush that rushed to her cheeks at his suggestive tone. 'We could delve into food pairing,' she suggested. 'Once you grasp the basics, we'll explore how flavours dance together.'

His smile turned teasing. 'Teach me how to taste?' he said, and the way he held her gaze made it clear he wasn't just talking about wine anymore. 'Something about your passion for all this tells me you'd be an amazing teacher.'

She knew she should keep her distance, but it was hard not to get drawn in by his open smile, laid-back demeanour and flirtatious banter. And the praise he lavished made her feel good about herself and her professional skills, perhaps for the first time since arriving in Devon. What was the harm in it? Would a little light flirtation really hurt anyone if it helped distract her from the mess she'd made of her life?

The door slammed against the wall, giving her an answer. Fiona spun round, meeting Ru's confident gaze.

'Fiona! I thought I'd find you in here,' Ru boomed, his presence like a summer storm. The light caught his sharp jawline and assured smile.

'Ruben,' she said, detecting her mouth suddenly go dry. 'Can't you see we're in the middle of something?'

He strode to the table, picked up her book, saying. 'Wine. Interesting.' He turned to Josh, eyes narrowing. 'George wants you back at the pots.'

Josh's chair scraped against the floor. He gave Ruben a mock salute and sauntered out.

Fiona sighed. When Ru was in the room, she felt like she was at the top of a rollercoaster about to plunge. It made it impossible to concentrate on anything else.

'Was that everything, Ru?'

'Just looking after you, Fi,' he said. 'If a head chef isn't good enough for you, then where does an Aussie pot washer come on the list?'

Fiona felt her hackles rise. Ru had never been the sort of person to be snide about junior roles in the kitchen. 'Let's not make this any more difficult than it already is. We said we'd keep it professional, remember?'

'Oh, I remember,' said Ru bitterly. He turned and walked back to the kitchen, taking a piece of her heart with him.

Fiona was in the staffroom pulling off her apron, her mind composing another tutorial for Josh, when she heard raised voices outside. Ignoring them, she grabbed her handbag, thinking that before they started tasting anything, she should cover the different types of wine in a bit more detail. She trotted through reception.

Outside, she paused on the top step. Below her, Ru was standing with his arms around two laughing women. He was smiling broadly, while a third woman snapped pictures on a phone.

'Autograph, autograph, please!' squealed one woman. Fiona

watched the scene unfold, her lips tightening involuntarily. It was all so familiar. The way Ru worked a crowd, being effortlessly charming while soaking up the attention – it was like watching a rerun of a show she knew by heart.

A memory came sharp and vivid: Ru in the open plan kitchen of the Fork & Cork, sweet-talking the guests as though they were old friends. She could see him there, leaning casually against the counter, his laugh loud and practised. Any time she had confronted him about his relentless flirting, he would brush it off with the same defence: 'It's part of the job, Fiona.'

The last time they'd had that argument, her patience had worn thin. Her retort had been biting, and she remembered it landing like a slap: 'But you don't have to look like you're enjoying it so much.'

His reply was instantaneous. 'Tell me how to flirt without doing that?'

She huffed. She didn't think it was just an act. Not anymore. Maybe a year ago when some of his fans started getting frisky, Ru had responded because he thought it was good for business, but recently she believed he was courting adulation, and thrived on it, addicted to his own fame.

His tone softened. 'Don't let the jealousy monster get to you, Fi. You know you're the only woman I love. Isn't that enough?'

Now, seeing him buzzing, she wondered what it must be like for Ru to work shut away, deprived of a stage. It was a bit like asking an opera singer to perform behind the stage curtains, muffling their voice.

Nearby, Rose and George stood watching the spectacle. 'Look at this – no one ever asks me for my photo,' said George.

Rose dug her husband in the ribs. 'Better learn how it's done, love. He won't be here forever.'

Fiona spoke in a sarcastic tone, 'Yes, all hail the great Ruben

. . . blessing us mere mortals with his gourmet touch.'

For a moment, Ru's smile seemed to fade, as if her words had stung him.

Rose turned, a look of astonishment on her face. 'Fiona!' she cried.

George frowned, 'Come on, no need to be so critical. The man's just doing his job.'

'Sure, George,' muttered Fiona. 'My mistake, I thought he was the sous chef. Here to help *you*.' She hesitated, not wanting to push past Ru's fans. Ru posed for one more photo, then shot Fiona a hurt look before jogging up the steps and slipping back inside.

She heard the door click shut. Marriage to Ru would have been a disaster. Once she was qualified, she would repay those debts and forge a new life without him . . . But she wished her heart didn't ache each time she set eyes on him. As the door clicked shut behind him, another voice called her name – warm, steady, the Australian accent omehow both familiar and new – making her heart flutter for reasons she wasn't ready to examine.

Ten

On Saturday evening, a new woman joined the serving team. Kim. She was the daughter of Rose's accountant. Kim's parents had invested in several local restaurants, and she was keen to learn all about fine dining. Kim was in her mid-twenties and physically reminded Fiona a little of herself, being short, with a round, pretty, smiley face. But unlike Fiona's curves, the new waitress was petite and evidently not short of money. Kim wore the sort of designer clothes Fiona was used to seeing customers wear, not the waiting staff. When Rose introduced the new team member to Josh, Ru and George, Fiona felt the pulse of testosterone shoot round the kitchen.

'Right,' said George, fastening a clean apron round his midriff, 'curtains up. Let's have a great service, everyone.'

That evening, the packed dining room buzzed with anticipation, as if everyone expected a rock star to entertain them. Against a backdrop of clinking glassware and the gentle scrape of cutlery on plates, Fiona soon forgot about who was cooking the food. Murmurs and gasps of appreciation rewarded each meal she delivered. She pasted on her professional smile, serving meticulously arranged plates, with the aromas of truffle oil and the familiar unctuous sauces Ruben was famous for, casting her back to life at the London restaurant.

Fiona was discussing the merits of the 2008 and 2009 claret

vintages with a customer when she caught the eye of another diner. It was difficult not to. He was waving both arms above his head in windmill fashion. She excused herself and switched tables.

'At last. Caught your attention,' said the windmilling man, a trace of irritation in his voice. 'My wife has changed her mind. She would like her steak blue, not rare.'

'Not a problem, sir.' Fiona said, smiling, 'I'll tell Chef now.'

'And could you find out what's happened to our wine?'

Fiona's smiled slipped. This was Kim's table. She told herself not to be critical. A busy restaurant was a tough place for a new waitress on her first night, and if the couple was waiting for a cellared wine, Kim wouldn't be able to fetch it. 'Let me investigate that for you now, sir.' Hoping to ease his tension, she verified the order, fetched the wine, then scanned the room. After a few moments, she concluded Kim must be in the kitchen.

Fiona pushed at the swing door, heard the hum of ovens, and inhaled the delicious smell of baking bread. At the service counter, Kim was fiddling with her hair, a moonstruck expression on her face. Fiona took a closer look; Kim was staring at the sous chef.

'Service!' Ru called out, sending a shiver of regret through Fiona. She dipped her head to avoid meeting his eyes, and said, 'Table 3 now wants their steak blue.'

Someone grunted. She looked up. Ru was pointing at the service bar: 'that's Table 3.'

'Is it blue?'

'No, it's rare, like the order slip says.'

Fiona swallowed, fixing her gaze on the plate. 'The wife wants blue.'

'The order slip says *rare*.'

Fiona lifted her eyes, meeting Ru's dark ones, which seemed to radiate misery. 'She changed her mind.'

'I'm good,' said Ru. 'I'm intuitive, but I am not telepathic.'

Fiona glared at Kim, who was smirking as she chirped. 'I didn't take the changed order, so don't expect me to take this to their table. They're friends of my parents. He will not react well to this mishap.'

Wiping his hands on his apron, George joined the crowd at the service bar. 'What's going on over here?'

Wanting to point out that if Kim knew the customers, it would be better for her to handle the incident, Fiona gritted her teeth. 'Let me try,' she said. Collecting the plates, she turned and, hearing a giggle, peeked out from the corner of her eye. Kim was leaning on the service counter, batting her eyes at Ru. Fiona stalked out.

Before she reached Table 3, the man called out, 'am I too late to change the wine order?'

What was it about this couple flip-flopping around with their order? Then she had a sudden thought – this was just the sort of sneaky tactics some restaurant critics used. 'No, sir,' she said, forcing herself to look at his florid face.

'Can you recommend something a little cheaper?'

She put the steak down in front of Mr Florid's wife, apologizing that she'd been too late to change it to blue.

'Well, you can take that back then, straight away,' the man snapped.

'Richard,' scolded his wife, 'it's my meal. I don't mind if it's rare. You know I only ask for it blue because I expect it to be overcooked.' The wife looked up at Fiona, 'If this is properly rare, it'll be just as I want it.'

Fiona spoke confidently; Ru would never over cook meat. 'Chef knows how to cook a rare steak, and the good news is that I have the perfect wine for you to try. If you want a great value Bordeaux blend, I recommend the Kanonkop Paul Sauer, from South Africa.'

The customer's face went from florid to red. 'I don't expect a sommelier to try flogging me a wine I can buy in the supermarket for a tenner.'

Realizing the customer had mistaken her recommendation for Kanonkop's signature wine for their entry-level Bordeaux blend, she lowered her voice, careful not to aggravate him further. 'The Paul Sauer is their flagship wine, sir, made from selected, mature vines that are over twenty-five years old. The older vines produce smaller fruit, which contribute to greater concentration, complexity and depth in the wine. It will only cost you £50, not the £125 your initial choice would have cost.'

As the man digested the news, internally Fiona ran through her reasons for pairing her selection with a rare steak.

'Sounds ideal doesn't it, darling?' said the wife. Fiona warmed to her. This woman endured her husband daily; Fiona could manage an evening.

After the last guest had left, Fiona cleared their coffee cups congratulating herself on defusing 'Steakgate'.

At a corner table, George and Rose were deep in discussion, a pile of credit card slips in front of them. Fiona took her loaded tray into the kitchen, where Ru was chopping fish bones, the knife flying up and down as fast as lightning striking the ground. Ru wiped his hands on a tea towel, a half-smile forming as Kim stood beside him untying her apron. 'Quick opinion – trying out a new halibut dish. You think it'd sing more with white wine, a splash of brandy, or maybe something citrusy?'

Kim froze mid-step, caught like a dropped plate. 'Oh! Uh . . . I'd say . . . brandy? Or citrus? Both?' Her voice wobbled into a laugh. 'Hard to say, really. I'm not great at . . . those kinds of details.'

Ru tilted his head, amused. 'Alright. I'll ask Fiona.'

Kim's smile faltered. She turned too fast, and as her eyes

caught Fiona's her jaw twitched. As Fiona passed Ru, carrying her tray to the washing area, he spoke, 'I need to marinade some meat. What wine do you suggest?'

It was a simple request; one he'd often made in London. Why have a trained sommelier and not seek advice? But she suspected he had been waiting all evening to corner her. She dumped the tray next to the sinks.

'Is that the last of it?' asked Josh, 'If not, I'm taking a vape break.'

'Last load,' she said confidently. 'What's this wine for, Ruben?'

Putting the knife down, he turned and gave her a challenging look. The familiar intensity in his gaze sent a shiver down her spine, a painful reminder of everything she had lost. Regret coiled in her chest; it was difficult letting go of someone so effortlessly charismatic. 'Boeuf Bourguignon.'

'Well, it has to be a red Burgundy then, doesn't it.'

'None of that in the kitchen.' He said flashing her a knowing smile.

'Come on then,' she said, opening the drawer and collecting the key. Reminding herself to stay brisk and professional she added, 'this way, Ruben,' and waited for him to follow.

In the corridor, they met George, and she mentioned they were fetching a Burgundy 'for Ruben's marinade'.

'As long as you only use the old stuff,' he quipped, chuckling to himself at his own joke.

Fiona unlocked the cellar and switched on the lights.

Halfway down the steps, feeling the cool damp of the cellar pressing against her skin, she stopped and sighed. With her eyes closed, the electric memory of their first kiss flickered through her mind. Like their anniversary date, their first kiss had been in a cellar, suffused with the same faint, earthy scent of aged pine and damp stone that she could smell now.

That night, hints of thyme and the aniseed scent of fennel had drifted down from the kitchen above – a kitchen where, until seconds earlier, Ru had been working. On a whim, they had slipped away, escaping the rattle of plates and the low drone of the exhaust fan. She could still feel the thrill of that stolen moment, the way the world had seemed to pause as they'd descended into the dim, quiet space together.

That night the only light had been from a single, dusty bulb that etched murky patterns along the stone walls. They paused by the tasting table, and he had taken a tentative step closer, before slowly raising a hand to touch her face with his thumb. Fiona had taken his other hand in hers, fingers stroking his palm, caressing the skin, rough from years of work. She'd pulled him towards her, felt the faint scratch of uneven bricks as she leaned back against the wall and drew him closer still. Their breath echoed softly in the small space, each exhale mingling with the still, damp air.

There was a pause, a quiet that seemed to stretch, filled with something both tender and electric. Fiona felt the heat radiating from him, warming her skin in the cellar's chill. Then, his lips had found hers, tentative yet sure, soft and tasting faintly of salt. The touch sent a spark down her spine, the faint aroma of herbs and wine lingering between them.

Fiona tried to blink away the image now as she walked down the stone steps, but with Ru behind her, his breath moist on her neck, the intense memory lingered. Was he remembering the moment too? Or had he now successfully closed his heart, and really did just need help choosing a Burgundy? She turned, looking up into his eyes. His lips parted, his mouth lowered towards hers. She could almost taste the salty tang of him.

'Yo!' came a voice, and they both turned toward the noise. Josh's broad frame filled the doorway. 'Got a minute to show your keenest pupil around the cellar?' he asked, clomping down the stairs.

Fiona snapped into action and led the way to the Burgundy section. If there had been a moment to ask Ruben what he had been really thinking, it was well and truly over.

Sunday was Fiona's day off. She stayed in bed, listening for the clunk of the front door, followed by Ivy's fading footsteps on the pathway. Moments later, an engine rumbled to life, and she listened as it gradually receded into silence, leaving the house unnervingly still.

She slipped out of bed, showered, dressed and collected her wine books, taking them out into the garden. A neatly mown lawn served as a green backdrop for the flower beds still bursting with colour in the gentle autumn sun. There were clusters of dahlias, asters and late-flowering roses. She scrunched her way over fallen leaves to an apple tree, kicked aside a few windfalls and spread a blanket beneath the canopy. The lingering sweet smell of ripening apples hinted at autumn and the cider making season, but Fiona was soon lost in Spain, exploring the Tempranillo grape. For several hours, she followed that grape's progress to South America and the excellent Chilean vineyards.

She was daydreaming about qualifying, paying Ru and her aunt back, and emigrating to work for one of the international hotels, travelling from one Michelin-starred restaurant to the next, when Ivy's voice interrupted her. 'I haven't seen you all week. How are things?'

Did her aunt know that Ru was working at the pub? 'Umm . . .' she muttered noncommittally.

'Coffee?' offered Ivy in a tone of voice Fiona recognized. Ivy might as well have added, 'We need to talk.'

Fiona closed her book. 'That would be lovely. Let me make it.'

'No,' said Ivy firmly. 'Put your studies away. I'll bring coffee and cake out in five.'

Fiona tidied her books into a pile, wishing it was as easy to assemble her thoughts and dreams. She felt adrift. If only Ru had listened to her, accepted her decision, allowed her to plot an alternative path after shattering her life plan. Being around him was confusing, sapping her energy and preventing her from moving on. She was focusing all her efforts on reinforcing the message that she was indifferent to him when, every time she saw him, she wanted to feel his arms encircle her.

Ivy returned with a tray and set it on a wooden table. Fiona joined her aunt, who passed her a mug and a plate with a large slice of cake. 'It's lemon drizzle. You always liked it as a child.'

'Rose paid me again. I've left you some money towards the bills.'

'I saw. You don't need to do that.'

'I do.' Fiona wasn't sponging off her retired aunt!

'I spoke to your parents last night. I didn't mention your finances, or your exam, of course, but I wish you would tell them. I know they would happily send you money.'

Fiona gritted her teeth. Ivy always thought the best of people, but this time she was wrong. Her parents were both incredibly successful in their field and they'd be terribly disappointed if they knew the truth: that their daughter was a failure. 'Why did you call them?'

'I didn't. They called me. You should speak to them. They'd love to hear from you.'

'Hmm.' She didn't want to talk to them until she had news worth sharing.

Deftly, Ivy changed the topic. 'How's it going?'

Fiona guessed her aunt was talking about Ru, hinting Fiona should contact him to sort out their affairs, but she didn't want to think about her ex right now. 'Well, I reckon I'm ready to apply to resit the exam.' Just saying those words was energizing and she felt a jolt of confidence. After weeks of solitary study, she was sure the CMS would let her resit. The sommelier who'd broken the news of her failure had hinted that Fiona had been a narrow miss – this time she would pass.

'Umm,' said Ivy, biting into her cake.

'You can't just sit it. They have to allow you to take it.'

'And what's this certificate for?'

'You make it sound so trivial!' Fiona tried not to mind. 'It's the Advanced Sommelier exam. It takes place a few times a year, and each time there's a limited number of candidates.'

Ivy put down her cake, wiping a crumb from her lip. 'When are you planning to sort this out?'

'I can apply to take the exam from anywhere.'

'I wasn't referring to the exam.'

Knowing Ivy would find out from Trish anyway, Fiona blurted out, 'Ru's working in the pub.'

'Ah. God moves in mysterious ways.' Ivy smiled. It was a knowing smile, the sort people gave when they were seeking another's acknowledgement of being bested, and it made Fiona question if her aunt had already known Ru was in Brambleton. Had the pair plotted this? Is that how Ru had discovered George was looking for an assistant?

'What's that supposed to mean?' demanded Fiona.

'Nothing.' said Ivy, clearing the plates. 'I'll take these in, so we don't attract insects. You can let me know when you want to talk. I only stopped off because I was gasping for a drink. I've got another service to cover. See you later.'

Fiona watched her aunt's retreating back. Ivy hadn't called in because she was thirsty. Coffee and biscuits followed every service, allowing the congregation to mingle. Had Ruben put her aunt up to this cosy little chat?

Eleven

On Monday afternoon, Fiona was sitting at the kitchen table in the upstairs flat. In front of her was a flurry of crayons, notebooks and scattered papers. George was at his desk, staring at his laptop and Rose lay on the sofa surrounded by credit card slips and stock sheets. There was a fire burning in the hearth, the logs crackling as if demonstrating they were working as hard as everyone else in the room. Beside Fiona, eight year old Timmy was struggling with his maths homework, his brow furrowed.

'Takings have jumped since your sous chef joined,' Rose said brightly. She got up and walked towards George, leaning over to look at his papers. He pushed her aside, slamming the screen shut with a crash.

'Don't pry,' he snapped.

Rose backed away. 'Sorry!' There was a pause before she added, 'How long is Ruben staying? How long does it take someone like that to get a yearning to cook fish fresh from the sea out of his system?'

Fiona smiled, now understanding Ru's cover story.

'No idea, love.' George barked a laugh. 'It's strange being with him in the kitchen. He's so talented, he makes me look a bit ham-fisted. When I stare at a basket of fish my mind comes up with what's already on the menu. He's spinning through alternatives faster than I can work out if I've got the ingredients for his last suggestion.'

'But it must be fun, working alongside someone so enthusiastic.'

'It is. I will miss him when he goes, but I don't think that will be before Easter. He's taken a six month winter let on a holiday flat, so fingers crossed . . .'

Fiona looked down at Timmy's maths problem. She leaned in, her voice gentle and encouraging, just as Aunt Ivy used to be when Fiona was struggling with homework. She guided Timmy, showing him how to break down the numbers and check his work. 'You try the next one alone,' she suggested, watching from the sidelines. She wondered if she should be making homework this much fun. Timmy and Becky must learn the importance of completing the task diligently like her parents had taught her. Rose's coughing interrupted her thoughts. It was a hacking sound that lasted nearly a minute and had Fiona scurrying to the tap for a glass of water.

She carried it to where George was leaning over his wife, a hand stroking her forehead.

'Here, have some water,' Fiona suggested.

George took the glass and held it up to his wife's lips. 'Take a sip, love. You okay?'

Rose took hold of the glass and drank thirstily. 'I think I might finish this lot tomorrow, and have a nap,' muttered Rose.

George rested his hand against Rose's forehead and frowned. 'You're a bit hot,' he said. 'Leave everything there. I'll finish them.'

'Is Mummy sick?' whined Becky.

'Come on, love, off to bed.' George held out a helping hand to his wife. 'I'll do the books. Ruben can start prep without me.'

Fiona watched Rose stumble out and George carry the

accounting records to his desk. They were a team, just like she and Ru used to be, but better balanced.

Walking back to the pub for evening service, the air was fresh and sliced through Fiona's raincoat. She would have to invest in a winter coat. None of Ivy's fitted and hers were in London. The sea breeze brushed against her face, bringing with it the faint smell of seaweed. She turned into the alleyway, shoving her hands into her pockets for warmth. By the back door, Josh was changing a pod on his vape. George was close by, dealing with another courier.

'Good evening, Josh,' Fiona called out cheerily. 'Got a few minutes for a chat about wine?'

Josh exhaled slowly then nodded enthusiastically.

'Meet you in the staffroom in five?' she suggested.

'Be right there,' said Josh.

George patted the courier on the back. 'Glad I've caught you, Fiona. Rose isn't well. Trish from Prosecco & Prose is coming in to help. Rose says you're in charge, please.'

Fiona felt a swell of pride. 'Great,' she said. The motorcyclist revved his engine and accelerated off up the hill. Wondering what was in George's plastic pouches, Fiona asked him.

George blushed. 'I sell herb rubs online for a bit of extra cash.' He coughed, barked a laugh, then added, 'But I might give that up now I'm working with a celebrity chef.'

This time, Fiona sat across from Josh. He leaned back in his chair, giving her an appreciative look that made her blush. She tucked a strand of hair behind her ear. 'I'll start with reds and whites – the basic grape varieties. I'll mention each, but often a wine is a combination of more than one type of grape. Understanding the characteristics of these grapes helps you to recognize flavours and identify which wines you enjoy.'

Josh nodded and gave her his full attention, though Fiona noticed his eyes flickering to her hands as she gestured.

'Let's start with Cabernet Sauvignon,' she said, her voice brimming with enthusiasm. 'It's grown in warmer places like Bordeaux in France, and it's strong, bold . . . the *king* of red grapes, you could say. Imagine dark, rich flavours – blackcurrant, cedar, even a hint of tobacco. It's a grape with high tannins, so it ages really well and gets better with time.'

Josh was scribbling in his notebook. He dropped his pen and looked up. 'Tannins? You get them in tea as well, right? What the heck are they?'

Hmm, how to explain tannins to a novice. 'Tannins are a group of chemical compounds. You're right that tea leaves contain tannin, and so do grapes. Tannins are extracted from grape skins, seeds and stems during the winemaking process, and tend to add a slightly bitter flavour. But in a high quality wine, they naturally soften over time and become more integrated, losing their harshness and developing a smoother, more velvety texture which balances the wine's flavour.'

'Neat! I'll fill in the gaps – in a shit wine they just taste nasty!'

She chuckled. 'Now back to grape varieties. Merlot is softer. Still bold, but a bit gentler around the edges. When I think of Merlot, I imagine flavours like plum, blackberry, maybe even a touch of chocolate. It's friendly, smooth and approachable.'

'Like a more *relaxed* Cabernet?' Josh asked, clearly intrigued.

'Exactly,' she agreed, buoyed by his enthusiasm. 'Then there's Pinot Noir – my personal favourite of the reds.' The door pushed open. 'Is this a private party or can anyone join?' asked Kim, wafting in. She was wearing cherry red lipstick, smoky eye make-up and loose-hanging hair. It wasn't the combination Fiona would have chosen for work, but then again, she wasn't twenty-four anymore.

'Fiona's explaining about different wine grapes. We're on Pinot Noir,' drawled Josh.

'Don't let me stop you,' said Kim, shrugging off a stunning jacket which Fiona guessed would have cost a month's wages, revealing a flame red dress that clung to her body. Fiona saw Josh giving Kim the same slow, appreciative look he had given her earlier. She resolved to keep her mind on the lesson.

'Pinot,' continued Fiona. 'It's delicate, almost shy, with soft tannins and red fruit flavours like cherry and strawberry. It's usually grown in cooler climates like Burgundy in France or Oregon in America. It's an earthy, floral wine.'

Josh smiled. 'Ah, a gentle wine.'

'Not for me then.' Kim raised an eyebrow and leaned over the table. Fiona couldn't help but notice how she squeezed her arms together as she did so, making her cleavage even more pronounced in her clinging dress. Kim peered at Josh's notebook. 'Gosh this looks dull. Waste of time studying, I just grab what I want from life. It's too short for swotting.'

'I hear you, mate,' said Josh. 'But Fiona here really makes it come alive.'

Fiona blushed again. 'Well, study and qualifications open up opportunities,' she said.

'Ha! Dad's wallet does that for me.' Kim snickered. 'Anyway, I just read the wine list – tells you if it's red or white and gives you the prices. That's all you need to know,' Kim said, pushing herself off the table.

Not wanting to delay Kim's departure, Fiona held her tongue. She watched the other woman secure an apron round her waist, and bit back her irritation when Kim then pulled a nail file from her handbag and sat back down at the table.

Fiona wasn't wild on teaching in front of Kim, so she wrapped up the reds quickly, zipping from Shiraz, with its intense full-bodied flavour and notes of black pepper, dark berries and spices, to Malbec, Argentina's star grape, bold and plush with a slightly smoky finish.

'Ready to move on to whites?' she asked awkwardly, looking at Kim, who was still filing her nails and pretending not to listen.

Josh nodded happily, seemingly oblivious to the tension between the two women.

'First, Chardonnay. This one changes depending on where it's grown and how it's aged. In Burgundy, it's often crisp and citrusy, but in California, it can be rich and buttery – especially if it's been aged in oak barrels.'

Josh's eyes widened. 'The same grape, but it can taste totally different?'

She gave a soft laugh. 'Yes,' she said, a glint of passion in her eyes. 'It's all about the climate and technique. Now, Sauvignon Blanc, that's fresh, often with bright acidity, tasting of green apple, citrus, sometimes even herbs or grass.'

The door opened. It was Ru, wearing a pinched expression. 'He's in here, George.'

Ru stood back and George walked in, wiping his hands on a towel. 'Come on, Josh, the pots are piling up. What's going on in here?' he asked.

Fiona rose, glancing at the clock. 'Sorry, my fault. We were discussing wine.'

'It's a little tutorial,' said Kim, standing up and smoothing her dress over her hips.

Ru's eyes widened. George puffed out his cheeks. 'Evening, Kim. You're dressed smartly tonight.'

'I like to make an effort for you, George,' she replied breezily. Fiona clenched her teeth. 'How many covers are we tonight, Chef?' asked Kim politely.

'Uh, Fiona will brief you, Rose isn't well. Trish from Prosecco & Prose is coming in to help.'

'Oh, I'm sorry to hear that,' purred Kim.

'Shall I go up and check on her before we open?' offered Fiona. 'Make her supper, if she's hungry?'

'I could come with you,' simpered Kim.

Fiona had a mental image of Becky's sticky fingers on Kim's red dress and hid a smile. George shot Fiona a grateful look. 'I've left Rose her supper, but maybe you could pop up and check the kids aren't being a nuisance. They're under strict instructions to take her the tray and then leave her alone.' He switched his attention to Kim. 'With Rose in bed, Fiona's in charge tonight.'

'The dream team,' said Kim, beaming.

George smiled at Kim, 'and Rose says please leave all the wine decisions to Fiona.'

As soon as the men left the staffroom, Kim turned to Fiona. 'Just because you've been put in charge, don't try ordering me around.'

Fiona watched the door shut behind the men, the sharp echo of Kim's words settling like a slap. For a moment, she said nothing, just blinked, her heart thudding a little harder than it should be. She didn't understand it. What had she done to deserve Kim's constant barbs? She was polite. Helpful. Never criticised. So why did it always feel like Fiona was walking into a fight that she hadn't started?

Ten minutes later, as Fiona nudged the door of the attic flat open, a smell greeted her. It was the pungent aftermath of cooking, but she couldn't pin down exactly what it was. She walked inside, feeling the squelch of something underfoot. Jam? Honey? She didn't want to think about it. A trail of sticky footprints led to the kitchen area. Fiona crossed to the sitting room, picking up cushions from the floor and retrieving a pink sock that dangled from a curtain rod. She heard footsteps and spun around. The perpetrators of the mess stood a few feet away.

'We've made Mummy's supper,' announced Timmy proudly.

'Yes. Daddy's meal didn't look very nice, so we've cooked, like Daddy does.'

Fiona picked up the tray, her nose wrinkling. Something offensive wafted from the plate. Eggs, certainly. But the sharp tang of burned butter and an undercurrent of something sweet suggested the children may have mixed in sugar.

Outside the master bedroom, she paused, tray balanced, then knocked, the tray wobbling.

'Come in!' croaked Rose, her voice muffled and rough.

Pushing open the bedroom door, Rose greeted her, sitting propped up against a mountain of pillows, her face pale but smiling.

'We made you eggs, Mummy!' Becky chirped, scrambling onto the bed and curling up beside her mother.

Timmy puffed out his chest. 'By ourselves!'

Fiona eyed the tray before setting it on Rose's lap. The plate of scrambled eggs shimmered with an unsettling greyish hue, flecked with blackened bits that might have once been onion – or charcoal.

Rose mustered maternal courage and took a tiny forkful. Fiona winced in sympathy as her boss chewed and swallowed, her eyes watering slightly. 'Mm,' Rose croaked. 'Delicious, darlings.' She smiled conspiratorially at Fiona. 'Shame I'm too ill to have more than one bite.'

Timmy beamed. Becky frowned, then fetched a cloth, and laid it, dripping, on Rose's face. 'Better now, Mummy?'

Fiona snorted softly, gently removed the cloth and stepped back, watching the scene. There was something oddly touching about the kids' pride in their food and Rose's sheer determination not to gag. Then the pang hit. Sudden, sharp and sad. This sticky, smelly mess was the sort of thing she might never have. No burned eggs lovingly cooked, no sticky footprints, no dripping cloth, no little faces looking at her with shining pride.

Rose's voice broke through her thoughts. 'Earth to Fiona?'

Fiona blinked. 'Sorry. Zoned out for a moment.'

'Thinking about escaping before they make you taste it?'

Fiona laughed and shook her head. 'I'm tougher than I look.'

She stayed a moment longer, watching the children's animated faces as they chattered over each other, then made her way out. A familiar ache settled in her chest, one she'd grown accustomed to carrying. The smell of burned eggs lingered behind her, along with the echo of small voices that followed her down the hall.

Twelve

That night, Fiona's sommelier skills were in demand. The fire was lit, filling the dining room with the smell of Applewood and casting flickering shadows along the walls. It was lovely hearing the gentle hiss of logs mingling with the hum of chatter and the booming sound of waves crashing against the harbour wall outside, but it made the staff, rushing around everywhere, feel hot and bothered.

Concentrating on wine, Fiona avoided the kitchen, allowing Trish and Kim to process orders. She was opening a bottle of Champagne as efficiently as she could, aware of more orders piling up in the kitchen, when she heard Trish deliver food to a nearby table.

'Duck confit for you, madam,' said Trish.

'No, I didn't order the duck, just my husband. I went for the risotto. And could we have our wine, please?'

While carefully pouring Champagne, Fiona tuned in. Duck was expensive. George would be cross if Trish had messed up and Rose wasn't here to soothe his temper.

'Let me check the order slip,' Trish said.

Fiona put the bottle in a chiller and turned, catching Trish's eye. It wasn't fair to let Trish face a moody George. 'Why don't I sort the food order, and you fetch their wine,' she smiled at the customers. 'It was the Chambertin-Clos de Bèze 2005, wasn't it?'

She slipped Trish the cellar key, telling her which drawer to return it to. 'I pulled their wine out earlier, you can't miss it. It's on the tasting table – I had too many bottles to bring it up with me.'

Fiona carried the plates of duck back to the kitchen, popping them on the serving counter. 'Chef, I need to check the order slip for Table 6.'

Trish's handwriting was clear: two duck. Fiona's pulse rate quickened. Was the mistake Trish's or the customers?

'Problem?' asked George tersely.

'Hopefully not,' said Fiona, picking up the plates. 'The wife claims she didn't order duck.'

'Service,' called Ruben, sliding three plates onto the counter. 'What's the matter with the duck?' Fiona chose her words carefully. 'Possible mistake on the order slip. Customer says they ordered risotto not duck.'

George huffed, but Ru smiled, slipped off his apron, and took the plates out of Fiona's hands. 'Let me see if I can sell this for you.'

As Fiona walked past tables, a hush fell, replaced by frantic whispering, finger pointing, and then inevitably, the phones started flashing. Customers swivelled in chairs, looking not at her, but at the man she was following. By the time she reached Table 6, the room was silent. Relieved to spot wine in their glasses, she leaned over the table and whispered, 'Madam, I am so sorry.'

Ru stood behind her, his leg brushing against hers. The faint contact sent a shiver through her, dragging her back three years. She'd been a nervous trainee sommelier then; he, the poised sous chef with four junior chefs under his command. That day, she'd bungled a food order – a slip she thought might spell disaster.

But Ru had swooped in effortlessly, turning calamity into

charm. That night he glided through the packed restaurant, his presence magnetic, and sold the unordered plate of scallops to a delighted customer.

Later that evening, he claimed his reward: their first date.

Now Ruben stepped forward. 'I believe the waitress made a mistake with your order, madam. The duck is one of our specialties. I'd recommend giving it a try – it's the best dish on our menu.'

Blushing, the woman nervously twirled a lock of her hair. 'Did you make this?' she asked, her voice soft with curiosity.

His face lit up. 'A kitchen is a team effort. We made the rub from scratch and cured the meat for twenty-four hours, then it's been slow cooking most of the day.' He smiled, his eyes alight with his enthusiasm. 'It's the same herb mixture we use in my London restaurant.'

There it was again. *My* restaurant. Fiona chewed on her lip.

'Well, if I'm trying the famous duck, could I get your autograph too?'

'Absolutely! My pleasure. Enjoy the meal, and I'll have that autograph ready.'

Ru stood, flashed Fiona a smile and whispered, 'I'll claim my reward later.'

'From Trish not me!' she hissed, scooting off, scolding herself for feeling relived it wasn't Kim who owed him a reward. But Ru was a free agent. He could date whoever he chose to. She just prayed he didn't flaunt his independence in front of her.

On Thursday, Fiona arrived at 11 a.m. to a ringing phone and a red-faced George scribbling in the appointments book.

'I've got it, George,' yelled Fiona, lunging for the phone, hoping it was a cancellation. 'The Smuggler's Inn.'

'Rose?' said a man's voice. 'It's Sam.'

'Rose isn't well I'm afraid. Can I help you? Sam, did you say?'

She lost grip of the phone as someone wrenched it away. 'Sam, hi – it's George.'

George covered the receiver with a hand. 'Need to squeeze a table for three in tonight. What time can we manage?'

Fiona threw her hands in the air. 'You choose. I might have to lay up a booth, as we're solid—'

George released his hand saying. 'That's fine, Sam. See you at eight. No, it's my pleasure. Thanks for the booking. Bye.'

He finished the call. 'Sorry, Sam Hastings is our best customer. Eats here at least once a week and he's bringing his brother – the Hastings family is our landlord.'

They will need looking after, Fiona thought. 'How's Rose? Is she up to working tonight?'

He clicked his tongue. 'No, and Trish can't help.'

Just her and Kim and an extra three VIP covers. That would be a challenge. 'Any other ideas for help?'

George rubbed his eyes. 'Pray?'

Fiona chuckled. 'That's an idea. I'll ask Ivy.'

Ivy was happy to help in the pub, and by 6.30p.m.was laying tables and polishing glasses alongside Fiona and Kim. George walked into the dining room, followed by his sous chef.

'Tonight's specials,' announced George. He ran his hands over his apron, fiddled with his chef's hat, then added, 'I'll let Ruben explain . . . they're both his ideas.'

'First, there's a pan-seared sea bass – crisp on the outside with a buttery, melt in your mouth texture inside. It's served with a zesty citrus beurre blanc sauce and complemented by a bed of roasted asparagus and a wild mushroom risotto.'

Listening to his enthusiastic voice, Fiona wanted to reach out and touch him. Her whole body tingled as she imagined kissing him, his lips lingering on hers. She diverted her mind, matching the complicated flavours with different grapes. She favoured a Sauvignon Blanc – the bright crispness would enhance the freshness of the sea bass and balance the richness of the sauce, without overpowering the delicate flavours of the fish. Or maybe an unoaked Chardonnay. Its crisp acidity and minerality would match both the fish and the rich wild mushroom risotto. Ru was still talking and Fiona realized she had missed what the second special was.

'For pudding,' said Ru, 'we've made a chocolate tart with autumn raspberries.' She darted a glance at him. He replied with a grin, sending a pulse of desire through her body. 'Thought we should set the sommelier a challenge.'

Ruben and George returned to the kitchen, leaving Fiona with an ache in her heart. How could she heal with him constantly reminding her of her loss?

Kim folded her arms over her chest. 'I reckon Ruben fancies you. Are you really a sommelier?' asked Kim.

'Yes.' She puffed out her chest. 'And I'm studying for the Advanced Sommelier qualification too.'

'What does that involve?' asked Kim rolling her eyes.

'A lot of hard work and a lot of experience. Blind tastings.'

'Blind tastings!' scoffed Kim, 'What's the point of that?' she asked and stalked off.

By opening time, Fiona was feeling nauseous and her head was pounding. She made herself an espresso and swallowed a couple of paracetamol. 'You okay, love?' asked Ivy, brushing a hair from Fiona's face. 'You're looking pale.'

'I'll be fine.' She gave a half laugh. She would soon be too busy to notice. The door opened and Fiona rushed to greet the customers, giving her head a shake to clear the brain fog. An hour later, her temples were still throbbing. Everyone sounded like they were shouting, and her hand felt too heavy to lift a pen to scribble down orders. Fiona was waiting at the serving counter when Kim joined her.

'Table 5 is asking for the sommelier. They can't decide between a *Margus* and a *Lynchy* something or other.'

Fiona smiled inwardly. 'I suspect it's a Margaux and a Lynch-Bages. I'll see to it.'

Ivy puffed over. 'Another wine request.' She panted, 'The Hastings table wants a bottle of Krug. Where can I find that?'

Fiona felt her chin tremble. The VIP table had ordered her favourite blended Champagne. Her chest felt tight and in front of her, Ivy's head seemed to blur.

'Service,' came a sharp command.

The room spun and Fiona collapsed.

Before losing consciousness, she registered a man's alarmed cry – 'Mousse!'

Fiona could smell him – a mixture of basil, caramelized onions and lemons – making her want to lie back in his arms and sleep. Her eyes flickered open and she saw his hands, chef's hands with the nails neatly trimmed and spotlessly clean. She felt his warm breath caress her ear.

'You fainted,' he murmured.

She looked beyond the hands, saw the floor tiles. 'I'm not feeling great.'

George lowered his head, his eyes narrowing as a quizzical expression spread across his face. 'Moose?' he said, addressing Ru. 'You cried *moose*. She fainted and you called her an animal?'

Fiona's mind churned, trying to unscramble the misunderstanding. How was Ru going to explain this slip-up?

'I said *move*, not *moose*,' Ru claimed hastily. 'I was trying to give her some space.'

George chuckled, his laughter breaking the tension. 'Ah,' he said with a smirk. 'I thought you said *moose*! I reckon she's got Rose's flu.'

'Sorry to be a bore, but where can I find a bottle of Krug?' asked Ivy.

Fiona groaned. All she wanted to do was crawl into bed, and she wasn't sure she even had the energy to manage that unaided. She lifted a hand – it felt as if someone had attached one of those ankle weights people used in gyms – and pointed at a drawer. 'Cellar key is in that drawer, Ivy,' she whispered. 'The Champagne is near the door, clearly labelled on the bin. There's a fast chiller behind the bar.'

'What do we do about Table 5's wine?' asked Kim.

'I'll deal with it,' said Ruben, pushing Fiona upright. 'George, if you can cope on your own for five minutes . . .? Kim, let's go and talk about fine wines, then I'll help you locate their choice.' As Josh helped Fiona onto her feet, she replayed the last few moments, drinking in the sensation of being cradled in the arms of the man she still – despite her best efforts – loved.

Thirteen

In her bedroom, Fiona lay propped up against a wall of pillows, her head heavy and her nose stuffy. It was difficult to concentrate on different wine scents with her nose swamped with the smell of menthol, eucalyptus and camphor from the rub slathered onto her chest. She lifted her eyes from her book. An early dusk seeped through the window, cold and damp. Outside, the countryside was awash with autumn's rich colours. She could see a mature acer tree, its delicate leaves a stunning shade of deep red, almost purple, and nearby a beech tree surrounded by a carpet of rusted leaves. She pulled the quilt tighter around herself, the soft fabric deliciously cool against her flushed skin, making her shiver.

The book lay open across her lap, but each word on the page seemed to blur. 'Tannins,' she murmured aloud, her throat scratchy and hoarse. 'High tannin wines . . . High tannin wines can taste . . . What?' She shut her eyes, picturing herself swirling a slither of wine around a highly polished tasting glass while customers waited with bated breath for her verdict. But tonight, the thought of a complex rich Bordeaux blend made her feel queasy.

Her mind wandered to Josh. He'd made it pretty clear in their lessons that he was interested in more than just wine. At first, despite their age gap, she'd felt a thrill of something in return, but then his eyes had roved over Kim as well, and she'd realized he was just one of those people who flirted with everyone. She smiled ruefully at herself now, wondering if her fever was making her overly sentimental.

Josh was good looking, but he wasn't a long-term prospect. 'A charming rogue,' is how her Aunt Ivy would describe him. He wasn't looking for a relationship, he was looking for a holiday fling before he headed on somewhere else to try out the surf. She thought of Ru – so full of charm, laughter and a natural charisma that drew everyone to him. The chemistry between him and Fiona had been like lighting a match; it crackled and surged. In comparison, Josh was more like a shaft of warm sunshine on a cold day. She sighed, feeling her eyelids grow heavy.

But maybe, to move on from Ru, and for him to understand it was really over, a holiday fling was just what was needed. She reached for the mug of hot toddy – a soothing blend of lemon, honey and whisky – which her aunt had left by the bedside. Wrapping her hands around its comforting warmth, she felt the heat seep into her aching fingers, easing the stiffness. Fiona took a sip, the tartness biting at her sore throat, though the honey's sweetness soothed a little. She hoped her aunt had used a cheap blended whisky in this concoction and hadn't sacrificed a malt.

Outside, the wind picked up, rattling the cottage's windows. Fiona closed her eyes, trying to picture Josh at her side. She imagined him strolling in, pulling the curtains, plumping up her pillows, then explaining he would be back later – 'Surf's up'. She winced. He wouldn't know how to reach her, to pull her from this melancholy like Ru would.

Ru would nurse her with food. Right now, Fiona couldn't imagine a single thing she wanted to eat, but he would think of something to tempt her with. He would have burst in, bringing with him tantalizing smells, and presented her with a tray of something irresistible. There would probably have been a rose in a bud vase on that tray. There would certainly have been an eager look in his eyes, waiting for her to congratulate him on his efforts.

Fiona allowed two tears to escape from her eyelids and snake down her cheeks. Then she snuggled down beneath the blankets. Each limb felt too heavy to move. The door opened and Ivy's voice drifted in. 'How are you, love? I've brought you another hot toddy for that throat.'

The soft shuffle of slippers on the hardwood floor, followed by the clink of a mug setting down on the bedside table signalled Ivy's approach. A chair scraped quietly against the wooden floor. Fiona wiped her eyes and heaved herself upright. Ivy clearly had something she wanted to discuss. She hoped it wasn't Ru.

But the chosen topic was worse. Without preamble, Ivy launched in. 'When did you last speak to your parents? I think you really should call them, tell them what you're going through with Ru and your studies.'

Fiona shifted on the bed, the sheet sticking to her damp skin. Call them? The thought left a sour taste in her mouth. She couldn't remember when she had last spoken to either of her parents. Her mother's voice had always been a strange thing – so formal, so distant, like they were two people in the same room but not quite sharing it. Fiona dredged around in her memory, deciding it was two years since she'd last spoken to them. Two years of WhatsApp messages with pictures of glorious sunsets, two years of dwindling invitations to visit Melbourne. That phone call had been to share the news she had passed her last wine exam.

'Mum, I passed,' Fiona had announced, trying to keep her voice light, hiding the triumph she secretly harboured.

'Darling, that's wonderful news. Your father will be so

pleased! You worked hard, and it paid off. A structured approach always yields results.'

Fiona closed her eyes, replaying her mother's words. A *structured approach*. Not pride, not love – just scientific cause and effect.

'I presume this puts you on a good trajectory?' her mother continued. 'It's fascinating how mastering a field is so often about disciplined study rather than innate talent. Though, of course, you have both. Darling, can I call you back? I'm late for a lecture.'

Fiona had carried around her mother's last words for days, trying to decide if that was her mother's way of telling her she was proud of Fiona's achievements, but concluded it was just her mother wanting to end the call so she could get back to work.

No, the last person Fiona wanted to speak to about Ru, or about any aspect of her life, was her mother.

'Ivy, please,' Fiona mumbled, her throat raw. 'I can't . . . I don't need to talk to them. Not now.' Perhaps not ever. It was always to Ivy she had turned to stitch together the parts of her life that felt too frayed. Fiona had the support of the relative she relied on. Why would she lean on her parents, when they had abandoned her?

'You need your parents, Fiona. That's what you need after a big break-up. Motherly love,' Ivy said, her tone both kind and insistent. 'I know you think you don't, but—'

Fiona exhaled a sharp breath, her hands clenching the sheet beneath her, the fabric cool against her feverish skin. 'Motherly love?' she repeated bitterly, her voice barely above a whisper. 'As if she knows what that is.'

Ivy's sigh came, heavy with years of history. She sat down on the end of the bed, her presence warm and familiar. 'She's my sister. I know she's not great on big shows of affection, but they *are* your parents, Fiona. You can't keep pretending they don't care.'

Fiona's chest tightened. Her parents wouldn't relish being disturbed from their academic worlds to discuss the mess their daughter was in. Anyway, Fiona knew what the solution was, and it wasn't *motherly love*. She turned her head towards the window, the blurry world outside her vision spinning gently. 'You've always helped me. Always. What do they even know about my life? They've never been here. Never helped me when I was struggling.'

The silence stretched out, a thick pause that drifted between them like smoke. Then Ivy's voice, softer now, but no less insistent: 'What you need, love, is someone who truly cares. Someone who's there. You need—'

'No,' Fiona interrupted, her voice sharp and desperate. 'What I need is to rely on myself. I need to study, and then I need to pass my exam. I don't need some . . . virtual *stranger* from Melbourne checking up on me. I'm fine. I don't need whatever they have to offer.'

Ivy didn't reply right away. Fiona could hear the faint rustle of her aunt's hand in her lap, the slight creak of her fingers tightening around a mug. After a long pause, Ivy whispered, 'Get some rest, but think about what I said.'

The heat in the room suddenly felt stifling. Fiona closed her eyes, listening to the steady rhythm of her own heartbeat. She smelled the soft scent of lavender and opened her eyes. Ivy leaned over and gently kissed her forehead. The faint creak of the door followed as she left, then her footsteps faded down the stairs, leaving a calm silence behind.

By Wednesday afternoon, Fiona's cold had receded to a sniffle. She felt better, so she joined Ivy and Kim for evening service. Kim seemed to have a new sparkle. Fiona wondered if something had blossomed between the youngster and Josh while she had been off ill.

The restaurant was full, and the bar area was heaving with lively customers. Fiona, holding a notepad with increasingly illegible scribbles, pushed through the crowd. Her cheeks were flushed, half from the warmth and half from having spotted Ru ten minutes earlier. Every time she was in the kitchen, he seemed to watch her. The sight of him still made her stomach flip.

She entered the kitchen stealthily, hoping to catch a glimpse of Ru unobserved. The bright lights and the warmth hit her. The smells were almost overpowering – sizzling meat, onions, a heady mix of spices. George was plating food with the precision of a surgeon, Ru was searing fish, while Josh was scrubbing pots at the sink. Kim was at the serving counter, somehow managing to look busy despite doing nothing.

'Ready with those fish?' boomed George.

'Yes, Chef,' said Ruben.

'Table 7,' called George. Four plates clattered onto the counter. Fiona picked them up, balancing two skilfully on each arm. But as she squeezed past Kim, she felt a sharp tug on her apron strings. The knot came undone. With her arms full, Fiona was powerless to prevent her apron slipping down, catching on her hip, and a cascade of pens, notepads and even her lipstick tumbled across the floor.

'Oh dear, you dropped something,' Kim murmured in a sugary tone, giving her a sly smile. Fiona replaced the plates, and knelt, feeling heat creep up her neck as she gathered her things in full view of Ru, who was chuckling, arms crossed, and one eyebrow arched. Josh skidded to a stop beside her, crouching down.

'Need some help?' he asked, handing her a stray pen. She shot him a grateful smile.

'Thanks, Josh,' she muttered, shoving her apron on with all

the dignity she could muster and making a mental note to double tie the knot in the future.

Half an hour later, Ivy pressed lightly on Fiona's arm. 'Customer's asking for the 2005 of this wine,' she said, holding up a bottle with a pink foil cap. 'I couldn't find it. I brought this instead. Will it do?'

From the distinctive pink cap, she was sure it would be Vieux Château Certan, but Fiona quickly checked the label. It was, but the vintage was 2017. 'It'll be lower down the rack. The older wines should be stored at the top, but I haven't had time to shuffle them around yet.'

Ivy frowned. 'Hmm, I did look. I'll try again, shall I?'

'Let me.' It would be faster. If the wine was misplaced, Ivy could be down there for hours. Her aunt handed over the key and Fiona trotted off.

Down in the cellar, Fiona flicked the light switch, illuminating rows of dusty pine cases and racks of bottles, allowing the cool, moist air to sooth her. She jogged down the steps and over to the correct bin. Crouching, she replaced the 2017 and took out the bottom bottle. It too was a 2017. Her mind raced, searching for explanations. She tried the next one up, and the one above that, but every bottle was from 2017. She was sure she'd counted half a dozen of the 2005 last week. Had there been a flurry of wine enthusiasts while she was ill, all wanting the same wine, from the same vintage?

Wondering what to propose as an alternative, she pushed herself onto her haunches. Her eyes fell on a nearby pine box of 2005 Château L'Évangile, one of the top wines of Pomerol. The top was askew. She nudged it aside and pulled out a bottle, wondering why the box was open but still full. At the top of the stairs, thinking she was about to sneeze, her hands rose instinctively, her nose twitched, and she caught sight of the label and froze.

The bottle shook. It wasn't a 2005 L'Évangile. It wasn't even a more recent vintage. This was the house red. Fiona felt dizzy. She retraced her steps, and collapsing beside the pine box labelled *L'Évangile*, setting the bottle down carefully on the floor. She pushed aside the lid and stared at the remaining five bottles. All were house red. With her heart racing she removed each one, peering through the slats at the six bottles stored below. Each should have been worth more than £250. None had the distinctive minimalist sketch of the famous château on their label. The entire box was full of bottles of house red wine.

She did a mental calculation: over £2000's worth of wine was missing. Fiona swept a shaky hand over her forehead. It was worse than that. This wine wasn't *missing*. Someone had removed expensive bottles and replaced them with cheaper ones. There was only one explanation – someone had stolen the wine and hidden the evidence. But who? Why? And was the sommelier going to be the prime suspect?

Fourteen

Fiona woke at dawn, after a night plagued by dreams in which bottles of wine were chasing her around a dark cellar. She decided to investigate before alerting her employers. It was possible that while she was away, someone had opened that case of fine wine and stored the precious bottles in a rack. She couldn't come up with an explanation for why the case was now full of bottles of house red wine, but she didn't care, provided she could locate the missing L'Évangile. She downed a cup of coffee and arrived at the pub's back entrance before 8.30 a.m.

Rose was on her way out, Timmy in one hand, Becky skipping down the steps after her brother, her shoes slapping on the stone, her pigtails dancing as she jumped.

'Fiona, when are you coming to play with us again?' squealed Becky, running over and throwing her arms round Fiona's thighs.

'Ooph, not now my love, you've got school.'

'School is silly. I'd rather play.'

'No,' Fiona said gently, kneeling to look Becky in the eyes. 'School is very important! It will teach you to work hard and pass your exams, and then you'll be free to lead whatever life you want.'

'Well, I want to lead a happy life, and I'm happy already,' replied Becky, wrinkling her nose, 'so I won't bother with exams.' She gave a triumphant smile.

'Out of the mouth of babes,' quipped Rose. 'You're in jolly early, Fiona.'

'Something I need to check in the cellar.'

'Problem?' asked Rose in a wary voice.

'Later.'

Rose gulped. 'Seriously?'

'It'll keep. You concentrate on the kids.'

'You've got me worried now,' said Rose, her eyebrows knitting together in a line, 'Damn! I've got to go straight into Barnstaple to see the accountant after the school run. Let's talk tomorrow morning. Do you mind coming to the flat at eight?'

Fiona nodded and crossed her fingers, hoping there wasn't a problem. At least if there was one, she had all day to size it.

'Yo, Fiona!' cried a loud male voice.

Unless Australia had invaded Brambleton, that voice must belong to Josh, but despite scanning the terrace, Fiona couldn't pin him down. 'Over here, on the beach.' She spun round. Clad in a wetsuit and looking every inch the professional surfer, Josh grinned across at her. 'Come on, what about that surfing lesson? You must have time; you're not on duty for hours.'

Which was true. How to wriggle out of this? 'I'm not exactly dressed for surfing.'

'That's easy to fix. Plenty of wetsuits in the surf school hut. Come on. I dare you. Take a gamble on life.'

Fiona hesitated. Spending time with Josh was easy and fun, and she had to admit the sea did look very inviting in the autumn sun. But despite what she'd been telling herself about having an innocent fling to try and get over Ru, she wasn't ready for anything that could be construed as a date. 'I've got a lot to do in the cellar.'

'Tomorrow morning then,' he tossed back.

'I'm busy. And before you suggest tomorrow afternoon, I'll

remind you that I've arranged to give someone a wine tutorial then.'

Josh grinned. 'Looking forward to that, but you can't be busy every day. Live a little.'

She smiled. Oh, why not? What was the harm? It wasn't a date, it was just a harmless lesson, in exchange for teaching him about wine. And she couldn't spend all her time moping around feeling sad about Ruben. 'Let me think about it.'

'Beauty!'

She was still smiling as she walked into the pub – Josh's constant upbeat approach to life seemed to have that effect on her. Inside, she grabbed a copy of the stock list and a felt-tip pen, then crept past the kitchen, where she could hear Ru and George discussing tonight's specials. Evidently there had been a fish delivery, and Ru was proposing roasting gurnard and matching the slightly sweet fish with caramelised fennel and a sea buckthorn butter sauce. It sounded great, but the waiting staff would need to be told what buckthorn berries were and that they would add a tart citrusy flavour to the sauce.

Not wanting anyone to question what she was doing, she dashed to the cellar, casting furtive glances back down the corridor. Fiona fumbled with the key, yanked the door open, and switched on the light. Her heart pounded; with Rose on the school run and George cooking breakfasts, this might be the perfect opportunity for the thief to strike. She took a deep breath, then locked herself in, leaving the key in the lock.

She started with the red burgundies. The most valuable bottles were worth over £500 each. An hour later and the scale of the disaster was starting to unfold. Where there should have been a half case of 2005 Chambertin-Clos de Bèze by a renowned grower, there were only two bottles. An entire pine case of Richebourg, worth even more, was missing. Bordeaux had also been plundered. At ten o'clock, she did a rough calculation: over £10,000's worth of wine was missing – and she had only skimmed the surface.

Fiona slumped to the floor, her fingers scrabbling in the dust. She heaved herself upright telling herself this wasn't her problem. Or was it? Who else with access to the cellar knew the value of those missing red burgundies?

The next morning when Fiona arrived for her breakfast meeting with Rose, Timmy let her into the flat wearing his school uniform and what looked like most of his breakfast. There was porridge clinging to his hair, neck and shirt.

'I didn't start it,' he announced triumphantly.

'Good morning to you too, Timmy,' she replied.

Rose appeared, the other culprit of the food fight wriggling in her grasp.

'Give me a hand getting these two changed, will you?'

'It wasn't me,' trilled Becky.

'It was so,' yelled Timmy.

'*Enough*!' shouted Rose, 'I don't want to hear about it. You're both in trouble.'

Fiona trailed behind the family. In the living room what remained of breakfast littered the carpet. 'If you strip their tops, I'll nip and get clean ones and a hairbrush,' muttered Rose.

'And a skirt for Becky,' said Fiona, spotting a clump of porridge stuck to the waistband. 'Come here you,' she said, grasping the girl by the hand. 'Arms up,' she instructed, then wriggled the top over Becky's head. 'I don't know how you cope, Rose. Two kids, the pub and the rooms . . .'

Rose sighed and tossed a clean shirt at Fiona. 'I think you're about to add to my workload. Please tell me the problem isn't that you're resigning.'

Fiona shook her head and threaded Becky's arms through the shirt sleeves. Unless Rose suspended her while she investigated the missing wine, Fiona wasn't going anywhere.

'I think there's some wine missing.'

Rose gasped. 'Expensive stuff?'

Fiona nodded. She had thought through her options. Rose knew how familiar her sommelier was with the cellar; down there Fiona was like a cat patrolling its territory. Rose would be slower, but if her investigation concluded the loss was worse than Fiona suggested, suspicion might fall on the sommelier. 'I don't know exactly how bad it is, not without doing a stock check, but it looks like there might be £10,000 worth of stock missing.'

Rose staggered backwards, dragging the hairbrush with her.

'Ow, that hurts, Mummy,' cried Timmy.

'Stand still then. I need to brush your hair.' Rose puffed out a sigh. 'A lot of bottles or a few expensive ones?'

Fiona picked a splodge of cold, sticky porridge from Becky's hair, telling herself this wasn't her problem to solve, any more than the food fight was. She was just helping Rose with both. 'Expensive ones.' *Very expensive.*

Rose's eyes met Fiona's, and there was an accusatory tone in her voice. 'The thief knows their way around the cellar then,' said Rose.

Fiona flinched, sensing the hairs stand up on her arms. 'Or they've seen the wine list,' she suggested.

A fleeting look of realization shot across her boss's face. 'Sorry, that sounded nasty.' Rose was holding out the hairbrush towards Fiona, as if offering an olive branch. 'It's not you – of course it's not. Anyway, why would you draw my attention to your own crime?'

Smiling weakly to acknowledge the apology, Fiona took the hairbrush and unthreaded Becky's plaits. 'Give your head a shake, that should dislodge the worst of it,' she instructed the child.

'We had this happen in London too. Champagne and spirits, no wine, thankfully we didn't have a fine wine list then,' Rose said.

'Is that why you moved here? Because of a thief.'

'No. It's tough making a living in a London pub, so when the lease on this came up, we leaped at it. A new start, a bit more support with the kids. What I want to know is, what is the thief doing with the stuff? I get how you can fence a case of spirits or a bottle of champagne, but' she screwed up her face, 'who buys stray bottles of fine wine?'

'Lots of places. There are dedicated auctions, or upmarket merchants will buy rare wine, provided it's been properly cellared. They have light filters which can detect if it's gone off.'

'Which this has not. George's uncle kept it in a temperature-controlled cellar. We left it where it was when we were in London.' Rose groaned, 'That wine was our nest egg. I wish we'd sold it.'

'Why didn't you?'

Rose licked a finger and rubbed at a splodge of porridge on Timmy's trousers. 'George wanted to sell it to a high-end merchant straightaway. But when he did the research, we discovered a bottle of top-notch wine costing £100 in a shop would only sell for £50 to a merchant, but I suspected we could charge £150 in a restaurant.' She sighed, 'It was my idea. When we knew we were moving somewhere with a reputation for fine dining, I suggested shifting it over time in the restaurant, and we arranged to have it delivered to the pub. I know it will take time, but the wines George inherited are from excellent vintages and won't go off any time soon.'

Fiona gave a slight headshake. 'It's not *all* good vintages. The 2017, for example—'

Fiona's thoughts froze. There was a fluttery sensation in her stomach. She was clearly much more knowledgeable about the contents of the cellar than her boss. 'Are you insured?'

'Yes, but I'm not sure they'll pay up. We've been a bit lax about security and too many people know where that key is hidden.'

Fiona blushed. Whichever way she looked at this, the prime suspect was the sommelier. 'Will you go to the police?'

'Not yet. I'd like to encourage the culprit to confess. Will you help me do a stock take when I get back from the school run?'

Fiona nodded. 'This one's ready,' she said, patting Becky on the back.

With a child in each hand, Rose strode towards the flat door, speaking over her shoulder, 'It's got to be Josh or Ruben from the kitchen.' Hearing Ru's name, Fiona winced. Rose ushered Fiona into the corridor. 'It's just you and me from the dining room. Kim and the bar staff don't know where the key is kept.'

Fiona grimaced. 'Sorry, Rose. That list is actually a bit longer. When you had the flu, Trish, Kim and Ivy were shown where that key lives.'

'Who took that decision?' barked Rose.

'Me.'

Rose tutted, then slammed the door shut behind them, leaving Fiona questioning how much longer her boss would believe her innocent.

As they descended the stairs, Fiona could see a sliver of light shining from the end of the corridor. The cellar door was ajar. She felt beads of sweat on her upper lip and stopped, clasping the stock list to her chest. Rose held a finger up to her mouth. 'Wait here,' she whispered, her voice wavering.

Conscious of her thumping heart, Fiona took quick, shallow breaths. Was the thief down there? Rose dashed to the door, yanked it wide and disappeared, her footsteps thudding on the stone steps. Fiona heard raised voices: Rose's and a man she couldn't identify, nor could she detect what either was saying.

Suddenly, George strode out, a bottle of wine in each hand, his face red and mutinous. 'It's a bog standard chardonnay.'

Rose followed her husband into the corridor, hands on hips. 'I messaged you – Fiona thinks there's some wine missing, and you promised you wouldn't take anything until after I'd checked.'

George marched towards Fiona, who flattened herself against the wall. 'I can't run a kitchen around the school run.' He held out the bottles of wine, jabbing his head at them. 'Ask our sommelier – this is just plonk. We need it to poach the halibut for tonight's fish special.'

'Nothing else?' demanded Rose.

He held his arms aloft. 'Frisk me. Fiona, satisfy the detective superintendent here.'

Rose muttered something under her breath. Poor woman. Like Fiona, she managed staff – a challenging role with its share of uncomfortable dilemmas. Fiona recalled suspecting one of her own employees of skimming cash tips. The experience had been awful. Doubting your team eroded trust and weighed heavily on the mind. She figured Rose must have handled the London theft and didn't envy her boss having to face an ordeal again.

Since Fiona knew much more about wine than her employer, Rose kept score – using Fiona's pen, after spending a fruitless five minutes looking for her own – while Fiona moved from bin to bin, calling out the contents. Each time missing bottles were identified, Fiona tried to ignore the sinking feeling in her stomach by concentrating on her ideas for Josh's wine tutorial this evening. By 11.30 a.m., they'd scoured Europe, identifying over £25,000 worth of missing wine. A chunk of that was a rare bottle of

Champagne by the famous house Krug, a Clos du Mesnil. The pale silver shiny wooden box was still on the shelf, but it was empty. 'I've got the replacement cost down as £750,' exclaimed Rose.

'Sounds about right,' Fiona confirmed.

'Who pays that sort of money for a bottle of fizz!'

Fiona winced. It was sacrilege to refer to any bottle of Krug as 'fizz'. In Fiona's expert opinion, Krug was the finest non-vintage Champagne; a complex, rich blend of over a hundred wines spanning over ten vintages, offering layers of flavour and a long, elegant finish. But the Clos du Mesnil was a vintage Champagne. The combination of high quality, limited availability and the Krug reputation made it a Champagne gem. 'It's pretty special, Rose.'

'Well, it *was* pretty special,' groaned her boss.

Footsteps thundered on the stone stairs, then George strode in. 'Rose, how much longer is this going to take? The blinking phone keeps ringing, and we can't keep interrupting prep to answer.'

Rose sighed. 'All right. Let's finish this off tomorrow, Fiona.'

In the space of a morning, the scale of the loss had more than doubled. But it was the pattern of disappearances, not just the value, that made Fiona's throat feel tight. Someone with intimate knowledge of the collection was behind this – someone who knew exactly which bottles were less likely to be missed. Yet another black mark against the sommelier.

Fifteen

When Fiona arrived at the pub to give Josh his wine lesson, he wasn't in the staffroom. She tried the kitchen. George was hunched over his computer screen, and Ru was filleting fish, making the task look as simple as peeling an orange.

'Where's Josh?' she asked.

Clearly absorbed in the culinary world, George didn't reply.

'Ruben?' she nudged. 'Seen Josh? I thought we'd arranged another wine tutorial.'

Ru scraped fish bones into a saucepan, adding a hand-tied bouquet garni of herbs, leaving the string dangling outside the pan. 'Yes, he did mention something about that. He's gone to fetch some more baking parchment – stocks are running a bit low.'

'Baking parchment?' she asked, rolling the words round her tongue. Why was that urgent?

'Yes,' said Ru in an offhand manner. 'I decided to cook the halibut 'en papillote' as one of tonight's specials.' He flashed her a smile. 'And to do that I need more baking parchment.'

Hmm, thought Fiona. This morning the plan had been to poach the fish in a wine-based stock. She was itching to ask if the inspiration to switch the recipe coincided with Ru's discovery of Josh's wine tutorial. 'Fine. Please tell him we'll reschedule.'

Deciding she might as well help Rose lay the tables, Fiona

marched out, leaving the door swinging behind her. Rose stood at the bar, the booking sheet in front of her.

'Anyone special in tonight, Rose.'

'You're in early,' mumbled the boss. 'And yes . . . now you ask – Richard and Cora Hastings. I've put them on Table 5. Cora made the booking and was very complimentary about you. Apparently, you recently recommended a very interesting wine to go with her rare steak.'

Fiona blushed, recalling Steakgate, and the man with the florid face. She hoped her boss would not ask her to look after the couple. The man had been rude and arrogant – the last person she wanted to serve again. 'Cora asked if you were on duty tonight, and when I told her you were, she asked for you to be on hand when they place their wine order.' Fiona's chest swelled with pride as her boss's praise echoed in her ears, a smile spread across her face and Fiona stood a little taller. She suspected Florid Face was a classic wine snob who assumed fine wine must hail from Europe, whereas his wife was more open to advice and delighted to drink similar wines at a cheaper price. 'That would be my pleasure,' Fiona responded beaming.

Later that evening, Fiona approached Table 5, where Kim, despite wearing an apron, and having an order pad tucked under an arm, looked more like a guest about to join the couple for dinner than a waitress.

Kim revealed both customers had ordered the fish special – halibut en papillote, with hazelnut butter and fresh thyme. 'I'll make sure Ruben himself prepares it for you,' Kim said, winking at the woman. 'I think he's got a crush on me.'

Fiona bit down on her lip. She hoped Ru would have better taste.

'I'll leave you in the capable hands of our sommelier,' said Kim, 'and I'll tell my Mum you said hi, Cora.'

The man spoke across the table at his wife. 'I think an aged white Burgundy will go well with that, don't you, Cora?'

Fiona might not like him, but she respected his wine knowledge; the rich, nutty, buttery flavours of an aged Chardonnay would pair beautifully with the fish, which was delicate enough to let the complexity of the wine shine. She ran mentally through the cellar, selecting a Chassagne-Montrachet.

A smile played at the corners of Cora's mouth as she sat back and caught Fiona's eye. '. . . unless our sommelier can recommend something from the New World at a fraction of the price?'

Sensing she was on treacherous ground, Fiona gushed, 'An aged white Burgundy is an excellent choice, sir, but there are several alternatives I could recommend, which are very cost-effective.'

The man took a breath. 'Go on.'

'There's one from South Africa, made also from the Chardonnay grape, called Palladius. And your wife is correct – although expensive, it's much cheaper than say a Chassagne-Montrachet, which is what I would recommend from Burgundy.' Should she mention that the South African winemaker followed biodynamic practices and fermented his wines in clay amphorae, which he believed allowed for purer expression of the terroir?

'Let me think about that,' said the man. 'Write down the details of both and I'll discuss them with my wife.'

Fiona did as asked, leaving the slip of paper with the couple while she went to fetch them some water.

She was returning with the jug of water when she bumped into Kim. 'Is that for Cora and Ricky?' asked Kim.

'It's for Table 5.'

'Mr and Mrs Hastings to you,' said Kim, sneering slightly. She tore a piece of paper in half, glanced at both pieces, then handed one to Fiona. 'Swap you. That's the wine they want.' Sauntering off, Kim added over her shoulder, 'Cora plays golf with Mummy, and Ricky is Daddy's bridge partner.'

Fiona glanced at her own handwriting; the couple had chosen the French wine. It was nearly three times the price of the South African. Rose would be thrilled. She had a sudden thought, and gulped – she hoped the wine was still in the cellar.

Five minutes later, with the precious bottle in her grasp, Fiona returned to Table 5, presenting the bottle label side up for the customer's approval.

He frowned, then waved it away. 'That's not the right wine.'

'Oh, I'm sorry, sir. This is the white Burgundy I recommended.' She checked the year. Yes, it was the correct vintage.

His face reddened. 'Exactly!' he hissed. 'We ordered the South African wine. You swapped it on purpose, didn't you? Trying to pull a fast one on us?'

Telling herself to speak calmly, and wishing the man would lower his voice, Fiona said, 'I assure you, sir, it was an honest mistake.' Except Fiona didn't think it was – she'd seen Kim check the paper before she handed it over.

'Can I help at all?' said a simpering voice. It was Kim, smiling sweetly. Fiona scraped a hand through her hair and adopted an authoritative tone. 'Thank you, Kim, I can handle this.'

But Kim didn't seem to want to leave.

'Here she is,' spluttered Mr Hastings. 'Kim, which wine did I choose? The South African or the French?'

'The South African. That's what I told the *sommelier*,' said Kim, managing to convey the impression there was something illicit in Fiona's profession. 'Has she made a mistake?'

'Thank you, Kim,' said Fiona through clenched teeth. 'Why don't you see what's happened to the starters.'

'Of course, Fiona.' Kim smiled.

Mrs Hastings reached out a steadying hand, covering one of her husband's. 'Richard let's not escalate this. It's just a mix-up. It hasn't even been opened yet.'

'A mix-up?' snapped Richard. 'She's deliberately trying to fool us into paying for a wine that's three times the price of the one we ordered. You heard Kim – I ordered the cheaper wine. This isn't my mistake. Why should I just gloss over this?'

'Because we're here to enjoy an evening together,' pleaded Cora, 'and I'd rather not start it off with a fight.'

Fiona risked joining the discussion. 'I can bring you the correct bottle right away, sir.'

'Fine but I'd better not be charged for this!'

The wife sighed. 'Let's just take a deep breath. It's just a mix-up over a bottle of wine.'

'Easy for you to say,' grumbled Richard.

'I'll take care of everything, sir. Thank you for your patience.' Fiona flashed a smile of thanks at the wife and escaped to the cellar.

For the rest of the evening Fiona kept her distance from Table 5. Anyway, she was superfluous. Kim was hanging round the table as if the couple were royalty, bending to pick up a dropped napkin, fetching a fresh jug of iced water when the one on the table was still half full.

By the end of service Fiona was still smarting – Kim had set her up. In the staffroom she pulled on her raincoat. Someone had left the windows open, and she could hear the rhythmic creaking of boat moorings in the harbour, the soft sound soothing her nerves. She leaned against the windowsill. Outside, a full moon shone, its reflection shimmering on the ocean's surface. She heard laughter, recognized Josh's gentle chuckle, and closed the window. She would rearrange their missed wine lesson.

Outside, she spotted three people standing close to the harbour wall. With the gentle shushing of the waves and the earthy smell from nearby pines, a romantic atmosphere seemed to envelope the small group. As she got closer, she identified Ru, Josh and finally Kim.

Kim's hair was loose, dancing lightly in the wind, and there was a sparkle in her eyes. 'When are you going to cook something special for me, Ruben?' she asked.

'What would you like to eat?' he asked in a teasing voice.

'Surprise me. I want a Ruben special.'

With his arms crossed, Josh watched the playful exchange. A flicker of annoyance crossed Fiona's face.

'Ah, Fiona!' Ru said, glancing over his shoulder. 'Join us! We're inventing specials and could do with some wine input.'

'From a sommelier,' said Kim, her tone mocking.

Fiona's brow furrowed and she struggled to suppress her irritation. 'Think I'll just head off, leave you three to cook up the specials. You don't need my skills,' she muttered, her voice edged with defensiveness.

'What skills might they be,' taunted Kim, 'when you can't tell the difference between a French wine and a South African?'

'What's this?' asked Ru, grinning.

Fiona's face burned and she shot Kim a sharp glare. Kim gave her version of the Table 5 wine debacle. Josh, to his credit, didn't seem to see the funny side of the story, but Ru and Kim found it amusing.

'That wasn't my fault, and you know it,' Fiona shot back, but her words felt weak against the laughter of the other two.

Ru chuckled, the sound mingling with that of waves hitting the rocks. 'Come on, Fiona! We all make mistakes! At least now we know who to send to the wine cellar,' he teased, nudging Kim playfully.

Kim burst into laughter, her joy echoing in the cool night air.

Fiona clenched her jaw, hurt surging through her as she tried to keep her composure. 'I'm not the only one who's ever messed up,' she managed, her voice steady but barely concealing her frustration.

'Come on, Fiona, don't be so sensitive!' Ru replied, his tone still light, yet it felt like a weight pressing down on her.

'Sorry I missed our lesson earlier,' said Josh. Fiona could have hugged him.

'No drama. I gather you were sent out on an errand. Same time tomorrow?'

'I reckon,' said Josh, 'so long as it's all good with the boss.' He raised his eyebrow slightly mockingly at Ruben. But Fiona didn't think he'd pull the same stunt twice in a row.

Sixteen

After spending her day off studying, Fiona slept in late on Tuesday morning. Just after nine, she woke to an email that made her heart race.

It was an alert from the CMS, announcing that new dates for the Advanced Sommelier exam were on their website. She clicked on the link, noting the date of the three day exam. It was in late November, only four weeks away, at a private members' club in London. The exam was always held in a restaurant; to test a candidate's ability to perform under pressure required a dining room setting. She would apply immediately, then request leave.

By the time she got downstairs for breakfast, the CMS had confirmed her place. Ivy insisted on making breakfast. She sat Fiona at the kitchen table with a cafetière of coffee. 'You sit while I cook,' said Ivy, beaming at her niece. 'It won't take me long.'

Fiona was still sipping her first cup of coffee, dreaming of being told she was being admitted to the CMS, when a steaming bowl of porridge appeared in front of her, together with a jar of golden honey. 'That's local,' Ivy said. 'I know the beekeeper.'

As Fiona watched honey drip languidly from her spoon, an unbidden memory surfaced: breakfast with Ru, the Sunday before her failed exam. As always, they had taken their time, like other couples would over a long, lovely dinner together. He had made salmon rillette that morning, poaching the fish delicately in stock, white wine and herbs. The rich, velvety mixture had been paired with warm, golden brioche fresh from the oven. Now, she stirred her porridge absently, the cloying texture on her tongue at odds with the memory of that decadent meal. She could almost taste the subtle tang of green peppercorns in the rillette, the buttery crispness of the brioche. They had sipped Krug with their breakfast, a perfect pairing to their life. Consumed by the art they both loved, they let work and play blur seamlessly – neither had wanted to draw a boundary. She knew that whoever she dated next would have a lot to live up to. Would her next boyfriend be like drinking a cheap boxed wine when she was used to a vintage claret?

She swallowed a mouthful of porridge. Once again, she wondered whether she had made a huge mistake breaking up with Ru. Would he have stuck with her for the long term after all, forgiving her flaws and accepting her as she was? After all, once she qualified, she would have earned his love. Briefly, she entertained a fantasy in which she passed her exam and they got back together. She shook herself out of her daydream; judging by how close he was getting to Kim, it appeared that Ru had managed to fall out of love with her faster than she could fall out of love with him.

The warm hum of the old radiators filled the staffroom. The tide was out, and Fiona could hear the distant murmur of the waves. Someone had left a window ajar, and the musky sweetness of fallen leaves drifted into the room.

Josh leaned forward. Fiona tucked her hair back behind her ears. This was about wine, not flirtation, but it was good to have her ego stroked. Her voice softened to her teaching tone. 'Tonight, we're going to discuss terroir,' Fiona said, watching

Josh's expression light up with interest, and she did her best to ignore how close he was, focusing instead on her notes.

'Terroir isn't just about the soil. Its climate, slope, altitude, the very essence of a place. It shapes the grapes,' she explained. 'That's why a Pinot Noir from Burgundy will taste so different from one from, say, America or New Zealand. The earth, the rainfall, even the wind – all of that plays into the character of the wine.'

Josh fired back at her. 'So that's why a Sancerre has that minerally edge I read about? Because of the chalky soils?'

A glimmer of approval sparked in Fiona's eyes. 'Exactly,' she replied, surprised and impressed. 'Sancerre's soil is full of limestone and flint, which gives those wines their crisp, almost steely quality.'

Josh grinned, 'And that's why Australian Chardonnay often tastes so . . .' He seemed to search for the right word, '*tropical*? Because of the warmer climate than they get in France.'

'Exactly,' she confirmed, genuinely pleased at his research. 'That warm sun ripens the grapes more fully, which can make for richer, fruitier wines. You're starting to sound like a sommelier yourself,' she teased, her voice a touch softer than she'd intended.

His gaze held hers, confidence radiating at her. 'Well, I have a good teacher,' he murmured, letting the words linger between them. She felt her cheeks warm but forced herself to continue.

'Anyway,' she said, clearing her throat, 'if you tasted a Pinot Noir from, for example, Central Otago in New Zealand, you'd notice it's very different from one made in Burgundy. The cooler climate there keeps the acidity high and the flavours intense.'

'More red fruit, more acidic?' Josh's eyes hadn't left her face. 'You see, I actually do read through the notes I take each time we meet.'

'Pleased to hear that!' And before she could hide it a smile curved her lips.

Josh held her gaze, his own smile deepening, making her blush.

The door pushed open. It was Kim. 'Not interrupting anything, am I?' she whispered loudly. 'Just wanted to leave my coat.'

'You're all right,' said Josh, gathering up his pen and pad and grinning broadly.

'Don't stop for me,' said Kim,

'So, when will you let me repay the favour, Fiona, and take you for that surf lesson?' asked Josh.

Fiona looked up, her heart fluttering. Was she really going to do this? An image of Kim giggling with Ru filled her mind. It was impossible being near him every day, but not able to be with him. She needed a distraction. 'Okay, Josh, you've worn me down.' She smiled. 'How about you take me surfing tomorrow?'

Kim sloughed off her coat. 'Brr it's chilly out there this evening. Don't you get cold in that raincoat of yours, Fiona?' asked Kim in a friendly tone.

A folded piece of paper slipped from Kim's coat pocket, dancing to the floor. Josh scooped it up. It was a handwritten page of notes.

'You dropped something' he said, studying the page with interest. His bronze face broke into a grin. 'Wine pairings? Fancy yourself a sommelier now?' he asked, holding it over for Fiona to look at. It was a meticulously detailed list of the house wines matched with different foods, complete with flavour descriptions. What caught Fiona's eye was how formulaic the descriptions seemed, almost like someone had memorized terms rather than experienced the flavours themselves.

Kim lunged for the notes, but Josh held them just out of reach.

'Hand it over,' Kim snapped, her tone brittle.

'Hang on now,' Josh teased. 'Is this for some posh dinner party you're hosting? Planning to impress with your 'sophisticated palate?

Fiona expected Kim to tear into him – it was what she'd do if she were alone with Fiona, after all. But something in her expression shifted, a crack in her carefully maintained façade. She looked younger suddenly, and surprisingly vulnerable.

'None of your business,' said Kim. Fiona recognized the bitterness in that voice – it was the same tone Kim used with her.

'Why are you working here Kim?' asked Josh.

'The younger woman snatched the page away from Josh. Her fingers smoothed over the creased paper with its carefully written descriptions, 'I just want my parents to be proud of me. I want to show them I can do this.' Then she tucked the page away, and her emotional barriers reappeared. Her spine straightened, her chin lifted, and she was once again the Kim that Fiona knew – beautiful, poised, confident. Unable to shake the image of the vulnerability which had flickered across Kim's face, Fiona called time on the wine lesson.

'Right, Josh, I think that's enough for one night,' said Fiona. 'Unless you've any more questions?' Snapping her book shut, Fiona rose and stowed it in her bag. All the talk of wine was reigniting her worries about the missing wine.

'Just one, Fiona,' Josh answered with a languid smile. 'Where shall we meet for our surf date?'

While Josh returned to the kitchen, Fiona and Kim joined Rose, who was laying up for the evening service.

'Are we full again tonight, boss?' asked Kim.

'We're fully booked every night. There's a waiting list for most evenings,' replied Rose, picking up a glass and holding it up to the light. 'This one has marks on it.'

'I'll fetch another,' said Kim, grabbing the dirty glass and rushing off.

'So helpful, that girl,' said Rose, examining another glass. 'I confess I was a little anxious when her father asked me to take her on. She's hardly from the classic waitressing background, but I was wrong. All the guests like her. She's got energy, enthusiasm and she's always got a smile on her face.'

Around everyone but me, thought Fiona, managing a weak smile. She wished Josh hadn't called the surfing lesson 'a date' in front of Kim. It wasn't a date, but she had an inkling Kim would find a way to spin the information to her advantage.

For a few minutes, Fiona and Rose moved around the tables, checking the glassware, straightening cutlery and folding napkins. Kim seemed to be taking an awfully long time finding a single glass.

'You know, I respect your wine knowledge,' Rose said. 'I need your help finishing the cellar stock take – you find everything so quickly. Can you come in around ten tomorrow morning?'

Fiona agreed, but part of her was questioning if her cellar knowledge was about to become a liability.

Kim trotted back into the dining room, carrying a glass. 'George says he'll be out shortly. They're a bit behind on preparations.' Kim angled her head towards Fiona while spinning the wineglass in her hands. Fiona blinked, suspecting she knew what was coming, and sure enough, Kim added tartly, 'Apparently Josh was a bit late for work.'

Rose's eyes flickered between the two younger women, as if sensing that one was willing her to enquire why Josh had been late for work and the other praying she wouldn't probe. Rose took a breath before speaking. 'I understand from Richard Hastings there was a mix-up over their wine on Saturday night, which Kim helped resolve.'

Fiona frowned; she would have preferred Rose to ask what caused Josh to be late for work. That wine incident was Kim's work, and Kim had done nothing to resolve it, but Fiona had no proof, and decided it was better to simply take the blame. 'I fetched the wrong bottle. Mrs Hastings was a lot more understanding than her husband.'

The kitchen door opened, and George strode out, followed by Ru, then Josh.

'Just be more careful next time, please. He is our landlord,' said Rose.

'It was quite a drama!' said Kim, in an unnecessarily loud voice, a smile twitching at her lips.

'What's this?' asked George scowling.

'Did someone say *drama*?' drawled Josh.

'We were just discussing Fiona's wine mistake on Saturday night,' said Kim.

'Orchestrated by you,' Fiona snapped. The words were out before she could stop herself, and she instantly regretted them.

There was a collective gasp. Rose trained her eyes on Fiona, then spoke gently. 'We're a team. Please don't be prickly with Kim.'

'Sorry,' mumbled Fiona.

'Once I explained to Cora and Ricky that she had failed her Advanced Sommelier exam they were very understanding,' said Kim in a sympathetic tone.

Biting her tongue, Fiona took the clean glass from Kim's hands, setting it down on the table a fraction more forcefully than she normally would.

'Shall we talk about the specials?' suggested Josh.

While George extolled the virtues of the evening specials, Kim scribbled notes with an attentive expression painted on her face and asked questions like the class swot. Was the fish from Brambleton

Harbour itself? How was the duck confit made? And which farm was the meat from? Fiona diverted her mind, focusing on pairing food flavours with wines.

'Any more questions?' asked George.

'Yes, can someone lend me a pen, please,' laughed Rose.

Josh plucked one from behind an ear and tossed it over.

Kim put up her hand, making Fiona cringe. 'Sorry, but Ruben, could you please run me through how that duck confit was made?' She waved her hands as if dismissing everyone else. 'I don't want to keep you all waiting, but it sounded amazing, and I didn't take proper notes.' She smiled at Ru. 'If you could spare a couple of minutes . . .?'

'Sure,' said Ru.

Fiona hesitated, watching Ru lean on the bar and hearing Kim chuckle at a shared joke. She noticed the other woman put out a hand to touch Ru's arm, and he didn't pull away. Kim tipped her head back and giggled. Fiona crossed her arms, feeling a burning sensation in her chest. If the key to a man's heart was through his stomach, the key to a chef's was through an interest in his cooking.

Fiona's interest in Ru's food had always been genuine, but it looked suspiciously like Kim was interested in the man, not the food. Despite her brain warning her to leave them alone, her heart dragged her towards them like a puppet tugged by strings it cannot see or sever.

'It's an interesting dish to pair a wine with,' said Fiona.

'Here she is,' said Kim light-heartedly, 'the woman who doesn't think wine under £50 is worth drinking.'

Ru laughed. The sound sliced Fiona's heart open like a wolf's claw raking across ice.

Fiona defended herself. This had been her undoing in her Advanced Sommelier exam, and she was now all over the topic of regional and New World wines.

'A Pinot Noir from Burgundy would be the classic pairing with duck confit, and you'd be lucky to get away with £50, but there are several excellent options that pair beautifully for a modest budget, such as a Pinot Noir from Oregon or New Zealand, which provide similar elegance and complexity at a more approachable price point. Of course, if a customer was open to sampling a different grape, I'd also recommend exploring reds from Italy's Trentino-Alto Adige region, such as wines made from the Teroldego grape. Or for a touch more tannin, try wines from Spain's Ribeira Sacra, where they grow the Mencía grape. All very cost-effective.'

There was a sour expression on Kim's face. 'Must be a huge cellar Rose has if they've got all those stored down there,' said Kim, the tension radiating from her. Ru's eyes swivelled between the two women as if concerned he might have to prevent a fist fight.

'Gotta get on,' he said, walking away, a subtle smirk tugging at the corner of his lips. He glanced over his shoulder, clearly savouring the flicker of competition between Kim and Fiona.

'Show off,' hissed Kim, her voice barely a whisper.

Fiona responded, 'Just let me do my job and you stick to yours,' she muttered, but goaded, her voice was louder than she intended, and Ru spun around.

'That was spiteful, and your earlier speech was frankly a bit arrogant, Fiona. We can't all spend our time swotting up on obscure grapes.'

Beside the counter Kim smiled coquettishly: 'Thanks for standing up for me, Ruben.'

Fiona's insides curled as the truth settled. Ru had moved on, and she'd missed the signs. His continued presence in Devon wasn't a symbol of lingering love; it was a sense of duty. Having promised to help George, he wouldn't renege.

A hollow ache spread through her as she accepted that he wasn't coming back – not for her, not anymore. She looked away. Being around him every day was tough. Their relationship had become like a decanted wine left too long – the initial complexity had separated, leaving only a harsh, bitter residue to endure.

At least she had her CMS exam booked, and this time she was not telling anyone.

As arranged, Fiona met Rose outside the cellar at 10 a.m. the next morning. Her boss unlocked the heavy wooden door with a methodical turn of the key, switched on the lights and the pair padded down the stone steps. For once, the familiar earthy dampness that usually whispered of hidden mysteries felt oppressive, clinging to Fiona's skin like a shroud. She was dreading what they might discover.

Rose, however, seemed in an ebullient mood. 'It's our anniversary soon. George wants to put a little table for two down here. He says he thinks its romantic.' She sighed. 'I hope he'll still think so when he learns how much of his precious wine is missing.'

Fiona closed her eyes and imagined the cellar bathed in warm candlelight. A couple sat at a small table, their quiet laughter echoing softly against the stone walls. Wine crates, repurposed as side tables, the couple holding elegant flutes filled with Champagne, the fine mousse unfurling like lace, trembling as it drifted, each delicate bubble a liquid prism shimmering in the soft, flickering candlelight. The image was easy to summon; that memory of sharing oysters and Champagne with Ru in the Fork & Cork's cellar still hovered, vivid and tender.

When Fiona opened her eyes, she could hardly bear it. In front of her were not Ru's strong hands shucking oysters, just a row of dusty wine bins. She shook the memory out of her head.

'Where do you want to start? Italy, Australia or America?' asked Fiona.

'Let's do the US.'

America took nearly an hour and revealed another £2000 discrepancy.

'Did you check your insurance policy?' asked Fiona.

'George did. He says we're not covered for cork fly, but it's not a pesky insect that's done this – there's more than the cork missing.'

Fiona laughed, then explained. 'Cork fly is not an insect. It's when corks are dislodged unexpectedly. It's quite a typical exclusion because cork fly is preventable through proper storage practices. Is that the only exclusion?'

'No,' said Rose through gritted teeth. '*Mysterious disappearance*. I guess that's exactly what we've got here. If someone had smashed down the cellar door and it was obvious there had been a break-in, we would be covered. Let's do South Africa, there's not too much of that, then finish off after lunch service,' suggested Rose.

Fiona crouched, her fingers brushing against a meticulously arranged stack of distinctive Vin de Constance black bottles. Their seventeenth-century style squat bodies and long necks caught the soft light – each one a testament to a legendary wine that had once graced the tables of Napoleon, charmed Charles Dickens and delighted Jane Austen. She started calling out the vintages: 'Two bottles of 2014.'

'Hold on. There should be a much earlier vintage. Three bottles of the 1986.'

Fiona's brow furrowed, and she stumbled over her words. 'Did you . . . Did you say 1986?'

'Yes. Three bottles.'

'Let me check,' she mumbled, acutely aware of Rose's piercing gaze watching her every move as she gently picked up each bottle, examining them one by one, a sinking feeling in her stomach. There wasn't a single bottle from the earlier vintage. She turned to face her boss and shook her head. 'Nope. Gone.'

'Strange. It doesn't say how much those are worth. The more recent vintages are listed at about the £40 mark, so I guess the others would be the same. Why would someone pinch bottles worth less than a blended Champagne?'

Unable to speak, Fiona massaged her throat. She wanted to sprint back upstairs. Things were moving too fast for her to process.

Her boss's eyes narrowed. 'You've gone a bit pale. Was 1986 a particularly good vintage?'

Fiona knew it was good, not exceptional. But that didn't matter. For over a century Vin de Constance hadn't been made. The vines had been killed by Phylloxera, a tiny insect that damaged the roots and leaves of the vines. In the nineteenth century the insects devastated European vineyards before spreading to South Africa. The estate had restarted making wine in 1986, and at the Nederburg wine auction in Cape Town, a bottle of their maiden vintage could easily fetch over £2000. Knowing Rose would soon uncover those facts for herself, Fiona told her. Rose wore a quizzical expression. 'Apart from a wine expert, who would know something as obscure as that?' Fiona's eyes flicked upstairs towards the kitchen involuntarily.

'I'll tell you who would know,' gasped Rose. 'A South African chef.

Seventeen

Fiona stood motionless as the metal hasp scraped against wood, the lock clicking into place with a finality that echoed the sudden fracture of her world. Until two months ago, Ru had been her business partner, her confidant, her lover . . . the man whose heartbeat she'd known as intimately as her own. Now he was suspected of a crime she could scarcely comprehend.

Her mind churned like a turbulent sea, memories colliding. Fragments of shared dreams, tender moments and professional ambitions, all splintered by nagging questions: Was Ru connected to the missing wine? How could she have been so spectacularly wrong? Her ability to read people, once a point of professional pride, now felt like a cruel joke.

It couldn't be Ru, could it? He was a success story. He had secured substantial financial backing for a new restaurant, and the success of the Fork & Cork suggested he was on the cusp of even greater achievements. There had even been talk of a book deal. Yet now, confronted with evidence of wine theft, everything she thought she knew about him was being called into question. Despite all her efforts to shut it out, a tiny, persistent voice in her mind wove an ugly narrative.

What if this wasn't a simple theft, but a calculated move? Ru had always been bold, dramatic – the type who might orchestrate an elaborate scheme. Was he framing her for the theft in revenge for her hurting him? Mentally she defended him: no, he had a heart of gold, he would never be that spiteful. His instinct was to protect not to punish. The only harsh words he'd ever uttered had been lashing out at her after she'd thrown equally nasty ones at him.

Then an even worse explanation occurred to her. What if, like her, he was in financial trouble, and the real reason Ru came to the pub was not to win her back, but to steal wine? Perhaps the investors for the new restaurant had pulled out? What if they'd questioned Ru's judgement for trying to include Fiona in his team, after her exam failure? What if the Fork & Cork was losing money? She recalled his nasty snap about wanting back the money he had loaned her. Was it possible that he needed money and had resorted to desperate tactics to get it?

She really didn't want to believe that Ru could be a thief. But who, other than Ru and herself, understood the significance of those South African wines?

Rose held up the key for a moment before slipping it into her trouser pocket. 'From now on I'm keeping this on me.'

Fiona stared blankly at her boss, wondering what Rose was thinking. She didn't dare ask. She was afraid to hear what she suspected – that Rose blamed Ru. Fiona felt powerless – it would look peculiar if she leaped to the defence of a colleague who she was supposed to have only known for a few weeks. Her mind raced. What should she do? Her relationship with Ru was over, but she didn't want him arrested. Without alerting their employers she must warn him. Give Ru time to replace the wine if it was him, and if it wasn't, give him a heads-up before someone accused him of theft.

Throughout lunch, the pub hummed with excited chatter and bursts of laughter. The space was packed with holidaymakers who'd stayed on despite the autumn drizzle, their faces flushed from coastal walks. Each time the front door opened Fiona felt a blast of cold wind. She pulled her apron tighter around her waist, feeling the crisp edge of a wine-stained piece of paper crumpled in her pocket. The numbers she'd scribbled earlier, tallied hastily when she and Rose had discovered the extra missing bottles, prickled at the back of her mind. Wine wasn't the only thing that seemed to be disappearing; her patience was fraying with each new table she greeted.

'Table 3's asking for another bottle of Chablis,' called Rose, giving her a look that was both sympathetic and exasperated. Today, worry shadowed Rose's usually serene face. The missing wine bottles were festering in both of their minds, and although Rose hadn't said it aloud, Fiona could tell her boss was itching to confront Ru.

Fiona crossed to Table 3, where four couples were crammed together. She wasn't surprised they needed another bottle. Fiona filled a tray with the empty glasses, acknowledging the two customers still drinking. 'I'll bring clean ones for the new bottle.'

That was one of her golden rules. Each bottle of fine wine was unique. She wouldn't risk mixing the fresh wine with the old.

Balancing the tray carefully, she wove between tables. The scent of rich food tangled with the salt air, setting her stomach rumbling. She hadn't been able to eat anything; not since that ghastly discovery in the cellar.

Just as she approached the bar, Kim brushed by, her shoulder nudging Fiona's arm and tilting the tray dangerously. Fiona steadied it, her fingers tightening around a glass, while Kim flashed her a tight smile.

'Careful, there,' Kim said with mock concern, placing a sugar bowl down at the next table. 'Wouldn't want you dropping anything.' Her tone was light, almost singsong, but there was a glint in her eye that made Fiona's cheeks flush. She bit her lip, swallowing down a retort. Kim was all silky words and soft smiles with customers and the other staff. With Fiona though, Kim's words often carried an edge.

A family at a corner table flagged Kim down and she immediately turned around, smiling and chatting with them effortlessly.

Fiona watched for a moment, sensing the knot of frustration tighten. Kim's soft voice drifted across the room as she laughed at a customer's joke. The warmth she projected was almost convincing enough for Fiona to doubt herself. But she could still feel the cold of Kim's shoulder brushing past her, her voice echoing in her head, taunting, and then Kim's gaze met hers over the heads of the diners, and Fiona saw that flash again – the barely concealed smirk, gone in an instant, but enough to remind her that there was something Kim was reserving just for her.

A loud crash echoed from the bar, followed by a muttered curse from Rose. Fiona turned, catching sight of her boss wiping down the counter with jerky, irritated motions. That was a second glass shattered. Rose was clearly rattled: she rarely broke things. Trying to shake off a sense of unease, Fiona, accompanied by Rose, went to fetch the wine for Table 3 from the cellar. Fiona couldn't stop thinking about the missing wine. She must warn Ru that he was a suspect. She owed him that much. But when would she catch him alone?

The autumn sun hung low, its pale honey light gilding the crests of the waves. Fiona squinted against the soft glare, the breeze tangling her fair hair as she adjusted the rope tethering her ankle to the board. The sand was cold beneath her bare feet and scattered with shells and dry seaweed that crunched softly when stepped on. She glanced at her 'instructor' – or at least that was how she'd described Josh in her head.

'You ready to get wet?' he asked, his accent lilting and warm.

Fiona forced a smile. 'Sure.' She gripped the waxy surface of the foam board, its bright yellow colour an almost cartoonish contrast to the muted blues and greens of the sea. Her stomach was roiling with nerves, or the lingering ache of love for Ru. It didn't matter which. Today was about distractions and Josh was a distraction wrapped in an Aussie drawl and taut muscles.

They waded into the water. The first icy wave splashed against her thighs, and she sucked in a sharp breath. 'Bloody cold,' she muttered.

Josh chuckled close behind her. 'It's bracing. Good for the soul.'

The waves tugged at her hips and her skin prickled with goosebumps as the wetsuit clung tighter to her body. Josh moved alongside her, his arm brushing hers as he steadied her on the board. She wasn't sure she needed the help, but he lingered, his hand resting a beat too long on her waist.

'Alright, now lie flat on your tummy,' he said, his voice soft yet insistent. She obeyed, feeling the slick chill of the board beneath her. Josh crouched beside her in the shallows, his hands running lightly over her hands. 'When you see the wave coming, you paddle like mad. Then pop up quick, yeah? Here, I'll show you.'

His hands guided her arms. His breath smelled faintly of coffee and saltwater, warm against her cheek as he leaned in to demonstrate. Her cheeks flushed, but she didn't pull away. She had to move on from Ru. She *had* to.

The ocean roared around them, waves breaking with hissing foam. She caught a faint whiff of something earthy and familiar, carried on the breeze – the scent of wood smoke evoking a memory of her and Ru sitting in front of a log fire grilling sardines on a beach in Portugal. She squeezed her eyes shut and focused on Josh's voice.

'Now paddle!'

She did as instructed, her arm muscles straining against the resistance of the water. A swell lifted the board, and she wobbled upright, balancing precariously as the wave propelled her toward the shore feeling a brief thrill of triumph before the inevitable tumble. The salt water rushed into her nose and mouth as she crashed.

Spluttering, she surfaced, pushing her wet hair from her face. Through stinging eyes, she spotted a figure on the shore, silhouetted against the sun. Ru.

Her breath caught. He stood still, arms crossed, watching her. Watching *them*.

Josh's laughter broke the moment. He swam to her, brushing hair from her face. 'You alright? First wipeout's always a bummer.'

Fiona forced a laugh, though her chest felt heavy. 'I'm fine,' she lied, her voice strained.

'Bet this is a ton more fun than swotting up for an exam you don't need, eh? Ready to catch another wave?'

Ru's presence burned at the edge of her vision. She couldn't look again. Guided by Josh's firm arms round her waist, Fiona waded out into the water again, her eyes searching for an incoming wave big enough to surf. She put Ru firmly out of her mind and caught herself smiling when the next wave washed through her. She couldn't think of the last time she had felt this invigorated.

When she passed that exam, maybe she *would* grab hold of a bit more of life.

The following afternoon, Fiona was sitting in a bay window at Prosecco & Prose, her laptop open in front of her. Frustrated by the constant interruptions of their wine lessons at the pub, Fiona had suggested meeting Josh here for their next lesson. It was a comfortable space, warm, busy, with the sweet aroma of baking pastries. The soft *whoosh* of the coffee machine punctuated the gentle purr of conversations. A bell tinkled, heralding another customer. Fiona looked up. Josh entered, a bright smile on his face, looking as excited as a trainee chef peering through the oven door, watching their first soufflé rise.

He pulled out a chair and sat. 'Great idea to meet here. Finally, no one can interrupt us.'

She forced a tight smile, her fingers curling around the edge of her coffee cup as she avoided his gaze.

'I'm glad you could make it,' she replied, her tone carefully neutral. Her eyes flickered briefly to the door, a faint tension settling on her shoulders. She hadn't expected him to sound quite so enthusiastic about this meeting – nor to feel so alone with him.

'What are we covering today?' he asked.

Fiona flipped through her notes, feeling the familiar surge of passion replace her wariness about them meeting in private. 'I thought we would explore some of the lesser-known wine regions.' She felt a stab of pride – this topic was not her bête noire any more. 'Everyone talks about France, Italy or South America, but places like Portugal's Douro Valley or Spain's Priorat region offer fantastic wines at much lower prices.'

She saw Josh's eyes widen.

'I've never heard of that place in Spain. Good reds?' he asked, leaning forward.

'Definitely! It's all about finding value.' Fiona smiled, watching his focus tighten on her words.

As she spoke, laughter erupted from a nearby table, adding a buzz to the café's warmth. Momentarily, Josh glanced over, but his gaze quickly returned to her, pen poised, intent. 'Now, all this talk about wine – when can we put it into practice in the real world? Can I take you out for a glass or two?'

Her smile faltered, just slightly. She had felt great in their surf lesson, but Josh was practically a boy, and she wasn't ready to date. She laughed it off. 'Maybe we could do some sampling together.'

Josh's grin grew wider, and he pulled his chair closer to the table, leaning over with his chin hovering so close to her hands so could feel his breath warm them. 'Sounds great,' he said.

She sat back, snapping her laptop shut and picking up her coffee with both hands. 'In the end, it's about experimenting and trusting your own tastes. Find what you like, regardless of price.'

Josh nodded, then set his pen down. 'Fiona, seriously, this has been amazing. How about letting me return the favour. Dinner? My treat.'

Fiona felt her cheeks flush. Dinner? That really was a date.

He pushed. 'Please. To say thank you.'

She shouldn't have taken up that surf lesson, or she should have done more to discourage his hands. Wishing she could stop herself, Fiona compared him to Ru; Josh felt like a supermarket fizz beside vintage Champagne. There was a sparkle to Josh, but no complexity, no depth. On the other hand, he was fun to be around and that was something she needed in her life right now.

'What are you worried about? That you might enjoy yourself again like you did in the surf? Come on, girl, lighten up. Live for life. It's just an evening out. I'm not asking you to marry me.'

Josh was right – it would be good to get out.

'Alright, but not dinner,' she said. 'I don't want you spending too much on me. Besides, I've enjoyed teaching you.'

'What about the movies?' he suggested. 'There's a really great little independent cinema in Barnstaple.'

That sounded quite safe, and not too expensive. She didn't

want to lead him on. 'Sounds lovely, you choose the film. Anything except for sci-fi or horror.'

'I'll check the website. Monday, when the restaurant is shut?'

She smiled, her heart tugging slightly. Not that Josh wasn't great, but he wasn't *Ru*. She knew she must stop clinging to the past. It felt too early for her to be interested in someone else, but going out on a date with Josh might be just what she needed. But as she nodded, a quiet voice in the back of her mind questioned if she was doing this for the right reasons – or if she was just running away from the shadows Ru had left behind.

Eighteen

That evening, Fiona leaned against the cool metal of the serving counter, her heart racing as she caught sight of Ru. He was prepping for the evening service, moving with a grace that belied the frenetic energy of the kitchen. His skin glistened under the bright fluorescent lights as he nimbly sliced vegetables, each motion precise and deliberate. The sweet aroma of caramelizing onions permeated the air. She waited briefly, checking for Josh or George in the stockroom. Once she was sure they were alone, she grabbed his attention. 'Ru!'

He looked up, his dark eyes locking onto hers for a fleeting moment before darting away, back to his work. 'Fiona, I've got a lot to do before service starts,' he replied, his tone clipped, as if the idea of conversation exhausted him.

Her heart twisted. 'It's important,' she insisted, her voice rising slightly above the kitchen clatter. 'I need to talk to you about something.'

'Can't it wait? I'm in the middle of prepping,' he replied coldly, not even looking around at her. His shoulders were tense. She could sense the wall he was putting up between them. It was what she'd asked for and what she knew she needed, yet she felt a pang of hurt, nonetheless. She pushed aside the sorrow. She was here to help him without going backwards in her attempt to fall out of love with him. He was making that part easier, at least. 'Ru, please put the knife down for a minute.' she said, her voice softer now, almost pleading.

Finally, he paused, setting down his knife and turning to face her fully. 'What do you want?' he shot back, his tone sharper than she expected.

Fiona felt warmth rise to her cheeks, the frustration bubbling inside her.

'I have something to say that will help you!'

Ru's gaze hardened, and she felt the air thicken between them. 'I saw you.'

She flinched. 'Saw me?'

'With Josh. First on the beach, then in Prosecco & Prose.'

'Oh that,' she blushed. 'It was a surf lesson – I was living life a little.'

He huffed. She tutted. 'And we were doing what most people do in a café – having coffee.'

'Looked like quite an intimate coffee to me. Didn't take you long to move on, did it.'

His words hit her like a physical blow, and she took a sharp breath, feeling the heat of the kitchen close in around her. She looked away. Although she knew she couldn't be with Ru, being near him every day was tough.

'It was just coffee!' she protested, her voice rising in a mixture of frustration and desperation. 'Not that it's any of your business, but we were discussing wine.'

'Right,' he said, sarcasm dripping from his voice. 'Discussing wine. Why not spend your spare time studying instead of flirting, so you can become fully qualified and repay your debts.' She gasped. The words cut deep, like the edge of a freshly sharpened knife, cold and precise, slicing through the quiet between them. She would show him – once qualified, and earning a chunky salary, she would repay his loan in full. Immediately.

'Ru, there isn't time to fight. Listen to me!' She felt the urgency of what she needed to say rising within her. 'I need to warn you.'

'About what?' His brow furrowed, and for a moment, she thought he might let her in, but then he turned away, grabbing another handful of herbs, massacring them like a vengeful gardener taking out years of repressed anger on an unsuspecting patch of greenery.

Determined to get through to him despite the growing distance, she took a step closer. 'It's serious! I think you might be in danger,'

'Danger?' His laugh was incredulous. 'From what? The kitchen porter?'

'Stop it!' she exclaimed, the words bursting from her. 'This isn't about us, me! It's about *you* – about something that could hurt you. Please, just listen!'

He looked at her then, really looked at her, and for a moment, the mask he wore cracked. She saw the hurt in his eyes, and a flash of something softer. Was there lingering affection buried beneath his layers of resentment? She wasn't sure. A part of her hoped desperately that there was, and another part knew it would be easier on them both if he had already snuffed out any flame of longing or love.

'Fine. What is it?' he asked, his voice suddenly low and intense, almost vulnerable.

Before she could elaborate, the swing door to the kitchen burst open and the words died on her lips. George strode in with a flourish, oblivious to the tension between his sommelier and the sous chef. 'Fiona! Rose is looking for you!' he said, sinking into a chair and flipping open his laptop.

'On my way,' she replied, her heart sinking as she stepped back. Fiona sensed the disappointment pooling inside her, the chance to protect Ru slipping away like the bouquet of a long decanted fine wine. She glanced back at him, but he was already lost in prep again. The warning that had felt so urgent just moments earlier was now eclipsed by the demands of the kitchen.

An hour later and Fiona was standing behind the bar, squeezing lime juice into a cocktail shaker. In front of her was a tray with three bowl-like glasses, their broad rims frosty with salt. As she began pouring in the margaritas, a hush fell over the busy restaurant, and she looked up. Ru. His presence was like a pulse of energy shooting round the room. She tracked him walking towards the table she was preparing drinks for, his progress shadowed by the irritating presence of Kim, once more clad top to toe in the sort of clothes Fiona would never be able to afford.

Fiona picked up the tray, balancing it carefully as she threaded through the crowded tables. Ru was deep in conversation with a customer. Kim's hand rested on his arm, and Fiona searched Ru's face for clues. Where once she could detect his thoughts from the subtle shift of his mouth or flicker of his eyes, now she couldn't read him. One thing she was certain of though: he wasn't pulling his arm free. Even though she knew this was best for both of them, her heart twisted, and she looked away, focusing on keeping her tray steady.

Nearing the table, Fiona swept her eyes over Ru, knowing that whatever his feelings towards her, he would always appreciate a perfectly prepared cocktail, and she still craved his approval, especially in front of Kim. Suddenly, a customer gestured animatedly, catching Fiona off guard. The tray tipped and, in a split second, Fiona watched in horror as one of the margaritas flew directly at Ru's chest. She heard a gasp, then stunned silence. Margarita dripped from Ru's white jacket. Fiona bit her lip – what a fiasco, all witnessed by Kim, and this time, it really was Fiona's fault.

'Oh my god, I'm so sorry,' she stammered, dumping her tray, ripping off her apron and moving towards Ru.

'It's fine,' he said, his eyes twinkling as he took the apron gently, dabbing his jacket. He didn't look angry; in fact, he looked almost amused. 'No harm done.'

Fiona became aware of how close they were standing. She caught a whiff of lime mingling with basil and oregano, the smell so comforting, familiar. For a moment, neither of them spoke.

Then Kim cleared her throat loudly, breaking the spell, and stepping between them with a clean napkin, shoving Fiona out of the way. 'How clumsy. Let me help you with that.'

Fiona stepped back, her heart sinking as she noticed the way Kim blotted Ru's jacket with unnecessary fuss, pressing her hands against muscles she knew to be toned – until recently she used to be the one to stroke them. He didn't move away, but he looked past Kim's shoulder, catching Fiona's eye for just a second and she felt a jolt of hope, certain she saw a spark there – something that looked almost like regret.

At five o'clock on Monday, the doorbell rang. 'That's your date,' said Ivy, smiling coyly. 'Are you going to invite him in to meet me?'

Fiona rolled her eyes. 'It's a thank you, not a date.'

'As you like.' said her aunt, kissing her cheek. 'Enjoy yourself.'

Fiona answered the door. Outside, Josh stood wearing a hoodie, with his hands thrust into his trouser pockets. 'Hi,' he said, grinning. 'Ready?'

She smiled. He opened the garden gate for her and pointed at a small white van, the words *The Smuggler's Inn, Brambleton* written above an artist's sketch of the pub. 'George let me borrow the van. Saves on taxis.'

She appreciated avoiding a long bus wait, but suspected George and Rose would paint this as a date and dreaded their teasing . . . and Ru's anger. She settled herself in the passenger seat, acutely conscious of Josh's presence. Today, sitting beside him felt awkward. She knew talking would help and asked him about surfing.

For the next fifteen minutes Fiona let him eulogize about his sport, interjecting with nods and probing questions.

'Sounds like I've got you hooked,' he ribbed. 'Fancy another lesson?'

Lulled by the comfortable atmosphere in the cabin, she asked why, if he loved the sport, he gave up being a professional. 'I know you said it was your parents' dream, but didn't it become yours too?'

'For a while,' he admitted, 'but then I discovered there's so much more to life.'

'As a teenager!' she mocked. 'Must have been a girl.'

He became serious. 'A woman, yes, but not a girl . . .'

'Sounds mysterious.'

'Remember I told you about my gran?'

She nodded.

'We were real close. She moved to Sydney when she realized we weren't coming back. When she died, she left me her diaries. All her working life – twenty years in Brambleton, then another fifteen in Sydney, she was a dinner lady. Those diaries. Amazing. They were chock full of happiness. Raising kids' confidence before tests, being told their results, sometimes before they'd even told their parents. Acting as the school agony aunt for teenage lovers' spats. And I kinda asked myself, if that woman got so much joy out of life by living every moment of every day doing something as unchallenging as being a dinner lady, what was I doing with my life? I couldn't recall being as happy as she had been. *Ever.* Challenged yes, proud, sure, exhausted, definitely, but happy? Nope. So, I asked myself why I was wasting my time doing the same bloody thing day after day if it never made me happy.'

'So that's why you're a KP.'

'Hey, don't knock it. I'm way happier than I was ten years ago. Gives me enough money to pay my way, and plenty of time off during the day to surf.'

He slung the van into a parking space. 'We're here.'

Josh led the way down a darkening street to the cinema. He paid for their tickets, then offered to buy her a bag of chocolates or a box of popcorn. Fiona tried to stay focused on the present, but she couldn't help it. Her mind drifted back to her first date with Ru, the memory flooding her senses like a rising tide.

They had met at Borough Market, where vendors' voices rose and fell in a rhythmic urban symphony, punctuated by the sharp chop of knives against wooden boards. Ru was waiting for her, his hands casually tucked into his jacket pockets, a confident smile playing on his lips. He exuded an unexpected warmth, softening the talented, focused chef she admired.

He had led her through the maze of food stalls and a tapestry of scents – succulent meat sputtering on open grills, releasing wisps of smoky fragrance; wild mushrooms oozing their earthy perfume; chestnuts crackling and caramelizing, discharging a sweet, nutty smell. Ru described each smell with the precision of someone who lived and breathed flavour. Fiona found herself spellbound, the sensory overload of the market intoxicating. Ru picked out a lamb kofta wrap for her, drizzled with creamy yogurt, while he selected a crispy, spicy empanada. With a mischievous grin, he dared her to try a bite of his choice. She did, laughing as the heat hit her tongue, then shared a bite of her wrap in return. It felt natural. Ru wasn't just a chef; he was someone who loved the comfort and community of food. He found joy in life's simplest moments.

Later, they strolled to a cosy craft beer pub. Fiona scanned the taps quickly, picking out a smoky stout for Ru and a lighter ale for herself. As they clinked glasses, she noticed the spark in his eyes – a mix of admiration and curiosity, filling her with a longing to prolong the evening, to spend more time with this intriguing man.

Now, sitting in the brightly lit cinema foyer with Josh, Fiona couldn't shake the contrast. The innocent offer of prepackaged chocolates and popcorn felt so distant from the vibrant, spontaneous energy of that evening with Ru. Josh's voice interrupted her musing. 'Would you like a drink? There's a bar upstairs, not sure I'd recommend the wine, but they might have a decent beer.'

She declined, wanting her senses sharp, aware of the difference between now and before. Josh wasn't *Ru* – not by a long shot.

The door to their screen opened and a stream of customers flooded into the foyer, blinking as their eyes adjusted to the harsh lights. Josh held the door open a second longer than necessary, smiling brightly as she slipped past him, her nostrils assaulted by the stale smell of a recently crowded room. They sank into their seats, the imitation velvet fabric squeaking as Josh fidgeted beside her. He offered her some popcorn, holding the tub slightly too close to her face. She waved it away, more curtly than she meant to. 'No, thanks.' She could feel him watching her in the low light, his gaze almost pressing down on her, and she exhaled, trying to focus on the trailer starting on the screen.

Josh leaned towards her. 'I've heard this movie is amazing.'

She forced a small smile, glancing at the flickering screen.

'Great,' she replied, wishing he'd relax, or, even better, stop talking altogether. She was thinking she'd made a mistake agreeing to this night out. Like Ru said, she should be revising.

She sat stiffly, her knees pressed together, arms crossed loosely over her bag. In front of her, the glossy trailers flickered, but she barely registered them. Josh's proximity gnawed at her – how he leaned slightly toward her to make a jokey comment, how his elbow hovered too close on the shared armrest. She told herself it wasn't a date. Yet the way his eyes lingered on her in the dim light told another story, one she didn't want to read. A sickly smell of vape clung to Josh, mixing with the salty aroma of the popcorn. He was fidgeting, and every time he moved a faint whoosh of air carried his scent over to her. She tried to ignore it, staring intently at the screen, but even the briefest shifts in his seat felt exaggerated to her senses.

He whispered something – was it about the upcoming movie? A joke about the adverts? She smiled vaguely, her attention fixed on the glowing *Exit* sign at the edge of her vision.

As the opening scenes of the film finally began, Fiona felt a surge of relief – an excuse to go quiet, to avoid the dance of polite engagement. Josh, however, kept glancing over at her, his face lighting up with every mildly funny line or dramatic moment, as if waiting for her to share in his enthusiasm. She realized that despite what he'd said about it being just an evening out, she might be leading him on. Perhaps it would have been better if she had declined his invitation and stayed in her room studying. Then she spotted the van keys in Josh's lap, and she swallowed.. By tomorrow, Ru would doubtless know all about this evening. She could already picture his wounded expression, hear the passive-aggressive snipes that would follow. Tonight might be innocent fun, but the ripples it would cause were anything but simple.

Nineteen

It wasn't until the evening shift on Tuesday that Fiona spotted another opportunity to speak to Ru. She arrived early, noticing George and Josh outside the back door chatting.

'I gather you two were on a date last night,' said George with a smirk.

Josh chuckled. 'We had a stellar night.'

Fiona smiled politely and rushed inside to the kitchen. The warm smell of toasting spices hit her. Ru had his back to her and was humming to himself as contentedly as he used to do in the flat when he was cooking for just the two of them. Tears pricked at her eyes as she remembered how she used to sneak up and wrap her arms around his waist. She reminded herself that she had come this far; with time, memories like that would become less poignant. She would fall out of love with him, just as he had fallen out of love with her. She had to set him free so that he could soar, and if that meant never holding him in her arms again, well, that was a sacrifice she must make.

'Ru,' she whispered.

He spun around, a hurt expression on his face. 'Enjoy your date last night?'

'It wasn't a date,' she hissed, her voice tight with mild annoyance. 'I went to the cinema. It was Josh's way of saying thank you for the wine lessons.' She crossed her arms, sensing the tension rise in her chest.

'That's not what he thinks,' Ru replied, his tone laced with something she couldn't quite place. This was awkward; the last thing she wanted was for Josh to have misinterpreted last night.

Fiona's eyes narrowed slightly, but her annoyance quickly gave way to a more urgent thought. There was no time to spar with him; they were alone, and she suspected they wouldn't be for long..

'I must talk to you. Can we meet?' she said, the words almost rushing out.

'I'm busy,' he spat, spinning away, removing the pan and shaking the toasted spices into a dish.

'Please. After work?'

'I'm busy after work too.' He paused, then said with a trace of a sneer, 'You're not the only one who's moved on.'

That hurt. She hadn't been on a date, but it sounded suspiciously like he was about to, and Fiona had a hunch she knew who with. But she still had to warn him. She owed him that much. How could she force him to meet her? She had a sudden idea. 'Ru, we need to discuss the flat. What to do with it . . . you know, now that we've split up?' She heard laughter and George's low, rumbling voice, and spoke urgently. 'Meet me at 7.30 tomorrow morning at Prosecco & Prose.' That was too early for the school run, and George would be busy cooking breakfasts.

He gave a slow nod. 'Fine.' With a thickness in her throat, Fiona scooted out of the room. Their relationship was over; she was just doing the honourable thing, warning a friend he may be in trouble.

In the morning, Fiona showered before her aunt rose, then dithered over what to wear. It was a choice between work clothes or summer holiday outfits, but those would be too cold for a late October morning. She compromised by taking extra care with her make-up. Wondering if Ru would notice, Fiona squirted *Gabrielle by Chanel* on her neck and wrists. For Fiona, the fragrance would forever be a memory of that day in Selfridges. She could still feel the warmth of Ru's hand clasping hers as he led her through the grand aisles, moving with his usual brash confidence, somehow fitting into the lush, polished world of luxury perfume like he was born into it.

In contrast, Fiona had been self-conscious and, watching other customers squirt and sniff knowledgably, was soon suffering from imposter syndrome. She fell into old habits: inhaling deeply, picking apart each fragrance with quiet reverence, whispering to Ru about top notes of jasmine and orange blossom, heart notes of sandalwood and lily. She closed her eyes, letting each scent unfurl in her mind like a delicate wine, identifying the underlying ingredients, the layers of sensuality and spice that lingered just beneath the surface.

But Ru wasn't listening to her wine-speak. 'Forget all that!' he said, laughing, a mischievous look in his eye. 'The only score that matters here, Fi, is how sexy it smells on you.' He picked up a sample bottle of perfume and squirted a cloud on her wrist, then with exaggerated seriousness, he took her hand and sniffed the pulse point, nodding thoughtfully before giving his verdict. They danced from one famous counter to the next, his energy infectious, his commentary blunt – he didn't care which perfume house he offended in his search for the perfect scent. Fiona's laugh rang through the hall as they tried one tester after another, each fragrance another opportunity for the simple pleasure of prolonging the memory.

Then they tried *Gabrielle*, Chanel's ode to freedom, and he fell quiet, inhaling as if struck. 'That's it,' he said, his voice suddenly soft. He said nothing else. He didn't need to; his silence said everything. *Gabrielle* was his Christmas present to her that year. She doubted he'd recognize it now, but for her, that scent would always be Ru, that particular Monday, the perfect mixture of wildness and warmth.

The café was less than two minutes' walk, and didn't open until 7.30 a.m., but determined not to be late, Fiona popped a small, blue box into her raincoat pocket, crept down the stairs and out of the house ten minutes before they were due to meet. She didn't want Ivy asking why she was up so early wearing a full face of make-up. A gentle breeze rustled the leaves, making a soothing, whispering sound that mingled with the distant rumble of waves against the shore. The air had a sharp, cool bite, and Fiona shivered in her thin raincoat as she hurried along the pavement. Sunlight filtered through the canopy of trees overhead, their leaves now faded to muted ambers and yellows, with the occasional splash of fiery red. As she walked, Fiona tried to tamp down the excitement of meeting Ru alone for the first time in six weeks.

When she reached the café, the lights were on inside and she could see Trish behind the counter, fiddling with the coffee machine. She huddled into her raincoat, wondering if they should meet on the terrace rather than inside, and glanced across at it. A hatless Ru was sitting at a table, as heartbreakingly beautiful as ever. Conscious of the rest of the team, she had been unable to look at him properly for weeks, and for a few moments she watched him rubbing his hands together and blowing on them, his breath forming little clouds. His dark skin looked warm against the chill of the autumn morning, his jawline sharper than she remembered, eyes thoughtful and distant. A part of her wanted to walk over and touch him, to feel that familiar warmth, but the calm, unreadable look on his face reminded her that his heart was no longer hers. She wrapped her arms around herself, holding back the ache, watching him.

'Ru!' she called. He stood and waved. 'You're early!' she said.

'Didn't want to be late.'

She laughed. 'How did you get out there?'

'I've been here since seven. Trish spotted me.' He pointed to a mug on the table. 'She took pity on a fellow chef.'

Fiona heard the key grating against the metal lock, then the sound of a tinkling bell, and the door opened. 'I'm not used to having a queue at this time of year,' said Trish. 'Come on inside. I presume you're meeting the other early bird. What can I get you?'

Fiona glanced at Ru, whose face was as expressionless as it had been yesterday. She guessed the barriers were still up. 'I'm having a smoked salmon bagel.'

Suddenly Fiona felt ravenous. 'Times two.'

They chose a small corner table. Her knees brushed against his, making her skin tingle and a peculiar sense of awkwardness came over her. She almost felt shy. He sniffed.

'You're wearing *Gabrielle*.' Then the mask began to crack; he sighed, and a wounded look came into his eyes making her heart clench, but she knew what she must do. She reached into her pocket, fingering the box, then, concerned he might storm out before she could warn him about the missing wine, she left the box where it was.

'Ru, something's happened at the pub.'

A confused look crossed his face. 'Right . . .'

Trish was walking towards their table. Keeping her eyes on the other woman, Fiona whispered, 'I've uncovered something. Thanks, Trish. This looks great.'

'What? What have you—?'

Fiona shot Ru a warning look.

'Anything else I can get for you?' asked Trish.

'Another coffee please,' said Ru, holding up his mug.

Fiona waited until Trish was out of earshot. 'A theft. Wine – very expensive wine,' she whispered.

His eyes popped wide. 'Wow, have you told Rose?'

She nodded, dipping her head to take a slurp of coffee. 'Yes. George knows too.'

'That explains . . .'

'Shush!' She pressed a finger to her lips then said brightly, 'Here comes your coffee, Ruben.'

He leaned towards her. She couldn't take her eyes off his lips, wanting to feel them pressing hard against her own, but he had made it clear yesterday he had other lips on his mind now – presumably Kim's. She dropped her gaze and picked up her bagel, nibbling at the edge. Trish placed a mug in front of Ru, then left. He glanced over his shoulder, waiting until Trish was out of earshot, then his eyes were on Fiona. 'That explains why George was so tetchy yesterday. How did they get in?'

She swallowed a mouthful of food, shaking her head. 'I don't think this was an outside job,' Ru's jaw dropped, and she rushed on, 'there's no sign of a break-in and it's been carefully planned. The thief targeted high-value wines. They knew exactly what to take.'

'Who, apart from you, knows about wine?'

She stopped herself from replying: 'You do'. She didn't want to spook him before she revealed the missing South African wines, but his reaction was so far convincing her that he'd had nothing to do with this. 'All they needed was the stock list – that makes it obvious what to pinch.'

'But without a knowledge of wine, how would they know what to do with it? It's not like selling knock-off Hermès handbags.'

'I haven't thought that far ahead. The thing is, I have a horrible feeling the thief is trying to frame someone for this crime.'

'You!'

'No,' she said, then added gently, 'you.'

'Me?' his head lurched forwards. 'How?'

'There are bottles of 1986 Vin de Constance missing.'

With a finger and thumb, he stroked his jaw, making her fingers itch to do the same. 'Their maiden year.'

'Yes.' She said, 'You have to know a lot about wine, or be seriously into South African wines to know how much those are worth.' He covered his face with his hands. 'It's just so predictable, isn't it – blame the black guy.'

She sighed. Race had never been an issue for either of them; Ru had been born into a post-apartheid South Africa, and Fiona's parents had instilled in her that the colour of one's skin didn't alter a person, a view reinforced by her Christian aunt – God was colour blind. 'That's not what I'm saying, and you know it. I just wanted to warn you . . .'

His eyes flashed anger at her and she flinched. 'That's what this meeting is about . . . to warn the man of colour he's about to be arrested for a crime he didn't even know existed?' he scoffed.

There was never going to be the perfect moment to do this, but she was determined she would do it today, so she pulled the little box out of her pocket, pushing it across the table. He winced, then spoke in a wavering voice: 'Keep— you keep it. I bought it for you.'

She spoke softly, 'No. That's not right.' She hadn't even accepted the ring. Pocketing it that day on the beach had been a mistake.

'I don't want it,' he said bitterly.

She felt a heaviness in her chest, but she would never move on without severing this last connection with him. 'Please, take it.'

He heaved a sigh, then pushed the box into his pocket. Shaking his head, he spoke softly. 'You told me you loved me. I don't understand why it went so wrong.'

At some point, they were always going to have this conversation, and she told herself she was strong enough, but her heart was in her mouth as she spoke. 'I'm not right for you, Ru. I drag you down. You're the most amazing chef, a social media star. Look what's happened to bookings at the pub since you arrived. Me –' she twisted her face, flicking her eyes at the ceiling '– I can't even pass my Advanced Sommelier exam.'

Saying those words, she pictured the email in her mind – the confirmation of her acceptance for the three day exam in less than two weeks. This time, she wasn't telling anyone; this time, she would pass. She had prepared relentlessly, and now success was within her grasp. This exam was the crucial step, the doorway to the financial independence she dreamed of. She was determined she would soon claim her place among the best sommeliers in the world. She might even get in touch with her parents – they would admire that sort of achievement. 'You've outgrown me, and I have to accept that.'

He leaned away from her. 'A healthy marriage isn't a competition, Fi. I respect your right to reject me. I just don't believe that's the real reason. I think you're terrified of failure, and you'd rather reject something that makes you happy than fear losing it one day.'

She felt herself well up and fought to stem the tears. 'So, you don't deny I'm right – that you're better than me?' She reached for his hand, and he held it briefly and then pulled away.

'I'm saying I don't care. I should be the judge of who I want to spend my life with. But I can't force you to be with me. You've made your decision. Now you've moved on, and so will I.'

She let out a strangled sob, then swallowed, raised her head and tried to laugh, but it sounded hollow. 'Right,' she sniffed, reminding herself that this was what she wanted, what she'd asked for. 'We're both moving on. And that's for the best.'

He sipped his coffee and avoided meeting her eye. 'Let's get back to the wine. I *am* grateful you told me. What's Rose going to do about it?'

She shrugged. 'I'm not sure, but it's too much money to ignore. I guess she'll call in the police ask them to investigate.'

'Will you help me prove my innocence?'

'Yes, of course.'

He passed her a napkin, and she dabbed at her eyes. 'Let's meet again tomorrow,' he suggested.

'Okay,' she said, swiping at her eyes. 'But this is business, okay? Professional, not personal.'

'Got it,' said Ru, and the look in his eyes had gone cold and distant again. 'Morning Prayers, then?'

She smiled at his choice of words, Morning Prayers used to be their term for staff meetings in London, always convened over breakfast.

'Morning prayers,' she agreed.

He angled his head at Trish. 'Not here.'

'Agreed.' And she didn't want to meet at Ivy's. 'Where then?'

'What about my flat? It's not far.'

Telling herself the venue didn't matter, it was just a business meeting after all, she smiled. 'Same time tomorrow. Give me the address.'

Twenty

At 7.30 a.m. the next day, Fiona stood in front of a row of Georgian terraced houses which were perched on the clifftop above Brambleton Beach. The sea stretched out in a vast, undulating expanse, its surface shimmering in the early dawn light. The sun was just beginning to rise, washing buttery light over the rippling waves and painting the Devon coast in shades of amber and rose. A stiff onshore breeze carried the distant cry of seagulls, echoing through the crisp autumn air. It was the kind of view one dreamed of waking up to beside someone you loved. But her fingers tightened around her typed agenda; this meeting was about helping an old friend.

Ru buzzed her in. 'First floor,' he said in a husky voice, making her heart flutter.

She jogged up, inhaling the spicy sweet scent of cinnamon bread as her mouth salivated. 'Thought we'd eat on the balcony, catch the sunrise. It's too beautiful to miss. Grab that blanket off the sofa if you're chilly.'

'Is that your cinnamon bread toasting?'

'Yup. And Eggs Benedict.'

She sighed, realizing how much she'd missed being cosseted by his cooking.

He picked up a tray and walked past her, whistling. She

smiled. His joy was infectious, but she had to try not to get too drawn in. 'I drew up an agenda.'

'Yes, Miss.'

Outside on the balcony, she threw a blanket over her shoulders, drinking in the view of the sun rising over the sea. Either side was a smudge of rose gold, as if someone had dipped a paintbrush in the sun and drawn a thick line on the horizon. She thrust her meeting plan onto the table, the crisp sound of paper cutting through the crackling tension she could sense between them. As she adjusted her posture, Fiona reminded herself that this was business, just like meetings in London. The only difference? No staff members were present. She exhaled slowly, trying to settle into the role, deciding to pretend there were others on the balcony with them, recalling how she had fought to keep her composure during the first breakfast meeting after waking up in Ru's arms.

Three years earlier, stepping into the professional kitchen where Ru was working as the sous chef, the lingering aroma of truffle oil and roasted garlic had greeted her, a rich reminder of the previous night's dinner service. The cooking scents mingled with the faint trace of his musky cologne still clinging to her skin. She felt his gaze from across the room – a silent dare in his dark, knowing eyes igniting memories of their night together that sent a shuddering shiver down her spine. She took a seat. He sat opposite, and she was acutely aware of him across the table, his sleeves rolled up, his forearms dusted with flour, his strong, capable hands that made her heart beat a little faster. Her mind longed to wander to the previous night, but she pinched the inside of her palm, forcing her focus back to the meeting.

She had tried to stay tuned in to the head chef's voice, hoping it would cut through the haze of desire, but it wasn't enough to keep her attention. Under the table, Ru's leg brushed hers, the touch so light she almost thought she'd imagined it. Her body responded, the reminder of the way his hands had traced her skin last night sending a flutter to her chest and a rush of warmth to her cheeks.

She recalled how a sharp voice had pierced her dreamy state. 'Fiona? Hello? Come in, Fiona!'

The chef's scowl brought her back to the meeting. Had he asked her a question? She straightened, guilt flashing across her face, then bit her lip, where the taste of last night's kisses still lingered, a thrilling, heady sweetness, rich and intoxicating like aged wine.

'Sorry, Chef, I didn't sleep well last night. What were you saying?'

Ru's eyes flickered, his gaze a private conversation, as if communicating silently through a lover's code. Their secret filled the space between them like static. Fiona wiped her sleeve over her face and refocused, offering a smile as he repeated his question.

This morning, Fiona feared that here, in Ru's flat, she might disappear into that same haze. She threw off the blanket, enabling the morning chill to distract her, then tried to pretend the entire London team from the Fork & Cork was sitting on the balcony, looking to her to lead the meeting professionally. 'How's Ben coping with you away?' she asked, dipping her fork into the velvety hollandaise sauce, letting the buttery richness coat her tongue.

'Ben's doing fine. We Zoom every day. He's normally at the new restaurant so we can keep track of the refurb.'

She cut into a poached egg, letting the buttercup yellow yolk blend with the sauce.

As Ru's best friend, not just his sous chef, Ben had probably known that Ru was planning to propose. Ben would hate Fiona for the hurt she had caused his friend. She shivered and pulled the blanket back around her, wanting to wrap her arms around Ru instead, feel his heart beating against her own, his warm body pressing against hers. But she knew she couldn't falter. If they got back together, it would make their eventual break-up so much harder. Besides, yesterday, Ru had made it clear that he had moved on. Adopting a business tone, she asked when the renovations would be complete.

'Kitchen will be finished in a month. All the wine you ordered is ready for delivery, but we don't have a sommelier to check it.'

That was a surprise, but not a problem. 'Easy enough to fix. Let's add that to the agenda for next time?'

His eyes clouded with something unreadable. 'There'll be a next time, will there?'

'Right, to Devon business.' She shook her page at him as if it was a weapon. 'The only way we can clear your name is by finding out who the thief is. Let's brainstorm.'

He seemed to brighten. 'How do you think the thief did this?'

'They must know where the cellar key is hidden.'

'Okay. Could you make a list of everyone who knows where it was kept?'

She glanced up. There was the tiniest blob of hollandaise sauce at the corner of his mouth. Her fingers itched to brush it away, but she dropped her eyes to the agenda instead. 'I've been thinking about how the thief is getting rid of the wine. I don't think they're using an auction house – it's not whole cases missing, and ad hoc bottles rarely make decent prices at auction. They could just be selling it through upmarket London wine merchants.'

'But wouldn't a good merchant ask questions? Check it wasn't knock-off stuff or stolen? That it had been properly cellared?'

'That's what I concluded too. They might be okay with a bottle or two, but with this volume I think they would be more wary about provenance.'

'If it was you . . .'

Fiona gasped.

'I mean hypothetically – of course it's not you! But if *you* had to sell it, how would you do it?'

She didn't hesitate. 'Oh, I know exactly what I would do.'

'What?'

Fiona explained that, spotting a gap in the market, some entrepreneurs had recently stepped in to solve a growing probate problem: people were inheriting boxes or bottles of wine, suspected they might be valuable, but had no idea how to value them or sell them on. Companies had sprung up which would buy the wine – despite not knowing how it had been cellared – using a special light filter to check for changes in a wine's chemical makeup, suggestive of spoilage. They then sold it on to private buyers, or restaurants.

'I've used them myself to source rare vintages. If the thief was aware of these companies, they could have sold the wine that way.' She paused, shaking her head slowly, a faint smile flickering and fading just as quickly. It was unsettling, sitting across from him like this, tossing ideas back and forth with the same easy rhythm they always had. The spark was still there, in the way their thoughts overlapped, in how quickly he picked up where she left off. They made a good team. They always had.

But the weight of what was missing pressed in around the edges. They weren't a couple anymore. No more shared mornings, no more inside jokes whispered in the dark. Just two people with a shared history and lingering warmth, trying to pretend it was simple.

She still loved him. And sitting here, watching him light up with an idea, admiring the way his mind worked, hurt in a way she hadn't prepared herself for.

'What is it?' he asked.

She shook her head dismissively, not wanting to explain her thoughts, then rustled her agenda for comfort, focusing her thoughts on her wine disposal theory. 'If they had sold the wine that way, the thief would have to contact the buying company, negotiate a price . . . probably leaving an email trail, and hopefully even their bank account details.'

'If you know these outfits, could you try and investigate?'

'How? Call each of them and ask them to breach client confidentiality by disclosing every person in Devon who's sold them wine in the last six months?'

'Hmmm. Good point.' He changed the subject. 'How are your eggs?'

'Perfect,' she said, cutting off a slice of cinnamon toast to dip into the golden yolk. Not wanting to think about Ru's gorgeous food, she flicked her eyes downwards to check what else she wanted to talk about.

'Next item, the Vin de Constance. Why would someone choose that? Rose had no idea of the value. Was it done to implicate you?'

'Could it just have been a lucky pick? Was it near the door, so an easy thing to grab and run?'

She shook her head. 'No. If they were after a quick getaway the obvious choice would be Champagne – that's closest to the door. The thief either knows their wine or is stealing to order from someone who does.'

'And then of course there's the South African element.'

'Yes. I suppose it could be coincidence, but assuming it was stolen after you joined, the thief would know that suspicion would fall on you. Have you upset anyone since you've been in Devon?'

He gave a wry laugh. 'Only you.'

Twenty-one

On Thursday evening Fiona arrived on the dot of 6.30 p.m. to discover a locksmith crouched by the cellar door, installing a new lock. Was every wine order to be passed up the chain to Rose? Given her boss's lack of familiarity with the cellar layout, that would slow service. Fiona walked into the staffroom where Kim was sitting at the table filing her nails. 'What's going on out there?' she asked Fiona.

Fiona was silent.

'What's going on? Tell me,' hissed Kim.

'I can't,' said Fiona. 'You'll have to ask Rose.'

Kim stood, walked to the coat rack and slipped her nail file into her handbag. Fiona eyed Kim's winter coat enviously. With winter just around the corner, Fiona had started jogging back up the hill after work in her raincoat to stay warm.

The staffroom door opened, admitting Ru and George, followed by Josh. 'What's Josh doing here?' whispered Kim. The men sat, Ru choosing the empty seat between Fiona and Kim. 'What's on the menu tonight Ruben?' asked Kim silkily.

Last to join, Rose pointedly shut the door behind her. 'Before the chefs brief us, I've got something to say. There's no nice way of putting this – we're a small team, and it appears there's a rotten apple in our basket.' Fiona sensed the tension in the room rising like a well-timed soufflé.

Rose ploughed on. 'It's been brought to my attention that there's some wine missing. Valuable wine, including some particularly expensive South African bottles.' She looked meaningfully at Ru, who kept his face blank. 'For now, we are not involving the police. George and I would prefer to deal with this privately, to give the culprit the opportunity to make amends.' Her eyes circled the team. Josh shuffled in his chair. Kim sat back in hers with her arms crossed over her chest. Outside, rain lashed against the windows, but inside the only sound was the gentle hiss of the old radiators.

Fiona wouldn't have handled it like Rose – publicly accusing a team member of theft in front of the entire team.

Oblivious to the charged atmosphere, Rose battled on: 'If anyone knows anything, please come and see me. I promise any information will be dealt with in the strictest confidence. As a precautionary measure, we've installed a new lock on the cellar. Only George and I know the combination. All wine orders other than house wine must come through me. Any questions?'

'Why are you so sure it's an inside job? What about a guest?' suggested Josh.

'The cellar is always locked,' said Rose, 'and there's no sign of forced entry. If it was a guest, someone on the inside must have helped them.'

Rose's eyes circled the room as if waiting for someone to confess. After a few moments, George broke the silence, clearing his throat and saying, 'Right, that's enough drama for one session. Tonight's specials: for the vegetarians . . .'

Fiona flipped open her notebook. She felt pressure against her thigh and glanced down. Ru's leg was pressed against her own. As if someone had dialled down the volume button on George, Fiona didn't register what the chef said, her mind wrestling with her conscience, wanting so much to respond to the pressure she felt.

'Ruben,' George continued, 'I'll let you explain the fish dish.'

As he stood up, his leg shifted sideways, making Fiona wonder if she'd imagined it, or if it had been an accident. But if it wasn't an accident, did that mean Ru hadn't moved on after all?

A shakshuka accompanied Friday's Morning Prayers, served with homemade flatbreads. Ru used autumnal vegetables – squashes, kale and Swiss chard – flavoured with a mixture of cumin and fennel.

Top of Fiona's agenda, which was really a summary of her worries, was Ru. Even a whiff of a crime could destroy his career. She wished she'd told Rose about her past with Ru. It was too late now; Rose might assume their secret had something to do with the theft. What if Ivy or Trish let something slip? She must ask them both to keep quiet.

Despite sniffing the food, her churning stomach prevented her from eating. 'Ru, I think you should go back up to London.'

He scoffed. 'Run away? That's like admitting guilt.'

She needed to get him to listen. This was her fault. If she had explained why she refused his proposal in August, then he wouldn't be here now. 'Ru, if someone connects us, realizes the reason you are here is not really because of your love of fish . . .'

'You mean, that the real reason is because I've planned an audacious wine heist?' he cracked. 'Come on, eat up. Those eggs were laid this morning.'

She frowned; he was being flippant. 'Ru, this isn't a game. If you're arrested, it could ruin your career. Social media can break you as quickly as it makes you.'

'*Eat!*'

She dipped her flatbread into an egg, using it to mop up the golden yolk before popping it in her mouth. She tried not to think about breakfasts in bed with Ru, where he would tell her to close her eyes, then feed her snippets of food, each mouthful a new sensation, until finally, instead of food, his mouth closed over her own. Just thinking about it was enough to make her want to plant her lips on his. She looked up at him, then tore her eyes away from his face and picked up her list of people who knew the location of the cellar key. How could she convince him to go? He was too much of a team player to leave George in the lurch.

She had a sudden idea. 'Please go back to London. Why not say you've got a crisis with the new kitchen and send Ben down to replace you here, while they find another junior?'

His face clouded; his eyes pinched together – at least he was considering her suggestion. Then he stared at her defiantly as he spoke. 'I can't leave Devon, not yet. There's someone I'm quite attached to here. I want to be where she is.'

Fiona swallowed. He really had moved on remarkably fast. If only she could. She hoped she wouldn't have to make that journey with Ru and Kim parading their new love in front of her. She bit her lip, trying to think of something to say. 'Where did you get these eggs?'

'From a local farmer, she keeps a flock of rescued battery hens.'

'Delicious.'

'I know how much you like fresh eggs,' he said

For a few minutes, they ate silently, listening to the waves crashing against the cliffs. Fiona broke the reverie by insisting they ran through her list of who knew where that key was kept. First to be eliminated was Ivy, followed by Trish, because neither of them could think of a motive for either of them. 'Has George said anything directly to you about the missing wine?' asked Fiona.

'Not a word.'

'Josh?'

'Nada.' He shot her a wounded look, then spoke sarcastically, 'But I'm not exactly close to him. Has he spoken to you?'

She shook her head. She had barely spoken to Josh about anything lately. With her exam date approaching, she'd cancelled their wine lessons to focus on her studies. Not that she was sharing that secret with anyone.

'What about Kim?' she asked, trying to keep her tone casual. 'Has she said anything to you?'

'No.'

'I don't think Rose's plan of getting the thief to confess is going to get her anywhere.' She felt her throat constrict – everyone believed either she or Ru were to blame. 'The police will be called in soon.'

'Stop worrying. I think this drama might blow over. When I was prepping a bone broth for an overnight simmer, I heard George and Rose talking. I think they assumed I'd left. He was one angry chef. Had a real go at her for accusing his staff. He wants to forget it, says it's their fault because they were too lax with security, and now that's been tightened he'd rather just get on with the business.'

That sounded promising. She locked eyes with his. 'And did Rose agree?'

'Not yet. She wants to interview everyone first. Says she can't concentrate, wondering which one of her team did it.'

'She should have thought of that before she accused us all,' said Fiona testily. 'It sounds like it's not over. She runs that business, not him.' Recalling the sensation of Ru's leg nudging hers at the staff meeting last night, she added a warning: 'Ru, stay away from me at work . . . please. We don't want anyone suspecting we're more than colleagues. They might think we planned this together.'

'Which would be ridiculous, because you've made it very clear there's nothing going on between us.'

She peeked up, met those dark eyes and sighed. 'Right.'

There was a moment of silence, until Ru changed the subject. 'What do you think of the shakshuka? Is the cumin too pronounced?' he asked.

'You know it isn't.'

'Good. Now, tell me what you would like for breakfast tomorrow.'

Concerned that either her aunt or Trish might let slip the reason Ru came to Brambleton, Fiona arranged to meet them both for coffee. As she pushed open the door of Prosecco & Prose, the bell above chimed softly, announcing her arrival. The place was buzzing with energy, a low hum of chatter filling the room. The rich scent of freshly ground coffee wrapped around her, just as it had when she'd met Ru there. Fiona spotted Ivy at a corner table, her silver hair gleaming in a sunbeam streaming through the window. Nearby, Trish leaned casually against the counter.

Fiona slid into the chair opposite Ivy, the cushion sinking beneath her, a slight comfort amid the tension tightening her chest. She had yet to mention the wine theft to her aunt. Trish joined them, bringing a steaming cup of coffee for Fiona.

'Ivy, Trish . . .' Fiona began, trying to steady the tremor she heard in her voice. The hum of the coffee machine and the clatter of plates became distant as she focused on the two women in front of her. 'Something's come up at work that makes it important for me and Ru to keep our past a secret.'

Ivy gasped, 'What's happened, love?'

Fiona swallowed, the words heavy in her throat. She told them about the wine theft, fielding their barrage of questions, explaining why Rose believed it had to be an inside job – and why, in her eyes, Fiona and Ru were the prime suspects. Hearing her aunt heave a sigh, Fiona glanced across, registering a thoughtful look cross Ivy's face. Ivy would never steal anything, but she might have seen something suspicious.

'Ivy?' she prompted.

'I was just thinking that must be why Rose wants to see me,' mumbled Ivy.

'Me too!' cried Trish. Fiona's eyes circled the room, taking in the bustle. It was thriving, even out of season. Trish wasn't short of money.

'Not that I would know what to take,' said Ivy.

Fiona grimaced. 'You could easily have found out from me.'

'I don't think I'm a prime suspect – some vicars lose their faith after they retire, rebel and act unethically, but that's not me and the whole village knows it. I adhere to the same values I did when I was their vicar.' Ivy looked at Fiona, her eyes full of sympathy. 'But that's not why you asked to meet us. You're worried Rose will discover Ruben's here because of you, and it will make him look dishonest, and the spotlight will fall on him?'

Fiona let out a breath she hadn't realized she was holding. 'Yes', she whispered. 'Either that or she'll suspect we planned it together.'

Ivy reached across the table, her hand brushing Fiona's in a reassuring gesture. 'Does this mean you and Ru are getting back together?' Ivy's eyes probed Fiona's for clues. Fiona picked up her mug, which felt warm and steady in her hands. She dipped her head to take a sip; she was not ready to discuss her confused feelings for Ru with someone as perceptive as her aunt.

'That's not what I'm saying. Just – please. Will you keep our history to yourselves?'

Trish tapped her fingers thoughtfully against the tabletop as if playing a tune. The melodic sound was soothing. 'We won't say a word,' said Trish. Ivy nodded in agreement, her grip tightening on Fiona's hand. 'You know I never break a confidence.'

Fiona looked at her aunt. Although glad her secret was safe with Ivy, that was a peculiar choice of words.

Twenty-two

Fiona was in the upstairs flat with Timmy and Becky. On the kitchen table, a pile of empty toilet rolls waited to be transformed into a spaceship.

'Can I do it?' squealed Timmy, standing up on his bar stool and lunging for the scissors.

Fiona pushed his hand away. 'I'll cut. You two are the artistic directors. Before we do anything, we must decide what the plan is. Let's draw a picture.'

The flat door opened, and George burst in. 'Rose! *Rose*? Where are you?' he shouted as he marched into the kitchen area.

'Daddy,' squealed Becky.

'Not now, honey,' said George, pausing to kiss his daughter's head. '*Rose*,' he yelled, stalking off and disappearing into the master bedroom.

'Right, you two,' said Fiona, picking up a crayon, 'now what sort of spaceship is this going to be?' She pushed the paper between the two children and gave them each a crayon.

'Timmy why don't you do the top half, and Becky the bottom?'

'But the nose is the best part,' squeaked Becky. Above the whining Fiona could hear raised voices. Not wanting the children to focus on their parents' row, Fiona lifted her own voice. 'No, the bottom is where the action will be. Come on, think about what shape you want the boosters to be – shall we have diamonds?'

Becky leaned her body over the picture, her tongue poking out, a crayon clutched in her fist. Rose, wearing a trouser suit, bustled into the open plan room, her eyes darting round. 'Mummy,' cried Becky.

'Not now, love. I need to find some papers.' She strode over to George's desk, trying to pull down the top.

George stormed over. 'That's private.'

Rose turned to face her husband, a curious expression on her face.

Fiona leaned over, hiding between the children. 'Why is it locked?' demanded Rose.

'Because it's private. That's got all my work papers in it, and I don't want them messed up by you or the kids. Promise me you will stop hounding the staff.'

'I'm not hounding anyone. I'm just going to ask everyone a few questions.'

'No. I won't let you speak to Ruben or Josh. They're my team, and there's no need. I'm sure it's neither of them.'

Fiona looked up. Rose was glaring at her husband. 'So, it's got to be one of my team, has it?'

'It's not one of mine,' said George evenly.

'I *will* get to the bottom of this, and you have to let me.'

He grunted, bunching his fists, 'Back off, Rose. They're in my team, and I'll handle them my way.'

Rose snatched up a file, her hands trembling as she pushed it into her bag. 'You mean, you *won't* handle it, just leave it all to me as usual!'

Rose struggled to fasten her handbag, her hands slipping on the lock. George paused, reached down and secured it for her. 'Come here you,' he said, reaching out for his wife. 'I'm sorry I'm tetchy. The kitchen's like working in a pressure cooker that's about to explode – everyone's jumpy, on the lookout for a thief skulking in the store cupboard. It's not a good creative space.'

Rose's shoulders relaxed as he hugged her close. Watching them, Fiona smiled wistfully. They had a special bond. 'I'd better go back down and let you get off to the accountants,' George said. 'I'll talk to my team. I promise.'

'Mummy, *pleeeeeease* help us with the spaceship,' begged Timmy.

Rose kissed George then walked into the kitchen area. 'Two minutes – show me what's going on then.' She turned to Fiona. 'I really do appreciate all this help with the kids. It's so kind of you.'

Fiona hesitated. 'Rose, can I ask you something?'

'Yup.'

'This might sound like an odd question, but . . . you and George . . . what makes things work between you two?'

Rose stroked her daughter's hair, a thoughtful expression on her face. 'It's a fair question, especially from someone recovering from a broken heart. Are you looking to date again?'

Fiona shook her head. 'I'm not ready yet. I'm just curious.'

'A tip from an older woman, then. Perfection doesn't exist. It's about accepting faults and flaws and giving your love freely. Even when, like this morning, your partner doesn't exactly behave like they deserve it.' Rose raised an eyebrow, but she was smiling. She glanced at her watch, kissed both the children, then said, 'And on that note, I should leave else I'll be late. Have fun, you lot.'

Fiona used the scissors to cut into an empty toilet roll, but her mind was elsewhere, once again thinking of Ru. His faults and flaws had been easy to live with, all adjuncts to his artistic temperament. Ru insisted on doing things 'the right way'. He wouldn't tolerate shortcuts or pre-made ingredients. At home, like at work, he controlled the kitchen, imposing strict rules about how to store, clean and organize items. He arranged everything precisely, making her nervous about offering to even make coffee. But those were barely flaws. No, the only real fault – if he had one – was that he could be a better listener. If he'd heard and understood that she wanted to stand up for herself, not shelter beneath his protection, he would never have warned the investors he thought she might fail her exam. Instead of 'protecting her' from the potential rejection of her wine-led restaurant concept, he should have told her directly that he didn't think her idea would work and that no one would back it. But she would soon be able to reinvent herself. The exam was only days away.

As the door closed behind Rose, Becky started wriggling in her seat. 'Timmy, I want to give Fiona her present. It took us ages to make.'

Timmy chewed his lip. 'Mummy said she wouldn't like it.'

Becky's lower lip began wobbling and Fiona spoke quickly. 'I'm sure I'd love it, Becky.' Whatever it was, Fiona was confident she could feign pleasure, just like Rose had done with that hideous scrambled egg.

Becky clambered off the stool and shot off, returning with a large sheet of paper flapping by her side. 'This is for you, because we love you, Fiona. We drew it together.'

Fiona took the paper. The drawing was a vibrant swirl of innocence and love, with stick figure people linked arm in arm, forming a cheerful, uneven circle. There was George with huge, oversized arms and a protruding tummy, Rose and the two children. In the centre stood Fiona, with an exaggerated smile and wild, colourful hair.

Becky bounced from foot to foot. 'Say something!' she demanded.

Timmy whispered. 'You see, we put you in the middle 'cos

Mummy says you've become the heart of the family. Mummy says she relies on you.'

They tugged at her hands and shouted, 'We love you, Fiona!'

Her chest swelled with gratitude. Children gave their love so freely, she thought, without hesitation or conditions, and being included in their little world felt like a special gift. But she was keenly aware of the holes in her own life – losing Ru, the unfulfilled dream of having her own children and the distant, muted love she'd experienced from her own parents. The picture was beautiful, but it spoke to her deepest desire, which she feared now she might never achieve.

The chill of the autumn breeze nipped at Fiona's cheeks when later that afternoon she and Josh strolled along Brambleton Beach. The sun hung low in the sky, its rays glinting off the water like scattered diamonds.

'Isn't this just beautiful?' Josh remarked as he kicked at a clump of seaweed, sending it tumbling across the sand.

'It is,' Fiona replied, her gaze drifting over the horizon. 'This beach is one of my favourite places. I've been coming here since I learned to walk.' The waves lapped gently against the shore, a soothing backdrop to their conversation.

Fiona had orchestrated this outing with care. Knowing it would be deserted in November, she'd chosen the beach instead of the staffroom or a café. Josh had hounded her for one last wine lesson and if he hadn't suggested one of her favourite topics – sparkling wine – she probably wouldn't have relented.

Fiona smiled. 'Let's start with Champagne, shall we?' She gestured toward the vast expanse of sky. 'Imagine we're in the Champagne region of France. It's cool and crisp, much like it is here. The grapes – Chardonnay, Pinot Noir and Pinot Meunier – thrive in that environment.'

As they walked, Fiona eulogized about Champagne. She could almost hear the faint hiss of a Champagne cork being teased out of the neck of the bottle, see the froth escaping. 'Champagne is made using the traditional method, or what we call the *méthode champenoise*. Each bottle undergoes a second fermentation, creating those fine bubbles.'

'Fine bubbles?' Josh teased. 'Can you get coarse ones?'

Fiona smiled. 'We call them 'larger bead' and you find them in lower quality fizz, like Prosecco, which has a much quicker carbonation process, usually in steel tanks. Fine bubbles are a hallmark of quality sparkling wine.'

'Do you ever think about pairing wines with seasons?' Josh asked, his eyes scanning the beach, looking for something to latch onto. 'Like, would you drink Champagne in autumn, or something heavier, like a rich red?'

'Absolutely,' Fiona said. 'Champagne is often seen as a celebratory drink, but it complements lots of foods.' She lifted her arms, as if to embrace the breeze that whipped past them. 'Imagine tonight, sitting in front of a glowing wood fire, eating apple crumble paired with a vintage Champagne. It's all about balance.'

Josh looked at her. 'You make it sound so romantic,' he said, his drawl dropping to a conspiratorial whisper. 'How about it? Just you, me and a bottle of Champagne?'

Fiona felt her cheeks warm but steered the conversation back on course. 'For me, wine is about sharing, learning and enjoying the moment.'

He nodded and grinned. 'Yes, boss.'

They approached a rocky outcrop where waves crashed more violently spraying a cool misty spray across her face. Josh fell silent for a moment, gazing out at the waves. Fiona felt the need to fill the silence. It was a habit she had developed over the years whenever conducting wine tastings – not trusting their own palate, guests were often too shy to voice an opinion.

She described how the different fermentation processes gave different characters to each sparkling wine, and ended with her favourite of the mass-produced fizzes, Prosecco. 'The simplicity of Prosecco comes from its focus on the Glera grape. It's less suited for ageing, but perfect for a bright, accessible sparkling wine. You can really taste the difference when you sip it.'

'Well, *you* can' he said, with a laugh.

Fiona chuckled softly, brushing a strand of hair behind her ear. 'Thanks. It's my job, but it's also a huge part of my life.'

'Nope. It *is* your life – I mean I appreciate you carving out time for this lesson, but why not carve some out for yourself? There's so much more to life than wine. I'm getting the vibe that you don't want to date me – and that's cool – but you should be having fun with someone. You're gorgeous, clever, passionate. Find someone who loves that!'

She gave a half laugh. For a cocky, Aussie KP he was a sweet guy, always trying to make her feel good about herself. 'I will do . . . just not yet.'

Josh took hold of her arm and stopped her. 'When, then? You only get one life, you know.'

She wasn't about to admit it, but she knew when. In a few days, when she was a member of the CMS, and could get a job in any restaurant she liked. 'Soon,' she hedged.

'Come on, Fiona. Isn't it time to live the life you want, not the one someone else dreams for you?'

She gaped at him. 'But being successful *is* my dream.'

'Is it? Seems to me like your dream is being a sommelier, and you're already doing a great job of that,' he said laughing. They walked in silence for a moment, the sound of the waves filling the space between them. 'Can I ask you something that's about wine, but not about wine?' he asked easily. She took a breath. Was he going to ask her out again, despite what he'd said earlier?

'Of course,' she said, trying to keep her tone light.

'This missing wine . . . do you think someone has stolen it?'

She drew in a deep breath, exhaling slowly. 'I'm afraid I do. Rose and I checked the cellar. It's not been misplaced, and it's worth too much for this to be a mistake. Why do you ask?'

'I'm kind of nervous about being interviewed. Can I tell you why?'

Twenty-three

Fiona was the first person to be interviewed. Rose walked into the staffroom carrying a tray with two steaming mugs and a plate of biscuits, which Fiona thought was a kind way to create a relaxing atmosphere. The boss held the tray effortlessly, while closing the door. Fiona crossed her legs, uncrossed them, re-crossed them, bounced her foot up and down . . . it was tough projecting innocence when hiding a secret. She should have told Rose about her history with Ru the day he'd shown up.

Rose set the tray down, picked up a mug and took a sip before speaking. 'I wanted to see you first because I know it wasn't you. In fact,' Rose shifted sideways, fishing something from her trouser pocket, 'this is the keycode for the cellar door – it's not practical me trying to find everything each evening. I trust you,' she said, passing over a slip of paper. Tucking the scrap inside her apron, Fiona felt a rush of relief, and her shoulders loosened. She concentrated on Rose's next words, 'Don't take this as me blaming you, I'm not, but you might have inadvertently given the idea to the culprit. Has anyone been quizzing you about wine?'

That one was easy to answer. 'People are naturally curious when they discover what I do for a living.'

A stern look crossed her employer's face. 'Who?'

Fiona thought back. Kim, Trish, Josh, the bar staff. The list was endless. She sipped her own tea, wondering how to respond. She didn't want suspicion to fall on Josh, not after what he'd told her on the beach.

Rose sat up. 'You can tell me in confidence. Who?'

'Everyone, except for Ivy and Ru for obvious reasons.'

Rose's eyes narrowed. 'Ru?'

Fiona could have screamed at her slip-up. In Devon no one shortened his name. With her heart beating faster, Fiona scrambled for an explanation, but her mind was blank. With no choice but to ignore it, she soldiered on, trying to keep her voice light. 'Yes. He's worked with lots of sommeliers.'

'What do you think of Ruben?' asked Rose, her eyes narrowing. 'Why is he here? If he wanted to experiment with fish why not go and work in one of the famous fish restaurants in Padstow? Why rural north Devon?'

Fiona shifted in her seat, her mind racing for ways to shift the subject onto someone other than Ru. 'Maybe that's exactly why he's here, to get away from other famous chefs?'

'So, he can shine?'

That wasn't Ru's style. He wasn't arrogant. When customers complimented the food, he praised the entire team. But defending his team spirit wasn't as important as deflecting attention from him as a suspect. She took another gulp of tea. 'Possibly.'

'I'm not sure,' muttered Rose, shaking her head. 'I think there's something suspicious about why he's here, something that's connected to London. Maybe something went wrong up there. George says he's often preoccupied, as if he's worried. What do you think?'

Fiona's eyes flitted round the room, bouncing off pictures, then her raincoat as if searching for something to lock onto. Rose was perceptive, and Fiona was unsure how to respond. 'I think he's an excellent chef. Always calm under pressure, polite, professional . . . treats the serving staff with respect.'

'Yes, Kim is quite taken with him,' said Rose, a crafty smile creasing her face. 'They'd make a great couple. She's a good worker, Kim. The customers like her – very efficient and polite.' Fiona kept her face impassive, as she remembered Rose scolding her about not pulling together with their small team.

'George is adamant it's no one in the kitchen, but those South African wines . . .' She pursed her lips. 'It would be a bit odd to steal them unless you know exactly what you're stealing, and how much it's worth.' She stood up, tapping a finger against her lip. 'I'll work it out, I never caught the thief in London, but I'll catch this one.'

Rose tipped up her mug and swallowed the remnants, before returning it to the tray. It looked like the meeting was over. It was on the tip of Fiona's tongue to ask about the London theft, but she didn't want to prolong the interview.

'See if Ruben can spare time to see me before he gets too busy, would you? And be a love . . . take these empties with you.'

Stepping into the bustling kitchen, the heat of the stoves instantly enveloped her. The room was alive with the crackle of oil, and the smoky hint of toasting cumin. Stainless steel counters gleamed under the bright kitchen lights, and Josh's whistling blended with the hiss of steam and the low hum of the extractor fan.

In the middle of it all, Kim was laughing – a lilting, flirty sound – as she leaned close to Ru, touching his arm lightly. Ru chuckled, meeting Kim's gaze, as his hands neatly chopped a bunch of flat leaf parsley, but his attention was clearly elsewhere. Even the simmering pots seemed to echo the pair's light-hearted mood, bubbling as though in on the joke. Fiona's breathing became faster and shallower.

Across the kitchen, Josh glanced up from the sink, exchanging a smirk with George. Both men seemed amused. George shook his head with a grin as he unfolded a fresh apron and secured it round his ample waist. Fiona could tell the men found Kim's flirtation entertaining, like some predictable kitchen show. Perhaps Ru viewed it thus, she mused. Missing his London stage, he was enjoying the opportunity to be the centre of attention.

But Fiona's fingers tightened on the tray handles as she forced herself to ignore the twinge of jealousy. She set the tray down harder than she'd intended, the *thunk* sharp against the softer kitchen sounds. The whistling stopped and Ru glanced up briefly. Quickly, Fiona looked away, hoping no one would comment. Forcing a calm expression, she carried the mugs to the dishwasher, but the playful laughter from the other end of the kitchen buzzed loudly in her ears.

She handed Josh the dirty crockery and walked towards the couple, her heart somersaulting at the sight of Kim stroking Ru's arm. Fiona fought to keep her face neutral, but when she spoke, there was a wobble in her voice. 'Ruben, sorry to disturb you, but Rose wants to see you in the staffroom.'

He gathered up the parsley, securing it between his fingers, then slid the knife up and down so fast the blade never seemed to lose contact with his board. He grunted but didn't take his eyes off the herbs. 'Now?' he asked.

'Yes. Now,' she said, allowing irritation to seep into her tone. 'She's waiting.'

Nonchalantly, he scraped the parsley into a bowl, removed his apron and sauntered past Fiona without even casting a glance her way. Fiona only hoped he could portray the same indifference during his interview. Over by the serving counter, Ru picked up a brown paper bag.

'For me?' squeaked Kim, rushing toward him.

Ru chuckled. 'For Rose.'

George raised his eyebrows. 'Oh, yes? Have I got a rival?'

'What is it?' asked Fiona politely.

The bag rustled as Ru withdrew a pen. Attached to the top was a cluster of six-inch long powder blue ostrich feathers. 'She's always losing hers – I thought this might help.'

'That, mate, is a beauty of a gift. She's not gonna lose that one!' said Josh.

Fiona smiled, recalling her bottle of perfume. Ru was generous with gifts and always so thoughtful. She hoped Kim appreciated those qualities as much as she had.

Fiona could smell baking pastry as she climbed the stairs up to Ru's flat the next morning. Her mouth salivated, hoping it was croissants – Ru was a skilled pastry chef. The front door was ajar, and she pushed it wider. The warmth hit her, making her realize how cold she was after just the short walk from Ivy's cottage; but in a few days' time she would be in London and could retrieve her coat. In a corner of the room a suspended wood-burning stove glowed. How long had Ru been preparing for Morning Prayers? She wished she had reciprocated by drawing up a detailed agenda, but today there were only two topics she wanted to discuss: Ru's interview, which she was sure he would tell her about; and whether there was something going on between him and Kim, which she knew wasn't any of her business.

'Hi Fi. Croissants will be ready soon. Take a seat.' He gestured at the sofa, positioned for a view of the spectacular coast. She sat at one end. On the coffee table in front of her were napkins, plates and knives; she pulled one set towards her, then moved the other to the far end of the table. 'How did your interview go?' she asked.

Behind her, she heard the oven door open, followed by a snatch of the humming fan, before it snapped shut. Moments later, Ru was standing beside her, a tray of croissants in one hand, a pat of butter in the other. 'This is made by a local dairy farmer. Just wait until you taste it. Expensive, but worth every penny. I'm trying to convince George to stock it,' he said, the enthusiasm clear in his voice.

She reached for a warm pastry, golden, crisp and flaky. As she broke off a piece she watched the steam rise. Slathering on butter, she let it melt, remembering how in London he used to rely on her to judge new products, making her smell, then taste things and score them out of ten. She took a bite, tasting the cream, the tang of salt . . . willing him to ask for her opinion. He was watching her face. She thought she detected a loving look in his eyes but knowing him, it could just as easily be for the butter, not her.

She swallowed her mouthful, taking her thoughts with the food. The butter was magnificent. Ru hadn't asked for her opinion because he didn't need it. In London, he had just been playing lip service to her skills. She broke off another piece of pastry, the comforting warmth a stark contrast to the dull ache settling in her chest.

'I saw you.' He spoke softly, the words more of a lament than a reproach. She glanced up. The sunlight danced through the window, accentuating the sharp line of his jaw and the slight curl of his hair. He looked effortlessly handsome in his well-fitted chef's jacket, the fabric just snug enough to hint at the strong shoulders beneath. 'Saw me?' she queried.

Ru's gaze was intense. 'On the beach . . . with Josh. Again. If you aren't a couple, I don't understand why you'd be out there with him,' Ru said, his voice steady but edged with an unmistakable anxiety. He hadn't taken a croissant, and the untouched tray of pastries sat in front of him like an accusation. 'It's not like you to go parading around the beach with a kitchen porter.'

Fiona's stomach tightened. 'We weren't parading, Ru. We were talking about sparkling wines,' she replied, trying to keep her tone light, but her heart raced under the weight of his scrutiny. 'You know how passionate Josh is to learn.'

'Passionate?' Ru echoed, the word as sharp as a paring knife. 'Is that what they're calling it now?'

As she met his gaze. Heat rose to her cheeks, 'You know I would—'

'Would what?' he interrupted, leaning forward slightly, his voice low but fierce.

'I was just—'

'Just what?' he shot back, the jealousy simmering just beneath the surface. 'Just enjoying the view? Just catching up on old times? Oh no, wait, you can't have been doing that because you've only known him for about two minutes.'

His bitterness stung. The silence roared louder than any words could, a warning as sharp as a scream, charged with unspoken emotions. Fiona looked down at her plate, tracing the outline of her croissant with a finger, caught in a whirlwind of memories and unspoken feelings. She ached to reach up, grasp his hand and reassure him it had only ever been him, but those hands weren't hers to hold anymore. That privilege belonged to another woman. It didn't really matter what he thought she was doing on the beach with Josh. She and Ru *weren't* a couple anymore. She must accept it and so must he.

'It was just a date,' she said, forcing the words out. 'You don't have to make it sound like . . .'

'Like what? Like I care?' His voice softened, a flicker of vulnerability flashing across his face. 'You've moved on remarkably quickly.'

'I haven't moved on,' she insisted. Her voice rose to match his. 'You know I still care about you. I always have.' And she feared she always would. He was too big a character to forget.

Ru's expression softened momentarily, a brief crack in his defences, but it snapped shut again. He shook his head, the movement as heavy as the weight of unspoken words.

'How did we get here, Mousse?'

She saw his jaw clench, his eyes narrowing with a mix of anger and hurt. For a moment, something vulnerable flickered beneath his sarcastic exterior – a raw, wounded look that made her heart ache. But she quickly hardened her expression, unwilling to pander to his jealous pride.

Fiona pushed her plate aside. 'I think I should go.' she muttered.

He whispered. 'No. I'm sorry. Of course you can see who you want. Don't rush off. Stay and enjoy your breakfast.'

Absentmindedly, she picked up the remains of her pastry, shredding it between her fingers. She'd lost her appetite. 'I'm not sure I should.'

He heaved a theatrical sigh. 'Don't go yet. I promise to behave like a rational human being.' He sat beside her. 'Now come on, tell me what you think of that butter. No one has a palate quite like yours.'

Although sure he knew the answer to his own question, she gave him a shy smile. 'The butter is a ten.'

He returned her smile, 'Do you want to hear about my interview with Rose?'

Twenty-four

The following morning as she approached the door of Ru's flat, Fiona paused, pulling her raincoat close against the wind as she listened to the distant crash of waves below. This morning it reminded her of a steady drumbeat, as if sounding an alert. Yesterday, they had wasted most the meeting dealing with Ru's jealousy. But she had learned that he had made it through his interview without raising any suspicion. Maybe it was the gift of that pen – simple, sincere, and so very him – that quietly spoke volumes about his character. Today, she was determined to run through the suspect list properly. The door was ajar, and she jogged up the stairs and into the flat. A kaleidoscope of aromas – cumin, coriander, and a hint of something buttery – filled the room. Ru had a knack for transforming simple ingredients into something special. Her heart fluttered at the sight of him. He had unfastened the top buttons of his chef's jacket, letting the front flap open and giving her a glimpse of his chest.

Ru was stirring something in a frying pan and the sound of sizzling potatoes permeated the space. Fiona leaned against the counter, pretending to be casual. Where once he had been the person she was most comfortable to be around, now she trod warily, watched what she said and how she spoke. It was a delicate balance, like pairing wine with food, wanting to experiment yet fearing that, instead of delighting the palate, it might clash.

To anchor herself, she placed her list of suspects on the kitchen counter.

'So, what's on the menu this morning?' she asked.

A flash of pride lit up his face. 'Aloo paratha – spiced potatoes stuffed in flaky bread. It's Indian comfort food really.'

She inhaled deeply again.

She had been right; the buttery smell wasn't butter but ghee. The absence of the salt was what she had detected. 'It smells incredible,' she said, letting her enthusiasm show.

As he skilfully flipped the parathas, the golden crust crackled, sending a burst of steam into the air. 'What do you think? Should I serve this with yogurt or the green chutney?' He raised an eyebrow, challenging her to choose.

'Why not both?'

Sprinkling fresh coriander over the finished parathas, he suggested they ate at the breakfast bar. He pushed a plate towards her, and she picked up her warm and flaky paratha. As she took a bite, flavours exploded on her tongue; cumin and coriander were a wonderful combination. Just like she and Ru used to be.

For a few minutes, their conversation danced around lightly, avoiding anything about feelings or either of their rivals, like a pair of novice skiers choosing the safe route down a slope.

Exhausted with small talk, Fiona asked Ru what he thought Rose would do now she'd interviewed most of her 'suspects.'

He shook his head as he tore a piece from his paratha. 'She's flailing about. I think she's just hoping someone will confess. What about you?'

'She told me she knows I'm not the thief.'

A look of relief crossed Ru's face, and Fiona wondered if he was worried his backers might hear of this drama. 'Well, that's good news,' he said.

She took a cautious bite of her paratha, the spices biting back as she chewed. Her eyes dipped to her suspect list. 'So, who did this?'

Ru's gaze shifted. 'Hmm. I have news.' He dunked his paratha in the yogurt sauce. 'You might not want to hear this, but your new boyfriend has a criminal record.'

Fiona shook her head dismissively. 'He's *not* my boyfriend! It was just a date. Anyway, I know it's not Josh.' She took another bite, the heat almost distracting her from her annoyance.

'He's suddenly become remarkably interested in wine, don't you think?' Ru's tone was casual, but his eyes were sharp. '. . . for a kitchen porter.'

Fiona put down her paratha, feeling the need to defend Josh. 'That's because he's working with a sommelier for the first time.'

Ru raised an eyebrow. 'Think a little less highly of him now?'

'Actually,' she said, wiping her fingers, 'Josh told me himself.' Wanting to avoid another trip down jealousy lane, Fiona didn't add that Josh had confided in her at the end of their walk on the beach. Josh had explained his one-off shop lifting had been an ill-thought-out act of rebellion; his way of forcing his parents to accept he would not waste his life pursuing their dream of him becoming a professional surfer. 'I was going to mention it last time we met,' Fiona said, 'but you got all huffy about me walking with him on the beach. I didn't think you'd be objective.' She took another defiant bite, the spices a comforting heat in her mouth as she locked eyes with him.

Ru looked at her a moment longer, then shrugged, taking a bite of his own. 'Well, Josh asked my advice. Apparently neither Rose nor George knows, and he's not sure if he should tell them.'

'No,' said Fiona, dabbing at her mouth with a napkin. 'I told him he should keep quiet about it unless asked directly. It doesn't help that he was prosecuted for shoplifting a bottle of whisky.'

'What if someone finds out and tells Rose?'

'I doubt that will happen; you won't shop him and neither will I. And anyway, nobody asked if he had a criminal record before thy hired him, so he hasn't lied.'

She peeled off another section of paratha, then bit into the gooey filling. She really had missed Ru's cooking. 'Do you think he did it?'

'No. The only time I recall him going to the cellar alone was when you were ill.'

'So, who did do it? I made a list of possibilities. Let's run through it and rank them.'

Ru leaned forward, an excited look on his face. He was so close she could smell the spices clinging to him. Mentally, she pulled his mouth closer, feeling his lips brush against hers. When he spoke, she felt his breath warm on her face.

'If we dismiss you, me Ivy and Trish, that only leaves Josh, and Kim.' Fiona tensed at the mention of her rival's name.

'What about the kids?' asked Ru.

At first, she didn't reply, startled that Ru hadn't leaped to defend Kim. She shook herself. 'The kids?'

'Yes. Do they know where the key is kept? Could this be a prank and they've hidden the stuff?' suggested Ru.

Picturing Timmy and Becky lugging around magnums of Châteauneuf-du-Pape, Fiona laughed. 'No. They're never left on their own – too young. But you raise a valid point – Rose and George should be on our list. By the way, Rose loves that new pen you gave her and hasn't managed to lose it yet!'

'Pleased to hear that,' he said, grinning, then he screwed up his face. 'Why would they steal their own wine?'

Fiona giggled. 'Do you think George might be financing a secret mistress?'

He raised his eyes to the ceiling. 'Not likely. He's a family man. He and Rose are a good team.' That made her wince. She and Ru were a good team once, until she became a failure, and he became a celebrity. 'Joking aside,' said Ru, 'he wouldn't have time. If he's not cooking, he's glued to a screen.'

'Doing what?'

'Dunno. I guess researching recipes and sourcing ingredients, like me? Time for another coffee?'

Fiona glanced at the sun rising over the horizon, a beautiful mix of soft pinks and purples. She let out a contented sigh, wishing she could curl up on the sofa for the day, but her books beckoned. 'Go on then.'

For two hours they discussed and rejected possible theories, each one more outlandish than the next. Was Kim flogging bottles to finance her incredible wardrobe? Was Trish trying to bring the pub into disrepute so that Prosecco & Prose could steal their customers? Was Josh smuggling fine wine out of the pub to his surfing mates? By the end they were in fits of giggles. They imagined the whole thing was an elaborate ruse – some London chef orchestrating everyone at the Smuggler's Inn in a grand sting operation. The goal? To bring down Ru and eliminate the threat of his soon-to-open second restaurant.

Coffee morphed into a light lunch of homemade pasta stuffed with wild mushrooms. Time evaporated until, with a start, Ru exclaimed, 'We've got to go – prep time for me; laying up for you!'

'Not for me,' she replied. Rose had given her the evening off as a thank you for helping with the cellar stock checks. Fiona would spend it studying.

Back at Ivy's cottage, Fiona trotted upstairs and pulled out her books. She chose one on South American wines and lay upside down on the bed, her feet resting on the pillows, propping herself up on her elbows with her chin resting in cupped hands. The words seemed to spin in front of her eyes. She blinked, focusing on the Malbec grape, running her tongue round her mouth, imagining the taste, but her mind kept drifting back to the delicate earthy flavour of the mushroom filling in her lunchtime pasta. A Malbec's bold tannic structure would smother that flavour, and the low acidity would be a mismatch for the elegant, earthy profile of the mushrooms.

She pushed herself off the bed and carried her books downstairs. Her aunt was in the kitchen, but she had lit a fire in the sitting room a bright orange reminder of her morning with Ru.

Fiona peeled off her jumper. It was too hot to concentrate on grape varieties. Trying to dislodge the muzzy feeling, she shook her head. After spending every morning playing amateur detective with Ru, studying was vital. She had booked enough time off work so she could travel to London the day before the three day exam and was intending to stay at the flat in Ladbroke Grove. She had her keys, Ru would never know, and anyway, she was still the joint owner and couldn't afford to stay anywhere else.

She counted the pages to the end of the chapter, promising herself a break when she reached it, then reread the same paragraph. Her eyelids felt heavy, and it was difficult reading about scent when her nostrils were full of the smell of Ivy's lemon drizzle cake.

'When's that cake going to be ready, Ivy?' she called.

Her aunt's voice floated back. 'Another five minutes, then time for it to cool. Fancy a coffee?'

Fiona closed her book and wandered into the kitchen. 'How did you get on with Rose?' she asked.

Ivy tutted. 'She interviewed Kim before me. That poor girl was shaking like a jelly so when I'd finished with Rose, I took her up to Trish's for a coffee to calm her down.'

Fiona's eyebrows furrowed. Kim wasn't her favourite person, but she didn't like to think of someone in distress, and Fiona didn't think Kim had stolen the wine, not with 'Daddy's wallet' available for treats. 'Why was Kim so nervous?'

Ivy held up a warning finger. 'None of your business.'

'Ivy!'

'No. Kim spoke to me in confidence.'

Listening to her aunt fill the kettle, Fiona moaned. 'Oh Ivy, you and your confidences. You make it sound as if you're a Catholic priest hearing confession.'

'I told Rose to hand this drama over to the professionals or drop it or she's going to start losing staff if she's not careful.'

Fiona laughed. 'She won't lose me; I need the money!'

'Yes, I told her that.'

Fiona straightened. 'What?'

'She was worried you might hand in your notice, and I wanted to reassure her.'

'You told someone who's investigating a theft that I'm short of money!'

'Don't be so dramatic,' said Ivy. She gave Fiona a playful shove. 'Off you go. I'll bring coffee and cake through shortly.'

Fiona slumped back on the sofa and picked up her book. She needed to concentrate. She was almost there now . . . just a few more days.

Snuggling down that night, Fiona wrestled with whether to share Ivy's revelation about Kim with Ru. Kim's anxiety after her interview provided a new lead, but Fiona didn't want to suggest that Ru investigate that line. She felt a stab of jealousy, imagining Kim's reaction if Ru suggested they meet for a walk on the beach, even though it was exactly what she'd done with Josh.

Perhaps it would be better to cancel the morning meeting and study instead? She had achieved virtually nothing today and she could always tell Ru about Kim another time, when there was something else to report – like Fiona being admitted to the CMS. She thumped her pillow into shape and turned the light off. She would sleep on it.

In the morning, Fiona picked up her phone and unblocked Ru's number. She typed out a message:

I've nothing to report, shall we skip?

How should she finish? Her finger hovered over the x button, then she scrolled through the emojis, selecting the female cop.

His reply was swift:

The menemen will be ready in twenty minutes.

Ru signed off with the chef emoji. It was the first message he had ever sent her without a beating heart as a full stop.

Fiona jabbed at the doorbell while stamping her feet up and down for warmth. The second it buzzed, she pushed it open, and the smell of cumin hit her. She glanced up at the flat door – ajar – wondering if he would have cooked simit, the crispy sesame seed crusted bread the Turkish dipped into their breakfast menemen. She bounded up the stairs, pausing briefly at the doorway to watch him unnoticed.

A faint smell of sizzling vegetables filled the air, and she noticed his shoulders relax as he tilted his head, inhaling the aroma with a small, satisfied smile. A sudden wave of nostalgia tugged at her. The simplicity of it all struck her: the way he cared for each step in his cooking, as if each dish was a small act of love.

She remembered how mornings like this used to belong to them – how he'd surprise her with breakfast, moving with the same effortless calm, the same easy warmth that used to make her feel so lucky to be loved and be in love with this man. She wondered if he missed her even a fraction as much as she missed him.

At the stove, Ru started crumbling cheese into a large sauté pan. She could smell yeast and spied a bottle of pomegranate molasses – she was getting simit.

'Hi,' she said.

'Two minutes. Make yourself comfortable. I've laid the table.'

In the bay window was a table covered in a white linen cloth. There was a single red rose in a bud vase, and resting on one chair was a package wrapped in tissue paper and secured with a pink ribbon. 'Aren't you going to open it?' he asked, pointing at the parcel.

She grinned. 'For me?'

He nodded.

She bounced over and prodded the parcel, which felt squidgy, like a cushion. She tugged at the ribbon, unfurled the paper and released a lavender coloured coat.

He was standing behind her, close enough for her to smell the musky shower gel he used, sending a shudder of pleasure through her body. 'It's too cold wandering round Brambleton in that raincoat,' he murmured, placing a hand on her shoulder. She stiffened, then relaxed, willing him to stroke her neck or better still, to kiss it. Instead, he gave her a gentle pat, like an owner would a faithful dog, then returned to the kitchen area.

'This is so thoughtful,' she said. Fiona recalled the novelty pen he'd given Rose – so like Ru. He didn't know she was heading to London tomorrow; he had no clue she'd be bringing her own winter coat back to Devon. The gift wasn't some calculated move – it was just Ru being Ru.

'Sit down.' He slipped a plate in front of her – a gutsy mixture of scrambled egg, sautéed onions, green peppers and tomatoes, seasoned with chilli flakes and cumin. Crumbled feta, black olives and a drizzle of olive oil garnished the top. 'Can I ask you a favour?'

'Sure,' she answered, smiling.

'The investors are huge gin fans. They want me to offer some interesting varieties. Who should I call for honest advice?'

'Oh, that's easy. Let me jot down a couple of my contacts. Got a piece of paper?'

He passed over a stack of Post-it notes and Fiona scribbled down two names, adding the details of the wine merchant each worked for and their phone numbers.

'How's life at Ivy's?' he asked.

'Busy; I'm spending all my free time studying.'

'How's that going?'

She grunted, chewing at her lip. Should she tell him where she was going tomorrow? His thoughtful present, coupled with asking her advice, persuaded her to trust him with her secret. 'I'm off to London tomorrow to retake my exam.'

His eyebrows rose. 'Why? You don't need any more certificates. You're good enough already.'

It was kind of him, but she knew better. The world of wine was cutthroat. To get ahead, she needed credentials. Had she been a CMS member three months earlier, the investors would have backed her. Would she have felt confident enough to accept Ru's marriage proposal if she hadn't failed that exam? Then again, perhaps he wouldn't have proposed if she had passed; perhaps that had been a sop to her hurt pride, a cack-handed attempt to keep his own plans for the restaurant – *his* restaurant – on track. '*I* need certificates. Everyone needs qualifications.'

He sat down opposite, picking up his fork and pointing it at her. 'I never did. I learned on the job.'

'But that's your raw talent shining through.' She didn't have any raw talent. She succeeded through hard work and passing exams. But tomorrow she would be back in London, and soon she would belong to the CMS. Finally, Fiona would be qualified. She would repay her debts and become someone!

She beamed at him, waiting, watching for his admiration, but his face was inscrutable. Eventually he put down his fork and spoke. 'What will you do if you fail again?'

Suddenly, the flat felt claustrophobic, an eery silence punctuated by the soft scrape of Ru's cutlery. Perched awkwardly on the edge of the sofa, her fingers twisting the hem of her jumper, Fiona couldn't eat another bite.

'You don't actually need this qualification,' Ru said quietly. 'Think about it rationally.'

Her head snapped up. 'How dare you!'

'I'm trying to help,' he insisted, his voice soft, but there was nothing reassuring about it.

'Help?' Fiona's laugh was brutal. 'You mean like you *helped* when you forewarned the investors you thought I wouldn't pass the first time?'

Ru's jaw tightened. 'If you fail again—'

'Which I won't,' she snapped.

'What's your actual plan?' he finished, a hint of genuine concern breaking through.

'My plan,' she hissed, 'is to pass, so I can prove to every single person who's ever doubted me that I am worth something. Starting with you.'

It was the kind of silence that filled every corner of the room, as if the air itself were replaying their words, which lingered – charged and unforgivable – exposing the raw, jagged edges of their broken history. 'I'm leaving,' declared Fiona.

'Fine,' spat Ru.

They rose together. Ru's face flushed with anger. He leaned over and for a moment she thought he was reaching for her, but he picked up the coat. 'Just take it. You'll freeze without one. It's dropping to minus five tonight.'

Snatching it up, she picked up the Post-it note too and shoved that into one of the coat pockets. 'You won't be wanting advice from a failure,' she muttered, then she stomped to the door and clomped down the stairs. She'd show him. Fail? Not this time.

Twenty-five

Running late, Fiona grimaced as she saw the team already assembled for the evening's briefing through the fogged-up kitchen window. She dashed up the steps, tearing off her new coat as she ran. Fiona tossed the coat onto the staffroom table and sprinted into the kitchen.

'Sorry I'm a bit late,' she puffed, sidling over to the serving counter where Kim and Rose stood with their hands clasped around notepads. Kim was wearing a short, figure-hugging emerald green dress, which Fiona thought was inappropriate for work, but perfect for attracting Ru's attention.

'Hi,' she whispered. Neither of the other women responded. She squeezed between them, and as she did, they both stepped sideways, distancing themselves as if she was contagious.

'The pheasant dish has poached chestnuts with it, so beware of nut allergies,' advised George.

'The sauce is thickened with a roux – that's a mixture of flour and butter, so contains gluten and dairy,' added Ru.

'Let me write that down, Ruben,' said Kim, fluttering her eyes at the sous chef. Fiona clamped her mouth shut. Kim wasn't very subtle.

'Any questions?' asked George.

Yes, thought Fiona. When was someone going to tell her why she felt as welcome as a wasp at a picnic? She shook her head and turned to follow Rose out, blanking out the sound of Kim's hurried footsteps thumping behind her. But Fiona couldn't ignore the younger woman's voice, loaded with venom, 'I've told Rose I saw you lurking round the cellar.'

Fiona spun round, laughing. If that explained her being cold-shouldered tonight, Fiona had nothing to fear. Rose trusted Fiona – she'd told her as much. 'Not a peculiar place to find a sommelier.'

'Sommeliers don't lurk . . . thieves do though . . .' Fiona's stomach sank. Then Kim's lip curled back, and she spat, 'I know you're having a relationship with Ruben. I clocked you coming out of his flat this morning. In this together, are you?'

Fiona didn't rise to the taunt, but wished she and Ru had been more careful. Evidently the sight of Fiona coming out of Ru's flat had goaded Kim into trying to finger Fiona for the wine thefts.

All evening, the pub thrummed with voices. Outside, waves rumbled against the harbour wall and the autumn winds blew against the windows. Fiona moved through the restaurant, offering smiles that hid her frayed nerves. She was good at her job – she knew that. But tonight, her thoughts were scattered. The pub was busy, and Fiona tried to concentrate, moving between tables, uncorking bottles with a flourish.

Across the room, Kim was laughing with Rose. The laughter was for show, Fiona knew that much. Whenever she thought no one was looking, Kim's eyes would flicker over to Fiona, her mouth set in a small, tight smirk. The idea of someone accusing Fiona of theft stung her, a barb planted by Kim that festered with every passing hour.

Rose was walking towards Fiona, her eyes flashing, making Fiona's throat constrict. Did her boss suspect her? She was innocent. Kim's accusations didn't carry any weight without evidence.

As she set down two empty cocktail glasses at the bar, she caught Rose giving her a pointed look, lips pursed, chin tilted. Fiona noticed the slight hesitation when Rose handed over a wine order, sliding the paper onto a nearby table rather than placing it in Fiona's hands, as if the simple act of touching them might taint her.

But Fiona kept her face neutral, her hands steady. Tonight, Kim's resentment seemed to linger just beneath the surface, like a bitter tannin that stayed in the mouth long after you swallowed. Fiona knew the source of the other woman's hostility – all those minor mishaps: the swapping of Mr Florid Face's wine order; the mysterious obstacle in Fiona's path when she was carrying a tray; her untied apron. They all stemmed from the same grudge. Kim must have detected an undercurrent of attraction between Fiona and Ru and, determined to have Ru for herself, she had set out to undermine her rival. Fiona bit her tongue. Snapping at Kim now would only give the younger woman more ammunition.

'Table 4 is asking for the sommelier, Fiona,' Rose called over her shoulder, voice clipped.

'On it,' she replied, grabbing a wine list and making her way to the table. She caught sight of Kim chatting with a couple at the bar. When Fiona brushed past her, Kim's smile didn't falter, but her gaze slipped sideways, just long enough for Fiona to feel the frostiness of it.

Discussing the merits of different wines with the couple at Table 4 steadied Fiona. But then Rose leaned over, muttering something low to Kim and glancing back at Fiona with narrowed eyes.

As the night wore on, the wind outside grew louder, howling around the pub as if echoing Fiona's storm of emotions. She continued pouring, smiling and describing each wine with the same careful dedication as always. But when the crowd thinned and the evening wound down, Fiona caught Rose alone, wiping down the bar.

She approached with measured steps, the words crystallizing in her mind. Surely, Fiona told herself, this was just a misunderstanding. She would explain that Kim's accusations stemmed from their long-standing rivalry. After all, Rose had trusted her enough to share the code to the new cellar lock – a gesture that spoke volumes. Kim's claims couldn't possibly have swayed the boss.

But when Rose looked up, her eyes reflected not understanding, but betrayal. Without a word, she stalked past, deliberately avoiding Fiona's outstretched hand. Kim followed in Rose's wake, a subtle smirk playing at the corners of her mouth.

Left alone, Fiona stood motionless in the deserted restaurant. The silence pressed in from all sides as the walls seemed to contract around her, trapping her with the weight of shattered trust. Thank goodness she was off to London in the morning. That would give time for Kim's accusations to blow over, although it might be better to hand in her notice when she returned. The Smuggler's Inn wouldn't have need of a member of the CMS.

Fiona plodded to the staffroom. Someone had hung up her coat. Probably Josh. Kim hadn't spoken to her all evening. Ru wouldn't look her in the eye. And Rose was barely civil. She removed it from the peg and slipped into it, the silky lining the only softness she'd encountered that night. The coat felt strangely heavy. Something thumped against her thigh, and she glanced down. A bottleneck was poking out of the pocket, its top covered in gold foil. She reached in, smiling as she pulled out a half bottle, with a simple yet striking gold label – Krug. Was this a peace offering from Ru after their harsh words, intended to calm her before her exam? He knew it was her favourite. It was thoughtful of him to choose a half bottle, so it fitted snugly in the pocket. A full bottle would be visible and might demand an explanation. She would chill it properly and enjoy it with Ivy to toast belonging to the CMS.

Hearing the door open, Fiona spun round. Rose stalked in wearing the same sullen expression she had been casting Fiona's way all evening. Good, she wanted to clear the air, defend herself from whatever poison Kim had dripped into Rose's ears. Behind her boss, Fiona spotted Josh, and then Kim, and beside her, Ru. Fiona's heart skipped a beat seeing Kim standing so close to him.

Then Fiona noticed Kim's eyes. They were alight, like a puppy who has just been tossed its favourite toy, and she felt a stirring of discomfort. Her whole body started tingling. Outside, the wind gave a drawn-out yowl as if prophesying danger.

'I can't tell you how disappointed I am, Fiona,' snapped Rose. Did Rose believe Kim's story? Fiona felt her body shaking. What was Kim doing here and why weren't Josh and Ru in the kitchen clearing up? Rose pointed at the bottle in Fiona's hands. 'Going somewhere with that, were you?' she sneered.

Fiona held the bottle out towards Ru with a pleading look in her eyes. There was a stunned expression on Ru's face, and limply, Fiona put the Krug on the table. If this wasn't a gift from Ru, what was it doing in her coat pocket?

Rose snapped around to face the audience. 'Please, leave us.'

Fiona's heart started pounding. She took a deep breath. Just as the door closed, she saw Kim stroking Ru's arm and gasped.

Ru's eyes narrowed to slits, and she shut her own, listening to his spiteful words as he spoke, 'How could you? That is pure evil.'

Feeling her insides shrivel, Fiona backed herself against the wall, clutching at the sides of her lavender coat for comfort. The door slammed shut and she gulped down her tears. An army of insects was crawling over her skin and she let out a soft sob; she wished Ru hadn't witnessed her being accused of theft and that she hadn't seen Kim comforting him. Was he congratulating himself on narrowly escaping marrying a thief?

When she opened her eyes, there was a grim expression on her boss's face. 'I'm going to give you a chance. Repay the money and I won't report you.'

Fiona's voice sounded whiny and desperate, 'But I haven't taken anything.' She put her hands up as if surrendering, 'I've no idea how the Champagne got in my pocket, I certainly didn't put it there.'

'I've made you my offer. Please leave that bottle where it is and go.'

Fiona's cheeks burned. She wasn't even being allowed to defend herself.

Someone had planted that wine, and everyone, including Ru, now thought she was guilty.

Twenty-six

Fiona slunk to the door, took a breath, wanting to turn and protest her innocence, but Rose's sharp words had shattered her confidence irreparably, like a ship's mast struck down in a powerful storm. She let herself out of the staffroom and crossed the silent reception area, thankful it was empty. Outside, an icy drizzle hit her cheeks. A thick layer of mist hung over the harbour. Fiona stood reeling from Rose's accusation, her world spinning. Each wispy tendril of fog seemed to shroud her in uncertainty and despair. She drew her coat around her and plodded down the steps. The lights were on in the kitchen, a brightness that seemed both to ooze comfort and emphasize her loneliness. She imagined the rest of the team gathered around the serving counter, gossiping about what they'd just witnessed. Passing by the window, she heard laughter. That stung. It would be Fiona they were laughing at.

Dragging her way back up the hill, tonight the silence seemed eerie. And then she remembered where she was going tomorrow. She told herself to forget about the Smuggler's Inn. She'd outgrown it.

Back at the cottage, she let herself in. There were no lights on, so she crept upstairs. Outside her aunt's bedroom door, she raised a hand to knock, then stopped and lowered it again. Why burden Ivy? She would slip away in the morning and return as a qualified Master Sommelier. Fiona crept back downstairs and scrawled a note for her aunt, reminding her she was taking a few days off to sort her things out at the London flat.

Brushing her teeth, she refused to allow the evening's events to dog her mind. She dodged her demons by conjuring up difficult flavours and challenging herself for pairing suggestions. It was good practice for the next few days: Szechuan duck with its bold chilli heat called for a Gewürztraminer – an aromatic wine whose floral sweetness and subtle spice notes created perfect harmony with the dish. Alternatively, a semi-sweet Riesling would work brilliantly, its natural acidity and delicate sweetness providing the ideal counterbalance to tame the fiery chilli while complementing the duck's rich flavour.

She clambered into bed, switched off the light and snuggled down, adding a third possibility to her pairing list: a rosé Champagne, but that sent her mind sprinting back to the half bottle of Krug. Who'd put it there? It had to be Kim. She didn't think Kim was the wine thief, but Fiona suspected her rival had set her up to convince Rose to fire her and clear the pitch for Kim to get together with Ruben. As if that was necessary after their row this morning! Ten minutes later, she sat up, turned on the light and picked up a wine book. If she couldn't sleep, she should study.

When Fiona woke up, the night was deep and thick, the sort of rural darkness that seemed to erase everything, as if someone had stolen the moon and stars. She sat up. Something hard and uncomfortable jabbed her thigh. She felt around. It was her wine book. She chucked it onto the bedside table and crawled across the bedclothes on her knees to the window. A chill wind was seeping through, and she shivered as she peered outside, seeing nothing, her mind filling with the memory of the scene in the staffroom: Rose's harsh accusation; Ru's spiteful words.

The wind, just a whisper against the window, rose suddenly

and carried with it an unexpected groan from the old wood of the house, a sound that seemed to come from the depths of the earth. An uneasy feeling crept over her, as though eyes were watching from the dense darkness beyond the window, eyes that accused her of theft. She flopped back onto the bed. She needed sleep.

Her fitness tracker flashed – six minutes past four. Fiona groaned, pulled the duvet up to her neck and tried to clear her mind. She flipped onto her side, then star fished onto her stomach, before trying her back once again, but her brain felt wired – it was like trying to nap in the middle of the day.

At 4.30 a.m. Fiona got up. A taxi would arrive within the hour.

It was still dark when the train left Barnstaple station for Exeter shortly before 6.30 a.m. Fiona switched off her phone, folded her coat inside out and rested it against the window, pulling one sleeve over her eyes to block out the stark train lights, then snuggled her cheek against the soft silky fabric lining. Soon, the gentle hum from the engine and the swaying of the carriage lulled her to sleep.

She woke an hour later as the train was pulling into Exeter, where she would catch a fast connection to London. She yawned, stretching her arms above her head. She felt refreshed. A flutter of nerves stirred in her stomach as she glanced out of the window, watching the outskirts of the city blur by. This was it – the trip she'd been preparing for. She checked her watch, mentally running through the route from the flat to the London club that was hosting the exam. Excitement and worry mingled, sharpening her focus. One step at a time. First task, catch that connecting train.

A faint scent of garlic hit Fiona the moment she stepped inside the flat. Their flat. The space she'd called home for two years.

She picked up weeks of mail from the rug, then closed the door softly, as if worried Ru might hear. Even after months away, it seemed as if the air still remembered her. She could almost hear Ru's voice from the kitchen, calling her to taste some new recipe he was experimenting with.

But he was in Devon. Fiona let out a long, silent breath and moved towards the lounge, eyes searching. She half-expected her shoes, that ancient pair of trainers he always teased her about, to be gone. But there they were, under the side table. Her heart skidded.

In the sitting room she tossed the mail onto the coffee table then took her overnight bag into the bedroom. Her gaze subconsciously gravitated to the chest of drawers. Her eyes narrowed. There should have been a gap, where the perfume bottle she took to Devon usually sat. But there wasn't. There was a full bottle in exactly the right spot, the faint, amber tinted liquid glinting against the glass like a drop of sunlight. She thought about the nearly empty one in Devon. Had Ru intended the perfume as a commiseration present to cheer her up after she failed her exam? If only he'd left it at the bottle of perfume and had never produced that beautiful engagement ring. That's when everything had started to unravel. Before then, it might have been possible to talk through why he'd approached the investors behind her back – she now believed his actions were a well-intentioned but misguided attempt to protect her.

Fiona swallowed. Unable to resist she reached out, picking it up, turning it over in her hand. She could still picture him watching her in the mirror as she sprayed it behind her ears, a half-smile tugging at his lips, the way he would so often lean over and inhale the scent. But why had he removed it from the packaging? Why hadn't he returned it and claimed a refund after she rejected his proposal?

And why were all her things still where she'd left them? She had expected everything to be gone, packed up into a box, waiting for her to collect. She thought he would have erased her presence. Her gaze flickered to her collection of wine books stacked precisely on her bedside table. She thought of their nightly ritual of winding down after a hectic service by reading next to each other, her murmuring wine notes into the silence while he scribbled ideas for new recipes. She pressed a hand against her mouth, as though it might silence the ache rising in her throat.

In the kitchen, Ru's presence seemed to hover like a ghost, filling the room with fragments of half-remembered laughter. She caught the faint, lingering smell of cinnamon and sighed. Randomly opening a cupboard, she saw spices neatly arranged, labelled in his precise handwriting. Her fingers hovered, hesitant, before moving on. She checked the freezer, discovering containers stacked meticulously, meals he'd prepped with care, all portioned for two. She pulled one out, noticing the date – a week before he'd shown up at the Smuggler's Inn. Had he been so confident of changing her mind that he'd kept on cooking for her? Or was the second portion intended for some other lucky woman?

She closed the freezer door softly, almost apologetically. Hunger gnawed at her, but a stronger sensation rose – she felt as if she was trespassing on a sacred space. Fiona leaned against the counter, the smell of herbs and spices clinging to it, a reminder that this was Ru's territory. Fiona didn't belong here anymore and that feeling lodged in her throat, making her almost queasy. She'd go for a stroll in Holland Park, then return to study.

Back in the flat and feeling refreshed, Fiona curled up on the sofa, her wine books by her side. On the coffee table was the stack of mail, and conscious there may be three months of bills waiting for her, she picked it up and rifled through the pile.

She stopped, her attention drawn to an envelope on the other side of the table. It was a handwritten letter with an Australian stamp, and it was already open. She recognized the writing at once and her eyes blurred as she tore at the letter. Why had Ru opened her post? And was this Ivy's work? Was this what she meant by not betraying a confidence? Had Ivy told her parents about her exam failure after all? Was Fiona about to read – second hand – a 'letter of condolence' from her parents? She felt her blood pumping as she slipped out the paper.

Her hand trembled as she unfolded the single page, crisp and thick, the two hallmarks of the quality writing paper she expected.

Her eyes skimmed the first lines, her eyes dancing over her father's familiar handwriting. Mid-sentence, she stopped, her breath catching in her throat. Fiona's fingers reflexively checked the envelope. It wasn't addressed to her. This was for Ru. Unable to stop herself, she unfolded the page again, and her father's voice emerged, measured, intellectual, yet something else was hiding beneath the academic veneer. Her eyes picked out a random sentence in the middle of the page.

We love Fiona deeply, but our expressions of that love were often scholarly . . .

Her throat tightened. A lifetime of proving her worth crystallized in those words. Her parents' love buried beneath academia.

Swallowing, she started back at the beginning.

I write in response to your recent letter requesting my daughter Fiona's hand in marriage.

First, let me commend you on the remarkable depth of understanding you have demonstrated regarding my daughter. Your astute observation that she incorrectly perceives love as something she must earn strikes me to the core. My wife and I have, I fear, inadvertently cultivated this perspective through our own dedication to academic achievements.

Our passion for our work – while never diminishing our love for our only child – created a home where intellectual achievement was perhaps encouraged a little too forcefully. We love Fiona deeply, but our expressions of that love were often scholarly: carefully chosen books, a rigorous debate, a moment of shared intellectual discovery.

Your recognition of this convinces me you understand Fiona and her need to prove her worth – and that you accept her and love her exactly as she is. One word of caution – she is an independent spirit, and whilst I respect your desire to protect her from the perils of forging too fast in her career, my suspicion is she will not thank you for that effort.

I am delighted by your traditional approach – formally requesting parental consent. Of course it is a formality only. Any decision made by our daughter should be hers alone to make. While we would love to come to England to celebrate your wedding, my wife and I would also be honoured to welcome you both to Melbourne. Your visit here would provide us a precious opportunity to reconnect with our daughter, to demonstrate our love.

With warmest regards

Fiona reread the letter; this time, with tears splashing freely over her face. She wasn't sure she understood exactly what her father was saying about love, but one thing she was certain of: Ru had understood her completely, he did truly love her, despite her flaws. He wasn't going to wake up one day thinking that she'd held him back. He wasn't going to trade her in for a better model as soon as he found one. He really had been trying to protect her by going behind her back to the investors. And he wasn't bulldozing her feelings with his suggestion to take her on honeymoon to Melbourne – that had been her parents' idea.

How could she have been so wrong? She'd had everything she could ever have wanted at her fingertips, and now it was gone for ever. Then in her mind, she heard Ru calling her 'pure evil'. Thank goodness her eyes were shut, and she'd not seen his expression.

There was no coming back from that. She had missed her opportunity to spend the rest of her life with a man she adored – and it was all her own fault.

By ten that evening Fiona's eyes were drooping. She took a shower, then sat on the edge of the bed, touching the cool sheet. Ru's head had left slight imprints on the pillow on his side of the bed. She leaned over, sniffing the faintest scent of his shampoo.

Fiona slipped under the duvet and closed her eyes, trying to recapture her earlier heavy eyelids, imagining that wonderful sense of drifting asleep, but she felt his absence like a missing shadow, an emptiness so solid it felt like an accusation. She sat bolt upright, her mind toying with the words in her father's letter, trying to understand them, but mostly replaying her last row with Ru, then the ghastly scene in the staffroom.

Fiona thumped the pillows into shape and settled down, focusing her mind on regional grape varieties.

Sleep didn't claim her. Thoughts kept circling her mind, like needles pricking through every attempt at sleep. Each time she shifted, she could feel him there. Her fingers kept drifting to the pillow beside her, tracing its edge in the dark. Did he really think she'd stolen that wine? She couldn't help but remember lying in this same bed the night before her last exam.

That night, her nerves had been a knot inside her chest, pulling tight no matter how many times she tried to shake it loose. But Ru had known. She remembered the weight of his hand stroking her arm as they lay tangled in the sheets. Fiona told him – stammered really – that she didn't think she could do it. She wasn't sure, but she thought she might have even whispered some nonsense about her tastebuds being on strike, her nose betraying her and her palate not being refined enough. The memory was so vivid. She recalled laughing weakly in the darkness, hoping her voice didn't give away how terrified she was.

And then he had kissed her. A slow, lingering kiss, one that left no doubt that he would listen to every doubt she was trying so hard to supress and help her chase those thoughts away, no matter how long it took. They made love that night, his hands and lips quieting her racing mind. His fingers gently tracing her shoulder, down her spine – soothing every worry, until she melted. That night, she finally drifted into sleep, cradled in his warmth, the faint smell of basil lingering on his skin. Her final thought was of him.

The next morning, when she had opened her eyes, she was alone. She slipped on his discarded shirt, rolling up the sleeves to her wrists and padded to the kitchen, drawn by the smell. The oven door clicked shut, Ru straightened and, seeing her, he had leaned against the counter with his arms crossed. She still remembered the smile spread across his face, warm and welcoming, just like the smell of baking pastry filling the air.

'What are we having?'

'It's a Burgundian cheese soufflé.'

She remembered its golden centre, sitting two inches proud of the short crust case. The pastry was crumbly, buttery, and the soufflé delicate, just browned at the edges and flecked with hints of Gruyère and Comté. 'Protein,' he said, sliding the plate before her, 'to make sure you're sharp. And that your tastebuds stay neutral.'

Fiona had laughed, tearing into the soufflé with a spoon. That morning tasted of Burgundy. Wine was the beating heart of Burgundy and gastronomy its soul. Each bite was light as a wisp of smoke, yet rich and filling. The cheese left a taste on her tongue, salty yet perfectly balanced. As she took one bite, then another, she felt the stirring of a gentle confidence in her chest. Ru had pasted it back together, like a master chef gathering sundry ingredients to craft a stunning dish.

That memory now slipped away like mist, leaving her staring at the ceiling in the dark. Her heart was still racing from a past that refused to stay buried. She turned onto her side, willing her thoughts to quiet, to obey, but her mind was too loud, looping the same fears over and over. Sleep hovered just out of reach, taunting her with what she couldn't have.

Let tomorrow come. She'd meet it, shaking if she had to, but standing all the same.

Twenty-seven

The location for the three day exam was a private members' club in Mayfair. At the reception desk, Fiona was met with a dignified hush, a stark contrast to the usual ringing phones and chattering families of a hotel. The silence felt intimidating and failed to calm her nerves – the next three days held the key to her future.

Following a dark-suited escort up the elegant staircase, her gaze wandered among the portraits of stern looking men – mostly in military uniform, who seemed to urge her on to victory. On the landing, Fiona closed her eyes and inhaled deeply. She calculated that she hadn't slept more than three hours last night, the same as the night before.

Her stomach twisted as she thought back to two nights ago. Ru's last words had convinced her that he believed what he'd seen – that Rose had caught the wine thief. Fiona might never see the man she loved again, or if she did, it would be the celebrity chef Ruben Nkosi she saw, not her Ru – the man who'd cooked for her just before her last exam.

Fiona pressed her palms to her eyes, forcing herself back to the present. But the memories clung to her like a fragrant old wine, a touch past its prime, but still beautiful. She wondered if she'd ever find another vintage quite like Ru.

Her escort showed her into what he referred to as the Coffee Room. It wasn't like any café Fiona had ever been in before. The dining room unfurled like an elegant canvas; its hundred-foot expanse punctuated by polished wooden tables. As someone guided her through the space, her fingertips traced the gleaming surface of a table rich with the subtle sheen of meticulously maintained antique wood. The chair she settled into embraced her, the supple leather whispering refinement.

Overhead, the high ceiling soared, and chunky, elaborate cornicing cascaded across the expanse. Massive sash windows lined one entire wall, their tall, pristine panes framing a view of St James's Square and its bare plane trees – a patchwork of grey and cream.

On the opposite side was a fireplace, flanked by two colossal portraits, one of the young Queen Victoria, the other of Prince Albert. Their sheer size amplified their presence, giving them a larger than-life quality which seemed to question Fiona's presence in this magnificent room. The royal couple didn't seem to be urging her on to greatness.

On a central table, in front of an elaborate artificial flower display, was a modern white digital plastic clock, looking incongruous in the room's splendour. On every other table was a pristine white tasting mat and rows of slender stemmed glasses. She glanced around at the other candidates, her fingers trembling.

From outside, Fiona heard the rumble of a taxi. She kept glancing around the room, her gaze skimming over faces she recognized from past industry events. These were all veterans of this brutal test, people who – unlike her – looked calm and collected. She recognized a few of the Master Sommeliers on the judging panel as well: Laurent, the inscrutable Frenchman, and Elsa, the Swedish sommelier with ice-blue eyes and an air of effortless composure.

Laurent stepped forward. 'Welcome to Day One,' he announced, his accent carrying an unmistakable Parisian lilt. 'Please check your phone is switched off.' Fiona didn't need to do that. Hers had been off since that ghastly night when Rose accused her of theft, and she had no intention of switching it back on anytime soon. 'You will begin with theory,' said Laurent. 'You have one hour.'

Fiona took a deep breath. A whiff of perfume, bold and spicy, reached her, immediately distracting her. She wondered what wine might pair with that scent. Then Laurent's voice cut in again. 'Begin.'

Each question was a daunting black block of text. Fiona's pulse quickened as she skimmed the first.

What specific winemaking technique is typically associated with white Burgundy?

She thought back to her revision notes, memories surfacing in fragments, her mind jumping from Chablis to Côte de Beaune to Montrachet. The answer came to her, and she smiled. She could do this. Everything was going to be fine: *bâtonnage and sur lie ageing.*

Less than half an hour later, her brain stalled. She stared at a question asking for the precise latitude of Tokaji, in Hungary. Fiona knew the general region, but the exact coordinates?

She swallowed, glanced sideways at the clock, then stared at the next question. The words seemed to blur for a second.

What's the key flavour profile of an Amarone?

Her mind raced, images of grape clusters and vineyard slopes surfacing. She'd studied this. She *knew* this. Just last night, when she saw her fitness tracker register 3 a.m., she was muttering to herself about drying racks and the perfect balance of cherry and spice. *Cherry, bitter almond, dried figs.*

'Twenty minutes left,' someone said in an official tone. Fiona's fingers spasmed with fear.

On the second morning, Fiona arrived ten minutes early, dark circles beneath her eyes. The other candidates around her looked equally bleary eyed. Clearly, she wasn't the only one finding sleep elusive.

This time, Elsa took charge, calling them to attention with her quiet, unhurried voice. 'Today is the tasting. You have six wines, two flights. Twelve minutes per flight.'

Her instructions were brisk, but her gaze softened briefly as she met Fiona's eye, something almost like encouragement in her expression. Fiona steeled herself. The glasses gleamed in front of her, each one a mystery waiting to be unlocked.

The first glass hovered just below her nose. She closed her eyes, inhaled and let the aroma fill her senses. *Cherries, definitely cherries . . . No, more like strawberry. And there's a hint of . . . tobacco?* A Pinot Noir, she was almost certain, but which region? Time was slipping. Her eyes flicked to Elsa, who was giving a nod to the next candidate. She pushed down her nerves and took a small sip. Earthy, bright acidity. Her mind raced through her notes. 'Oregon,' she whispered.

The next wine was a white. Honey and apples met her tongue, and her confidence sharpened. *Sauternes? Or could it be a Tokaji?*

The next was also white. Fiona hunched over, inhaling deeply, catching notes of green apple, citrus and a faint touch of something herbal. She scribbled quickly: *grassy, hint of elderflower, moderate acidity*. As the minutes ticked by, she worked her way through each glass with systematic precision, inhaling, swirling, sipping, spitting, taking furious notes.

But by the time she reached the penultimate wine, her senses felt muddled, the scents and tastes blending in her mind. She inhaled, trying to pinpoint the aroma, but her thoughts were jumbled. *Was it lychee? No, pear. Or was it quince?*

Across the room, she noticed Elsa's pale gaze lingering on her for a fraction too long, like she could sense the struggle from her examiner's seat. She scribbled hastily and picked up the last glass. *Crisp acidity, high minerality.* When the buzzer sounded, her heart skipped, realizing she'd missed the structure for the last wine. She hadn't noted the wine's finish, a crucial detail. Fiona's heart sank, but it was too late. Laurent and Elsa were already moving around the room, quietly collecting the tasting notes.

Laurent paused by Fiona's table, leaning in to scrutinize her tasting sheet. He frowned almost imperceptibly, then glanced over at her with a raised brow. 'I see you have identified a Californian Sauvignon Blanc. Curious location.' His voice was maddeningly calm, giving nothing away, but Fiona felt a chill creep down her spine.

'I . . . I was confident with that one,' she stammered, though her cheeks grew hot. She clenched her teeth, mentally retracing her tasting notes.

A tangle of citrus, wet stone and freshly cut grass. Was the wine from Sancerre in Laurent's native France, and not from America? Hadn't she nailed the acidity? The minerality?

Laurent gave her a curt nod and moved on. Fiona's mind churned with doubt. She'd spent years perfecting her palate, studying with laser focus, yet here she was, messing up on what should've been an easy call. She watched him walk away, frustration flickering beneath her exhaustion.

On the third morning, Fiona took her overnight bag with her. She didn't want to spend another night in the flat, every inch offering a different memory of Ru.

A restaurant setting replaced the exam room today. The tables were occupied, but the diners did not fool Fiona. Every one of them was a member of the elite CMS. In front of each person, polished silverware gleamed against the white tablecloth, and ranks of glasses stood ready for service. Fiona felt like a ghost of herself. She'd tossed and turned all night, the previous day's tasting misstep haunting her. She couldn't afford another mistake.

Three stern faces looked up at her. 'We're in the mood for something delicate yet bold, perhaps an unusual pairing,' said a male voice, his gaze steely. *Delicate and bold*, she mused. That was a tricky combination to satisfy.

She inclined her head, hoping it gave her a studious air. 'Might I suggest a Nebbiolo? It has the body to stand alone, yet it's delicate enough in its floral notes to pair well with richer dishes.' The examiner's eyes narrowed, and he challenged, 'But what would you suggest if we were eating spicy lamb?' She hesitated a split second, her pulse quickening. 'In that case, perhaps a light, slightly chilled Grenache to complement the heat without overpowering.'

In the corner, Laurent and Elsa sat with another examiner, a German with a stern expression and wire-rimmed glasses. They watched her approach with an unsettling calmness.

Laurent began, a hint of mischief in his eye. 'Imagine you are serving a party of four who have ordered the tasting menu. They would like recommendations on pairing.' His voice held a faint hint of amusement, as if he knew she'd barely slept a wink. She wondered if he harboured a sense of hurt pride after yesterday's mistake of identifying a French wine for what his Gallic pride might label a 'New World imposter'.

She glanced at the imaginary tasting menu, straightened her spine and forced a smile. 'Of course, sir. May I suggest starting with a vintage Champagne for the oyster course? Its acidity and fine mousse will cut through the richness.' She hoped her suggestion would please the Frenchman.

She made her way through the courses adeptly. The panel listened with unreadable expressions, but Fiona felt a bit of her confidence return.

'What if one guest were vegetarian and not interested in oysters?' Elsa challenged.

Fiona wanted to ask what the principal flavours of the vegetarian alternative were but stopped herself. *Think general, probably nuts or cheese.* Fiona's heart skipped, but she composed herself. 'Then perhaps a crisp Chablis with a bit of age. The subtle minerality would complement a vegetarian dish without overpowering it.'

Elsa nodded approvingly and Fiona's chest eased slightly. But Laurent wasn't done with her.

'And if the guest requested something from . . . let's say, a lesser-known region?' His lips quirked, enjoying her discomfort.

Of course he'd test her on obscurities, Fiona thought. That had been her downfall last time. Her mind scrambled for a solution. 'I'd suggest a Grüner Veltliner from the Kremstal region. It has an herbaceous character that's versatile and pairs well with food, with bright acidity to cut through richer flavours.'

She saw Laurent's eyes narrow in faint amusement, but he nodded, evidently satisfied. Yet, Fiona's hand trembled ever so slightly as she poured their glasses, a small bead of wine dribbling down the side of the bottle.

When she finished, Laurent rose. 'Thank you. Please wait outside in the corridor. We will deliver the results shortly.'

Elsa looked at Fiona with a slight smile, sending a flicker of hope through her, but Fiona didn't dare let it grow too much. Her heart thudded painfully in her chest.

'It's a brutal test, I know. It's meant to be.' Elsa's eyes softened, and she placed a reassuring hand on Fiona's shoulder. 'But you held your ground.'

Fiona managed a small smile in return, heartened by the unexpected kindness. 'I guess we'll see,' she replied, her voice thick with exhaustion.

'We won't keep you long.'

Silently Fiona shuffled out to join the other candidates, her brain buzzing with everything that had gone wrong: yesterday's misplaced wine, today the slip of her hand, the tricky questions on that first day. She slumped into a chair and exhaled loudly. She stared at the club members and smartly dressed staff, all moving with easy purpose, oblivious to the tension clinging to those waiting in the corridor. She had given her all. Not perfect, but who was? Surely, they allowed for a few missteps.

Her heart pounded louder with every second, a steady thrum of rising panic. She replayed answers, second-guessed her wine choices. Still, the door across from her stayed shut.

She sat rigid on the edge of the leather armchair, fingers tapping her knee. The silence pressed in, broken now and then by laughter or muffled conversations drifting from other rooms, carefree voices that only reminded her how much she stood to lose.

The door opened. 'Come in and take a seat,' said Elsa, a faint smile ticking at her lips. Was that a condolence or a congratulation? With her heart pounding, Fiona stepped inside. Her palms were clammy, and she clasped them tightly in her lap, hoping to steady herself as she searched Elsa's face, trying to read any hint of what was coming, torn between anticipation and dread. Hardly daring to breathe, her brain was racing, feeding her snapshots of every minor mistake she thought she'd made, calculating if she had done enough.

Elsa was shifting on her feet, her hands neatly by her side, every inch of her composed yet carrying a hint of sorrow in her eyes. She took a step forward, her heels sinking into the thick rug, and finally spoke, her voice low and steady.

'Fiona,' Elsa said, her accent adding a gentle rhythm to each word, 'I'm so sorry . . . but you haven't passed.'

Fiona felt the words strike like a deep, sickening blow. Her hands bunched, her knuckles were white. Reality settled in. Each shallow breath was full of the scents of beeswax and faint notes of wine, the remnants of the recent exam, the aromas clinging, a reminder of her failure.

'No,' she whispered, almost as if trying to deny it. 'Not again.' Her voice faltered.

Elsa's expression softened. 'You were close, Fiona. Closer than last time,' she said carefully. 'But the panel felt there wasn't enough consistency in the tasting portion.'

Somewhere down the hall a door clicked shut, the muted sound magnified in the silent room. Fiona's eyes flicked up for a brief second, following the noise, wishing she could disappear into the hallway and out into the crisp London air, distancing herself from the scene of her failure.

She took a shaky breath, blinking back the sting in her eyes. 'I did everything I could, Elsa,' she whispered, her voice thick with emotion. 'I studied, I worked . . .' Her words choked off, the desperation catching in her throat. 'I needed this. I needed to prove I could do this. That I'm good enough. And now . . .' Her voice faded as she looked down, the intricate, tangled pattern of the rug a cruel reminder of how lost she felt.

As she took another step closer, Elsa sighed, the sound soft, carrying a hint of empathy. 'You're not alone. The exam . . . it sees everything, Fiona. Every tiny slip, every hesitation.'

Although meant to reassure, there was a cool finality in those words, making Fiona feel the loss more keenly. A silence settled uncomfortably between them as they stood there, just inches apart yet worlds away. Elsa was a member of the elite CMS, Fiona a mere wannabe. She closed her eyes, sensing Elsa's presence, a mirror image of the life she'd glimpsed and lost.

Fiona collected her bag from the luggage room. It felt heavier than when she'd left it that morning. She trudged outside. Drizzle settled on her coat and the damp wind bit into her cheeks as if in sympathy with her despondency. She wasn't catching a cab or even taking the Tube; not after today. Not after everything she'd spent, both in money she couldn't afford to repay, and time preparing for that exam. She forced herself to walk, heading down Piccadilly towards Hyde Park and ultimately Paddington Station, each step through a mist-laden London full of couples and families reminding her how utterly alone she felt.

She tracked the side of St. James's Park, deserted, save for a few joggers and a couple huddling under a lamp post, whispering to each other. She averted her eyes from them; this wasn't a night to be thinking of love. Every bone in her body was numb with disappointment. There was no resounding applause, no tearful, celebratory call to Ivy explaining what Fiona had really been doing in London. No picking up the phone to call her parents either. No one would be proud of her today. She'd failed. Again.

Fiona clutched the strap of her bag tightly as if it could somehow hold her together.

By the time she reached the station, the crowd had thinned, leaving behind a scattering of tired commuters and droopy-eyed travellers waiting to catch the Heathrow Express, their faces showing the same weariness she felt. She took out her phone, intending to turn it back on, but then replaced it. There was no reason to call Ivy before she had pulled herself together and made a plan.

It was close to nine, and she had half an hour to wait for the next train, so she bought herself a coffee and sat staring up at the display board in front of her, hearing the gentle rattle each time the information was updated. Noting her platform, she stood mechanically, plodding to the ticket barrier, then boarded her train and slid into an empty seat by the window. She barely registered the world hurtling past outside. She wouldn't get back to Barnstaple until after midnight, but it didn't matter. There would be no one waiting for her.

She felt something rise within her, a flicker of a question, a murmur of doubt. Had all of this been worth it? All the studying, the mountain of debt, the hope? Had she always been bound to fail – just like Ru prophesised in their last heated row? Had she misjudged her own potential? Fiona squeezed her eyes shut, letting the rhythmic sway of the train lull her. For now, there were no answers. Just the hollow ache, and the last scraps of a dream she wasn't ready to let go of.

Twenty-eight

As the first pale light of dawn crept over the horizon, Fiona dawdled along the beach, trying to clear her head after yet another sleepless night. Her footsteps were soft, barely disturbing the quiet. She moved closer to the water's edge, where the waves lapped lazily at the shore. There was a pleasant woody fragrance, which she attributed to a mixture of decaying autumn leaves and driftwood, but it didn't soothe her nerves.

She needed to come up with a plan. She had failed her exam for a second time, but in the cold light of the Devon morning, she recognized that might be the least of her problems. Fiona had debts. She was unemployed and accused of theft. She shuddered, recalling Ru's expression upon seeing the half bottle of Krug that night. A picture of pure disgust. Fiona hugged her lavender coat closer – Ru's last gift – wishing it was his arms embracing her instead.

As a newly crowned member of the elite CMS, she believed she would have convinced him of her innocence. Now, he wouldn't want anything to do with her; but he would want his money back.

She trudged on, her shoes kicking up clods of wet sand. How could she escape this mess? Paying her way out wouldn't resolve her predicament. Her former boss didn't mean paying just for the Champagne. A half bottle of Krug would set her back nearly £100, a tall order, but Rose meant the tens of thousands of pounds of missing wine. It was one thing borrowing money from Ivy to retake her exams – she certainly wouldn't borrow it to pay for wine she hadn't stolen.

What on earth could she do? If only she had spent all of her spare time studying, not playing amateur detective. After she'd discovered the wine theft and started meeting Ru, she'd hardly looked at her books. That exam had been her ticket to a secure future, and she had squandered her chance. She'd pretended it was to solve the crime, but she knew deep down it had been because she'd wanted to spend time with Ru – the man who could once have been her husband, but now, through her own fault, would never be. His last bitter words to her – *How could you? That is pure evil* – seemed to echo across the deserted beach, settling like an overaged vintage, left stale and undrunk.

In the distance, the sky was awash with shades of muted pinks and greys, while the sea reflected the dim, waking light of the sun, casting a silver sheen over the water. It was a gorgeous sight and lifted Fiona's spirits. She gave herself a talking to. Things were not that bleak. Even if Rose reported her, the police would probably not arrest her. She knew she was innocent and there was only circumstantial evidence to implicate her. Kim had only reported seeing Fiona near the cellar: that was not grounds for arrest.

Rose would encourage the team not to gossip; she wouldn't want the scandal. And even if someone did talk, the Smuggler's Inn was in rural North Devon. Rumours wouldn't travel far. She could resurface in a big city like Manchester or Glasgow, start again as a junior sommelier and work her way up.

Why had Rose refused to let Fiona explain? Her boss had trusted her with the cellar lock code, yet somehow now believed that someone who'd supervised her children's homework was a thief. And Ru – he'd accepted her guilt without question, washing his hands of her completely. How could he be so superficial?

He knew her, had even loved her once, yet Ru wasn't curious about Fiona's side of the story.

She picked up a pebble and tossed it, trying to make it skim across the water, but it sank, taking her optimism with it. What if Kim gave a false statement, claiming she had actually witnessed Fiona stealing wine? If she also shared the fact that Ru and Fiona had been meeting secretly in Ru's flat, which was true, their previous relationship would be discovered and then perhaps the whole of Kim's story would be believed. If it was, the bottle of Champagne might tip the weight of circumstantial evidence against Fiona. And if they charged her, Ru would be affected too. She couldn't risk that.

There was only one solution. Fiona must persuade Rose that she was innocent before she left Brambleton. Then she should follow Josh's example: find a modest job far away, leave this behind. Put Ru behind her too. Except she couldn't work out how to achieve that and couldn't think of anyone to ask for help. The person she had turned to for advice over the past three years had always been Ru, and he wouldn't help her now. A brick had been hurled into their relationship, shattering it like glass, scattering their romance into pieces too sharp to pick up.

Out at sea, the silhouettes of small fishing boats bobbed on the horizon, their shapes blurry in the misty dawn. She could see the faint movements of the fishermen, casting their nets into the sea as they began their day's work, their figures outlined against the soft glow of the morning sky. The scene felt timeless, a daily rhythm of toil and nature that carried on, oblivious to the changing seasons. Fiona stopped, watching them in quiet reverie, her breath hanging like smoke in the icy air as she listened to the distant sounds of the waves mingling with the faint hum of boat engines. She needed to get her own life back in rhythm.

Fiona rubbed her hands down her face, trying to summon her energy. She owed money to Ru, and to Ivy, and without that final qualification, she had no prospect of earning much. She should give that exam one more try, but the thought of studying filled her with dread.

She dragged herself back up through the village, let herself into the cottage and sat cross-legged on the faded bedspread. An hour later, and although her books lay scattered around her, she had yet to open one. Outside, the golden leaves swirled in the autumn breeze, their vibrant colours glowing against the overcast sky. The distant sound of a woodpecker echoed from somewhere in the trees. It resembled a scene from a storybook, but the sting of yesterday's failure was a gaping wound.

By mid-morning, unable to concentrate on wine, and needing to keep her mind occupied, Fiona stripped her bed, then Ivy's. In the bathroom, she grabbed the laundry basket and dumped the soiled linen on the floor. She heard her aunt's footsteps on the stairs, followed by her calling out in surprise: 'Fiona, you're back.'

'Thought I'd put some washing on,' Fiona said, concentrating on separating the darks from the whites.

Ivy leaned round the bathroom door. Her face was pale and drawn, and she looked exhausted, as if she had slept little more than Fiona in the last few nights.

'I've been so worried. Why did you switch your phone off?'

Fiona squeezed her eyes shut, realizing her phone had been switched off for four days. She had no intention of changing that. There was no one she wanted to contact, and there were several people she didn't want to contact her. Like Rose, George or the police. 'I left you a note. You knew where I was.'

'But why didn't you say goodbye before you left, or hello when you got home? And why *is* your phone switched off?'

Feeling herself well up, Fiona screwed up her eyes; her aunt walked into the room, holding her arms wide and Fiona crumpled into them sobbing. Ivy stroked her hair. 'What's happened, love?'

Struggling to stem her tears, Fiona sniffed. She took a breath, stepped away, then explained the real reason she had gone to London, and that she'd failed her exam. All the while the tears fell. When she finished, she wiped the back of her hand over her eyes, then across her mouth, tasting the salty tears, a reminder of her failure to identify that blasted Sancerre wine.

Ivy spoke gently, concern etched on her face, 'Do you want me to call Rose and let her know you're not well enough for work today?'

Fiona stifled a laugh. 'No,' she spluttered. 'No need. I've been fired. Accused of theft. Somebody set me up.'

Ivy swayed, clutching at the doorframe. 'Who would do something as wicked as that?' she gasped.

Fiona wanted to name the culprit, but although certain who it was, she had no proof it was Kim. Blinking back the tears, she told herself to do something. She couldn't collapse in a heap of misery. She picked up the pile of whites, tying the ends of a sheet round the bundle, then stumbled past Ivy and down the stairs, hearing her aunt thumping her way down behind her.

She hurled the linen into the washing machine and snapped the door shut. 'Why would anyone want you to take the blame, and how did they do it?' asked Ivy.

While stabbing at the dial to choose a cycle, Fiona told her aunt about the bottle of Krug. When Ivy didn't respond, Fiona spun around. Her aunt was chewing her lip, clutching at the cross at her neck.

'Ivy, if you know something . . . please, I beg you, help me!'

'All I can say is . . .' Ivy heaved a sigh. 'Someone has a problem.'

'Who?'

Ivy clutched at her cross again.

'Who?'

'I never break a confidence.' Listening to those words, Fiona recalled Ivy saying how Kim had been upset after being interviewed and that she had taken her for a coffee and a chat. Had Kim confided in Ivy, confessed some secret? Maybe Kim *was* the thief. Fiona had read about wealthy people shoplifting for the thrill of the crime. Had Kim done this as a dare and planted the evidence against Fiona, not just to remove her from the 'love playing field' but to deflect suspicion away from herself? Fiona's heart started pounding, and she raised her voice, 'It's Kim, isn't it?'

Ivy dropped her gaze. 'I think you should talk to Rose. I'll come with you if you like. She may be more receptive after a few days reflecting on this. She must know you're not a thief.'

Hearing the comforting sound of water gurgling into the washing machine behind her, Fiona shook her head. 'I'm going upstairs to study.'

She stormed upstairs and slammed the bedroom door behind her. Grabbing her *World Atlas of Wine*, she sank onto the bed, opened the book and flicked through the pages, seeing neither the pictures nor the words. Instead, her mind tortured her, feeding her visions of Kim stroking Ru's arm, and echoes of his voice accusing Fiona of being evil. She couldn't let Kim win. She snapped the book shut, then hurled it at the wall. What was the point of studying? If she was a convicted thief, she'd be lucky to get a job washing pots. She must convince Rose of her innocence. Fiona didn't need help from anyone; she could fight her own battles. She'd work out a script, then confront Rose.

Later that afternoon, determined to clear her name, Fiona marched through Brambleton, her jaw clenched. Rose had accused her of being a *thief*. That word was lodged in her mind like the bitter aftertaste of an immature glass of fine wine.

Emerging from the alley, the cool onshore breeze hit her. She paused, to gather her confidence and spotted Josh leaning against the wall by the back steps. He looked up, his eyes widening slightly at the sight of her.

'Fiona!' he said, the warmth in his voice juxtaposed with the autumn chill. 'Where've ya been? Are you working tonight?'

'London and no,' she replied tersely. She didn't want to engage in small talk. Not now.

He exhaled a cloud of vape which curled up towards the pub sign which was swaying gently in the wind. Josh sauntered closer, a serious expression spreading across his face. 'Just wanted to say, I reckon you're innocent.' Just for a moment, the brash confidence in his voice made her pause. She glanced at him, taking in his swagger, the way he stood with an exaggerated casual stance that screamed Australian bravado. 'If you need any help proving it, I'm your guy,' he added, hooking a thumb into his belt loop.

'I don't need anyone's help, Josh,' she said, her tone sharper than intended. 'I need to speak to Rose. Do you know where she is?'

He shrugged. 'Dunno. Are you sure I can't help? I could—'

'I'm sure.' She cut him off, the firmness of her voice echoing around the empty terrace.

'Okay. If you change your mind, need anything . . . any backup or . . .'

He was standing there, vape smoke trailing up around his face, creating a cloud that momentarily obscured his expression. Gazing at him, so self-assured, the only person to stand up for her, she felt a deep warmth towards him. He had always made her feel good about herself, but despite the flirting, had never expected anything in return. He was uncomplicated and fun. He would make someone a special partner one day.

'No,' she said firmly, shaking her head. 'I must do this myself.' The wind picked up slightly, rustling the leaves of the nearby trees and carrying the scent of impending rain.

He laughed, then nodded. 'Dive right in. I'm here if you need me.'

Smiling for the first time in days, she turned her back on him, making her way up the steps. She took a deep breath and pushed the door open, ready to fight for her reputation.

As she hoped, her former boss stood behind the reception desk, phone cradled against her shoulder as she scribbled in the diary. Becky perched on the edge, her skinny legs drumming against the wood.

Alerted by the door opening, mother and daughter looked up. Rose frowned, reaching out a protective hand toward her child. 'Fiona', cried out Becky, her face bright with excitement. Becky wriggled her little body around so she could scramble down backwards to the floor, then hurtled toward Fiona, gabbling as she ran.

'Mummy said you weren't coming to see us anymore, and she said it was something bad you'd done, but I knew she was fibbing 'cos you wouldn't do bad things.' Becky threw her arms around Fiona's thighs and spoke the last words into Fiona's coat. 'It's just Timmy and me who do naughty things.' Her mother spoke hurriedly into the receiver, 'All booked, sir. We look forward to welcoming you.' Rose placed the phone gently back on the cradle and barked, 'Becky, run along upstairs to Granny now, please.'

'Can Fiona come with me?'

'No,' said Rose softly. 'We need some grown-up time.'

The child groaned, gave Fiona's legs a last squeeze, then

chirped, 'Come and see us again soon, Fiona. We love you.' Fiona's heart skipped a beat. She couldn't think of anything she had done to deserve Becky's adulation, but she was grateful for the child's love, given so freely, and thankful, too, that Rose had not poisoned it. Maybe there was still a chance to regain Rose's trust.

Rose watched her daughter disappearing up the stairs before speaking. 'I'm surprised to see you here.'

It wasn't a reassuring line, and Fiona felt her confidence crumble like a sandcastle hit by a wave. 'I'd like a word, please. In private.' Rose scratched her head, then tutted. 'Let's do this in the staffroom.'

Marvellous, thought Fiona, just mentioning that room sent a chill through her, but she followed her former boss, mentally running through her speech. Closing the door, Rose took hold of a chairback. 'Have you come to repay the money?'

That hurt. No pretence that she had second thoughts about Fiona's guilt. Abandoning her carefully rehearsed script, Fiona fought back. 'No, because I didn't steal anything.'

Rose spluttered, shaking her head.

'I am *not* a thief.'

Rose drummed her fingers on the chairback, huffed a sigh and without looking at Fiona, said, 'Just go, and expect a call from the police.'

Her voice sounding desperate, Fiona struggled on. 'Please, let me speak.'

'I think you've said enough,' Rose raised her head, glaring at Fiona, a mixture of disappointment and anger in her eyes. 'You knew that wine was our nest egg. We helped you. I trusted you, let you into our family. Now look at how you've repaid that kindness.'

'Rose, I promise you—'

'Stop. If that bottle of Champagne wasn't enough to convince me of your guilt, the next morning—'

Fiona swallowed. What was Rose about to say? Her mind raced as she struggled to keep her face calm, but her pulse betrayed her, quickening with every second that passed. By her side, she clenched her fists, willing herself not to flinch. *More proof*? Impossible. She had done nothing. But the look in Rose's eyes told her that her innocence might be irrelevant.

Fiona forced herself to meet Rose's gaze and an icy wave of dread washed over her. 'You've forgotten what you did, haven't you? For someone usually so meticulous, you've been quite careless. I was too upset that night to think straight. I left the bottle of Krug in here – after all, I'd found the thief, I knew it would be safe.' Rose's eyes narrowed, then she added, 'In the morning when I came to fetch the Champagne—'

Fiona interrupted. 'I wasn't here in the morning.' Fiona had been nowhere near Devon that day. Fiona had been on her way to London. To fail that exam. She dug her hands into her coat pockets, sensing a flicker of hope as she clutched the battered train tickets, her fingers pressing into the paper. She had an alibi. Proof. Her voice trembled with a mixture of relief and defiance. 'What is it I'm supposed to have done?'

Rose pulled a yellow sticky tab from her pocket. 'This,' she said bitterly.

Fiona's mouth felt so dry it was like sandpaper rubbing against itself. Her voice cracking, she asked, 'What is that?'

'Don't play the innocent with me. These are the contact details for two top London wine merchants. You left it stuck to the bottle of Champagne.' Rose's tone switched to sarcastic. 'They knew who you were. Oh, they both denied you'd been in touch with them in the last few months, but they would, wouldn't they.'

Fiona felt her temples throbbing. More damning evidence. What Rose had in her hands must be the Post-it note with the contact details Fiona had written down for Ru; Kim must have found it when she'd planted the Champagne in Fiona's coat pocket. That ghastly night there had been nothing attached to the bottle of Krug. Fiona would have seen it. Kim must have spotted an opportunity later that evening to attach the incriminating note to the bottle.

'You are so wrong, Rose.' She said, her voice wavering. Fiona rushed out of the staffroom, wanting to sprint outside, to feel the cool of the autumn evening wind smart her face, but her eyes were drawn to a couple.

His back was towards her, a well-built frame and a rush of familiarity washed over her – the way he held himself, the curve of his shoulders, and the distinct style of his hair. Her heart skipped a beat. Ru. The woman had her hand on his arm, and glanced over her shoulder, her eyes shining with the unmistakable lustre of newfound love.

Kim.

Jealousy surged and Fiona bolted for the back door.

Twenty-nine

Fiona sprinted down the steps and bumped into a motorcyclist encased in shiny black leather.

The man spoke in a cheerful voice, at odds with Fiona's emotions. 'Hey careful there.'

'Sorry,' she mumbled. The man wasn't responsible for her imploding life. Although desperate to get away, something in the man's demeanour halted her. He was unassuming at first glance, perhaps in his late twenties, with tousled brown hair that fell over his forehead and an earnest look in his blue eyes. Yet, beneath that disarming exterior was an air of secrecy, a tension that belied his amiable smile. He shifted his weight from one foot to another, glancing over his shoulder as if expecting someone to emerge from the shadows.

'Do you know where I can find Fiona?'

'That's me,' she said cautiously.

'Can I give you this?' he asked, his voice brimming with casual indifference as he picked up a cardboard box and thrust it her way. Fiona squinted at him, her instincts on high alert. The box felt light, almost as if empty, and curiosity gnawed at her. 'How long will you be?' he asked.

She read the labels. There were two. The larger label gave the pub's address and a smaller one just said 'Fiona', with no surname. 'How long will I be?' she asked curiously.

'Yes,' he said, rolling his eyes at her, 'I've got a long drive back up to London.'

'To where precisely?'

As he mentioned the name of a wine company – one known for acquiring rare and valuable wine – her throat tightened, and she fought for breath. The injustice boiled within her. Someone was definitely trying to frame her.

'What's in the box?' she asked, trying to keep her voice steady despite the growing urgency in her chest.

He shrugged, a nonchalant gesture that only deepened her suspicions. 'Just a delivery. Nothing special.'

The words lingered between them, heavy with what he had not said.

'Why are you really here? Who are you really looking for?' she pressed, her instincts screaming at her to be cautious.

He hesitated, the corners of his mouth twitching. 'Look, I'm just doing my job,' he replied, but there was a flicker of uncertainty in his eyes.

In a moment of clarity, she realized she needed to check the contents of the box. She shook it, then felt his hands snatch it back from her.

'You're part of this, aren't you?' she accused, her voice sharp. But before she could say anything more, he and his motorcycle had roared off, taking the evidence with them.

Without thinking, she sprinted down the alley, her breath coming in quick bursts. She had to get away. As she ran, adrenaline coursed through her veins, dulling the surrounding cold. The sound of her heart thundering in her ears drowned out the world.

Halfway up the hill, she cursed herself for not trying harder to hold on to that box. She should have destroyed it. Or at least opened it to find out what was inside. What if the courier turned around again and delivered it to the pub, when she was safely out of range?

She panted up the rest of the hill. At the top of the village, she paused and stared at her aunt's cottage, before rushing past, out onto a footpath she had often taken with Ivy – the Tarka Trail, which meandered around the coast, then snaked inland through the glorious Devon countryside. For over an hour, Fiona wandered, listening to the waves crash with a steady beat.

She now understood how the thief had disposed of the wine. When she'd shaken the box, she had felt the rattle of light but bulky plastic inside, confirming her suspicions. There would have been thick protective plastic pouches inside the box for someone to stuff with wine bottles. Despite his shifty look, the courier was most probably an innocent pawn. There was no hint that the wine was stolen – it was just being collected from a pub which wanted to sell surplus stock.

The thief must have requested Fiona's name be added to the address slip, and had presumably been planning for Rose to take delivery of the box, see Fiona's name and put the final nail in the sommelier's coffin. Fiona wished she had grabbed that box and destroyed it. If he hadn't already done so, the courier would return later, planting more evidence linking Fiona to the crime.

She turned to retrace her steps, mulling over what she had discovered. A brisk wind whipped her hair round her face, and she stopped to untangle it. She might have unravelled the clues regarding how the thief was selling on the wine, but that brought her no closer to unmasking the culprit. She slowed her pace and looked down at Brambleton Beach, where seashells and driftwood littered the golden sand. The summer crowds were gone, leaving the shoreline peaceful and serene. At the far end of the bay, a group armed with litter pickers were collecting washed-up plastic.

Fishing a strand of hair from her mouth, Fiona watched the litter team pick its way along the shoreline. If only clearing away her own mess was as simple. She lumbered on, listening to the waves crash with a steady beat, the wind whipping her hair round her face. She pictured the police knocking on Ivy's door and fear gripped her. Fiona had tried, but she couldn't do this alone; she needed help. Surely now Ivy would break her confidence and rescue her niece. She switched on her phone, intending to warn Ivy, but she let out a groan: no signal.

As she walked into the village, Fiona's phone pinged. She pulled it out and saw a message sent an hour earlier from Ivy. 'Where are you?' There were also four missed calls. All from Ru. Her heart dropped like a stone through dark water. Too late to return his calls now. He would be prepping for evening service and have his own phone switched off. In her mind's eye, she saw them: Ru and Kim on the narrow staircase, her hand on his arm. A hollow ache settled in her chest.

The phone vibrated in her hand. She glanced down. A message from Ru. Was this a vitriolic parting shot before *he* blocked *her* number? How ironic that the tables were now turned. She crossed her fingers, knowing that wouldn't be like him. Maybe he didn't want to part badly either. Fiona opened the message.

Once George has found a replacement, I'm heading back to London.

That was it. No beating heart emoji, not a single kiss, no request she meet him before he left, or a suggestion she go with him. The pain in her heart felt unbearable and she slumped, clutching the phone, tears coursing down her cheeks.

She loved him so much and she'd been so wrong. Ru should never have gone behind her back to the investors, but his motive for doing that was his instinct to protect *her*, not to protect his career. Ru had accepted that what he had done was wrong, and then he had put his own future on the line, risked upsetting his backers to come and work in Devon, not because he wouldn't take no for an answer, but because he really loved her. She hadn't needed to earn his love by passing that exam; he had given it freely. Now she had lost it forever, but what cut deeper was that she had lost his respect.

Before she could turn her key in the lock, the front door opened, and Fiona found herself looking into Ivy's troubled face. Had the police already been? 'I've been worried. Where have you been all afternoon?'

Fiona pushed past her, tore off her coat and threw it at a peg. 'I went for a walk. I need to break free from this. I can't study!'

Ivy pulled a sceptical face. 'Well, that's no bad thing. Burying yourself in books won't solve your problems.'

'I tried.' Fiona could feel tears pricking at her eyelids. She gulped. 'I went to see Rose.'

'And?' prompted her aunt.

Fiona's teeth caught on her lower lip, a tremor of frustration threading through her.

'The real thief has planted more evidence against me,' she said, her voice tight. Each syllable seemed weighted with the exhaustion of being cornered, of watching the truth slip away like smoke between grasping fingers. 'You'd better be prepared for a knock on the door. She warned me to expect the police.'

Ivy's face drained of colour. 'I don't believe for a second you're a thief.' Ivy squinted at her, then took hold of Fiona's arm, steering her to the sofa. 'Sit down and tell me what's happened.'

Fiona replayed her earlier encounter with Rose, then told Ivy about the courier, explaining the significance. Her aunt started toying with the cross at her neck. 'Please, Ivy, I need you to help me.'

Ivy spoke in a hushed reverie. 'I never break a confidence.'

Fiona scowled. 'Is it right to keep the secret of someone who's framing your niece for a crime she didn't commit?'

Ivy blushed, then averted her gaze. Fiona reached for her aunt's hands. 'Ivy, I'm begging you.' Slowly Ivy lifted her head. 'If I vow to keep a secret, it goes with me to the grave.'

'I need your help.' She looked pointedly at Ivy. 'You know something. Are you going to allow me to be branded a thief?'

Ivy closed her eyes, her lips moving in silent prayer. 'Please don't ask me.'

Fiona trembled; desperation carved lines around her mouth as she stared at her aunt.

'Ivy,' Fiona's plea was scraped from her throat, 'tell me something – just give me a hint. I can figure out the rest.'

Ivy's gaze softened, a fleeting tenderness, but her lips remained pressed together, a sealed vault of secrets. Before a single word could escape, the doorbell sliced through the cottage's quiet, its metallic chime lingering in the air like a threat.

Fiona's pulse thundered. Her voice wavered. 'They've come for me, haven't they?'

Thirty

Ivy rested a hand on her niece's shoulder, her gaze calm but steely. 'Wait in the kitchen, where you can't be seen,' she instructed, her tone leaving no room for debate.

Fiona scuttled into the kitchen, listening to her aunt's footsteps recede. She heard the door open. Her chest heaved as she listened to muffled voices. Fiona strained to hear what was being said, every creak of the cottage amplifying her anxiety. She forced herself to stay still, gripping the edge of the counter, her knuckles white. Her mind was racing, totting up the evidence planted against her. If the courier had circled back and delivered the box to the pub, there was probably enough to justify arresting her.

She heard the front door click shut, then the sound of footsteps echoing from the hallway – multiple footsteps, each heavy with purpose. Fiona went numb and a chill prickled down her spine. She stood frozen by the kitchen window, staring blankly at the garden. Outside, leaves skittered against the windows, tapping like a thousand accusing fingers. Her hands gripped the edge of the sink. She couldn't bring herself to turn around. She knew who it was, she could feel it in the air.

The police.

The footsteps stopped. Then came a voice, clear, commanding and tinged with authority. 'Fiona.' The female voice was familiar and unmistakable, yet it was subtly different. She hadn't heard it for years. It was older and faintly accented with something that took her a moment to place: Melbourne.

She spun around so fast that the world tilted, her pulse pounding in her ears. Her aunt was standing in the doorway . . . and behind her were Fiona's parents.

'Fiona,' her mother said again, a hesitant smile playing on her lips, but the friendly face and words didn't ease the tension.

Fiona's inner demons raged. After all these years, her parents had reappeared. Why now, of all times? She'd spent that time protecting herself, putting up barriers and becoming self-sufficient so that their absence and their distance couldn't hurt her anymore. Now, with her life in pieces, when her guard was down, their sudden presence pierced to her core, churning up all the feelings of abandonment and sorrow she thought she had put a lid on long ago.

Was Ivy responsible for her parents' sudden reappearance? Fiona needed time to recover, work through her emotions. Ivy's soft voice intruded on her thoughts. 'I'll make some tea, then I'm going out for a walk. Let you three catch up – in private.'

Once the tea had been served, Ivy left. Fiona sat across from her parents, feeling the weight of their presence like a heavy fog. Her mother, poised and elegant, cradled a cup of tea in her hands with the same careful precision she applied to every aspect of her life. Her father sat stiffly, adjusting his glasses, his eyes flicking over the room in a way that suggested he was mentally cataloguing the furniture. They were academics – cool, distant, and cerebral – and they always would be.

The tea was too hot. Fiona's cup radiated heat into her hands. Taking a sip, the liquid seemed to scald her throat. Her mother sat up straighter, then carefully placed her cup down on the saucer, her lips pursed as if unsure what to say.

'So . . . jet lag,' her mother said, her voice clipped and formal as ever. 'It's hard to adjust, isn't it?'

'Yes,' Fiona's father answered. 'Not the easiest trip, and the weather here . . . quite a change from a Melbourne spring.'

Fiona's eyes drifted to the garden, tracing the sad shapes of the drooping dahlias and asters, mirroring the load settling in her chest. The rosemary bush sprawled across the path, untamed and unkempt, and she thought of her own life unravelling: the accusations hanging over her, the exam she couldn't pass, and now the unwelcome, jagged edges of her non-relationship with her parents. The silence hung thickly in the room.

'But at least it's dry,' added her mother. 'I was always glad of a dry English autumn day.'

Fiona couldn't tolerate the uncomfortable small talk any longer.

'What are you doing here?' she blurted, the words tumbling from her lips before she could stop them. 'Did you know I'd be here?'

Her mother's eyes met hers, and there was a flicker of something she hadn't expected. Something close to . . . *compassion*? Her mother's voice was soft, almost tender as she spoke. 'Of course we did. Ivy is my only sister. When she says something is important, I listen.' She paused, her gaze shifting to her husband for a moment. 'When Ivy asked us to come, we came. You know, we would have listened to you too – if you'd have asked us.'

Fiona stared at them, speechless. This baffled her. All her life, she'd been left to fend for herself. Her parents, always so absorbed in their world of academia, had never really involved themselves much in her life. It was Ivy whose shoulder she'd cried on when her first boyfriend dumped her; Ivy with whom she'd discussed her dreams of becoming a sommelier; Ivy who'd driven her to college, the back seat of the car stacked with the contents of Fiona's bedroom – from Ivy's rectory. Her parents were always too busy, their thoughts on higher things. Yet now, they were here after years of absence, because Ivy had asked them to come. Seriously?

Then, fragments of the letter her father had written to Ru floated into her memory, bobbing like pieces of a broken cork. She had spent her life building a protective wall of hurt self-righteousness, convinced their love was conditional on her academic achievements. Had she been wrong about that, just as she had been wrong about Ru? The anger still burned within her, but it was now tinged with confusion. It was as if she had dismissed a complex wine after a hasty sip, only to find her palette detecting subtle hints of depth and complexity she had initially missed.

'All the way from Melbourne?' Fiona's voice was shaky, almost a whisper.

'Yes,' her father said, his voice firm. 'You're our only child, Fiona. I know we can get wrapped up in our work, and you made it obvious you valued your independence and did not want us smothering you with love, but if you're in trouble, we would go to the moon for you.'

The words hit her like a punch to the chest. For the first time in her life, Fiona felt the strength of their love. A love she had never understood. What her father had written in that letter to Ru was true. They'd always seemed so distant, so wrapped up in their books and papers. But their love had been there all along, just hidden beneath a layer of academia. She had been responsible for pushing them away, just as she had alienated Ru. At least it wasn't too late to fix her relationship with her parents.

Her father shifted, his usual reserved manner slipping for just a moment. 'Ruben . . . came to visit us, a few months back . . . Actually, he was the first to tell us he thought you might need us.'

Fiona felt the blood drain from her face. Her hands shook, the cup rattling against its saucer. 'What?' she asked, barely able to keep the tremor from her voice.

'Yes,' her father said, nodding with an air of approval. 'He came all the way to Melbourne. He wanted to meet us even though you'd turned down his proposal. Ruben said you'd been going through a rough time, thought you might need us. We've been trying to speak to you, but Ivy kept saying you weren't yet ready to listen to what we had to say.'

Fiona froze, her thoughts racing. She had expected Ru to go to Melbourne in lieu of the honeymoon, rather than wasting the money, but why had he bothered to visit her parents after she'd rejected his marriage proposal?

Her father continued, oblivious to the turmoil in Fiona's mind. 'He's a good man, Fiona. We liked him.'

Fiona winced. She forced herself to speak, but her throat felt tight. 'Yes. I . . . I . . .' But it was too late. Ru had moved on. Her mother's gaze softened again. 'What did Ivy mean when she said you were in trouble?'

Fiona hesitated. The room seemed to shrink around her. The tea had gone cold, but her fingers were too numb to notice. She stared at her parents, their faces earnest, waiting for her to speak. Eventually, she told them about the break-up with Ru, and the missing wine.

'I . . . I didn't steal anything,' she said, her voice barely audible. 'But someone is framing me for it.'

Her parents' expressions shifted. They weren't academics now. They were parents: worried, protective, alert.

'When the doorbell rang earlier,' Fiona continued, her voice growing more strained, 'I thought it was the police. I thought they'd come for me. I didn't know what to do.'

Her mother got up first. Then her father. They moved toward

her with surprising speed, wrapping their arms around her in unison. The embrace was unexpected, yet it felt so right, something she hadn't realized she wanted until it was happening. Fiona closed her eyes, trying to hold back the tears. She couldn't remember the last time they'd hugged her, not since she was a young child. Yet cradled in their arms, she felt safe.

The pressure in her chest eased. She didn't even try to hold back the tears, but let them fall, blubbing like a baby, and all the while she felt the grip of their arms, holding her tight. She sniffed, wiping her eyes, summoning the courage to speak again. 'I failed my Advanced Sommelier exams. Twice.'

Her father didn't hesitate. 'It doesn't matter, Fiona. You don't need a piece of paper to succeed. Ru told us you're the best sommelier he's ever worked with.'

That was when Fiona realized her parents had always loved her deeply. They just hadn't known how to show it. But now, she could feel it in their arms, see it in their eyes and she began to think she would not have to fight her battle alone.

That evening, Fiona, her parents and Ivy gathered around the small kitchen table. The scent of roasted vegetables drifted through the room, tinged with the smell from Ivy's wilting basil plant. In pride of place on the table, wrapped in a white linen napkin, was a bottle of Leeuwin Estate Art Series Chardonnay, chilled to just the right temperature. Her parents had brought it all the way from Australia.

At Fiona's suggestion, they had built the meal around the iconic wine; she had explained how the creamy texture and vibrant acidity of the wine would balance beautifully with the natural sweetness and umami of roasted vegetables. Her words flowed freely; she was sharing her passion, not delivering a lecture. Her shoulders lifted as she watched her parents' expressions absorb every detail. Was that maternal pride in her mother's smile?

Fiona moved quietly, pouring wine with a contented, almost shy smile. 'I still can't believe you're staying all week,' Fiona murmured, glancing at her parents before taking her seat.

Her mother's hand found hers across the table. 'And longer if we need to. We are staying until this is resolved,' she replied softly. Ivy had insisted on giving up her bedroom for her sister, content to sleep on the sofa bed – she didn't need to announce her satisfaction at finally reuniting parents and daughter.

The meal passed with comfortable chatter, her father sharing a spirited debate with Ivy about how to fight ageing, her mother chiming in with her theories. Fiona felt herself relax; she didn't fear a knock on the door anymore – not with her support team.

Once the plates were cleared, her father's expression grew serious. 'Now,' he said, looking at Fiona, 'how can we help figure out what really happened?'

Fiona tensed slightly and glanced at her aunt. Was it fair to press Ivy? Only as a last resort.

There was one other person she could try first . . . unless he had already gone. She would message him and ask for one final Morning Prayers.

As Fiona was settling into bed, she took a moment to check her emails one final time. Her eyes scanned the subject lines. One stood out, pulling her out of her sleepy haze:

New exam date confirmed

It was from the CMS. She sat up straighter, her heart leaping. This was it – a fresh chance! A rush of excitement surged through her, like the first crisp sip of Sauvignon Blanc on a summer afternoon.

She clicked on the email, a pulse of anticipation in her fingertips. Her mind leaped ahead, imagining herself being congratulated by Elsa, or better still, Laurent. But as her eyes traced down the screen, the thrill ebbed, slowly replaced by a creeping doubt. Her hands hesitated above the keyboard. *Could she really go through this again?*

All those hours of study, going further into debt, the relentless tasting sessions . . . She remembered the quiet dread that had knotted in her stomach just days earlier in the exam room. The thought of returning to that pressure felt suffocating, as if her ambitions were pressing her down.

Fiona took a shaky breath as the joy she'd felt only moments before slipped away like the last drops of a glass of fine wine. She closed her eyes and leaned back against the headboard, trying to find comfort from her memories of the evening: the gentle laughter of her family, all four of them lingering over the coffee cups, reluctant to end a memorable night. All evening, she had felt safe, cocooned, untouched by the exalted demands of the CMS.

In her mind, she pictured Josh coasting in on a board, pulsing with the thrill of surfing a perfect wave, and his words that day on the beach came back to her. 'You only get one life. Live the life you want, not the one someone else dreams for you.'

Fiona felt a tear slip down her cheek, though it wasn't from sadness. She brushed it away with the back of her hand. With a small, shaky sigh, she realized maybe she didn't need to pursue this exam. That was a dream conjured by a mistaken need to keep achieving academic milestones. She loved wine, but there was no need to belong to the CMS to live her dream. She knew so much about wine already and found genuine joy in sharing that knowledge – in watching people's faces light up as they discovered a perfect pairing or a hidden gem from a lesser-known region. Being an Advanced Sommelier might boost her ego and her salary, but it wouldn't enhance her true passion. She didn't need money; her parents had offered to repay her debts, and her job satisfaction had never come from credentials. She closed her laptop, feeling both lighter and warmer, as if her decision was settling around her like a soft blanket. Fiona shut her eyes and drifted off to sleep in minutes.

When Fiona arrived at Ru's early the next morning, a light shone in the bay window. She stood outside, the wind nipping at her cheeks. Her gaze lingered on the horizon, where the water met the sky in a dull grey line. Below her, waves broke gently against the cliffs, but the soft sound did little to calm her nerves.

Would Ru listen to her, believe her, maybe even help her? Was he inside right now, wrestling with ways to identify the actual thief? Or had the accusations shattered his trust in her, and his agreement to meet nothing but a nod to their shared romance, a chance to say goodbye politely after their last bitter argument?

The ocean stretched endlessly before her and, in its vastness, she imagined her life stretching out without Ru's love. The autumn winds seemed to mirror her thoughts, swirling unpredictably as she stood there, slivers of amber, yellow and red fluttering around her legs before drifting towards the cliff edge.

Uncertain of her reception, she traipsed up and down with her mind whirling, eroding her confidence, like a wildfire spreading across dry grass scorching the vegetation.

As Fiona paced, she thought of the irony: after all these years, she finally felt part of a family. Her parents' subtle, quiet pride emerging in their careful questions about last night's wine, their encouraging nods as she answered their questions about the theft. Now, just as she was finally embracing their support, she was losing the respect of the man she used to rely on and, despite her best efforts, still adored. A shiver ran through her, and she wrapped her coat tighter, feeling as though her heart were fraying with each gust of wind.

She glanced upwards and saw him looking down. His face looked taut. No smile. Her heart twisted. She had come to terms with the loss of his love, but she had clung to the fragile hope that she could preserve his respect. Now, even that felt lost. Fiona strode to the door, hearing the buzzer sound on the lock's release.

Thirty-one

Closing her eyes, Fiona took a calming breath, telling herself that Ru would help. He wouldn't have agreed to meet if he didn't intend to at least listen to her, but she couldn't dislodge his judgemental rebuke five nights earlier, nor the distant look in his eyes she'd just seen. Ru would help her because it was in his interest too. With their names linked, if she fell from grace, he would surely follow.

The flat door was open. She climbed the stairs, counting each one as she plodded upwards. Halfway up, she smelled cinnamon toast and her spirits rose. She lifted her face. He was standing in the doorway, his arms open wide. His eyes locked onto hers radiating the same longing she'd been suppressing for weeks. Without a second thought, she ran to him, her heart pounding, drowning out the sound of her feet against the stairs. The moment she reached him, he pulled her close as if he never wanted to let go. She melted into him, her head resting against his chest, breathing him in, feeling the warmth and safety of his embrace. Gently he lifted her chin, his eyes searching hers for permission before he leaned down and kissed her, softly and tenderly at first, then deeper, full of all the unspoken words and emotions they hadn't shared for months. Time seemed to stop, and in that moment, nothing else mattered but them.

He murmured into her hair, 'What took you so long to get in touch?'

'I . . . I . . . I thought you believed Rose,' she sobbed into his shirt.

Gently, he pushed her head away from his shoulder, his dark eyes looking down into hers. 'How could you possibly think I would believe you were a thief?'

'That night,' she paused, trying to shake away the image, 'you looked daggers at me, and then you snapped "that is pure evil" at me. But I have no idea how that Champagne got into my coat pocket – I thought it was a present from you!'

He reached out a hand and caressed her cheek. 'Fi, I wasn't looking at you when I said that. I was looking at the person who framed you. Those words were aimed at Kim.'

Fiona's head crashed against his shoulder. Of course. She had heard those words with her eyes shut and, in her panic, had assumed they were aimed at her. 'Kim? I guessed it was her who put the bottle in my pocket, but why? I don't think she's the thief – she doesn't know the first thing about wine.'

'Let's not play detective now. We can do all that later.'

Fiona leaned against Ru. He was right. The only thing that mattered just now was the two of them. She tilted her face up towards him and he kissed her long and hard, moving his body against hers, sending shockwaves of desire through hers. She sighed. 'Ru, I've missed you so much. I was so stupid to push you away. I'm so sorry.'

He pulled away, and his voice was tender as he said, 'Fi, you're not just saying that are you?' he whispered, 'I don't want you to do something you'll regret later.'

How could she ever regret making love with the man she adored?

When she woke, the first thing Fiona saw was the face of the person she loved most, and his eyes were smiling down at her.

Her heart soared. She could never match Ru's talent or his success, but that wasn't what had driven them apart. She saw now what she couldn't before: his protection had started as something beautiful – shielding her from a world he knew would wound her fragile confidence. But that protection had slowly morphed into something else – decisions made on her behalf, opportunities quietly redirected, her voice gradually muted. What began as shelter became a cage, with Ru standing as both guardian and gatekeeper. And to prevent herself either disappearing completely into his shadow or becoming an anchor weighing down his brilliance she had been forced to break free. Their break-up enabled them both to change: for him to recognize that his way of loving her had kept her from discovering her own strength, and for her to discover that strength.

Ru stroked her face, tracing a line over her cheek. 'You've been asleep for nearly an hour.'

Recalling how quickly she'd fallen asleep at Ivy's the night before, she realized it was becoming remarkably easy to sleep. But then she did have quite a lot of sleep to catch up on.

'Hungry?' he asked.

'You bet.'

'Breakfast in bed?'

She grinned.

He unwound himself from her body and sat up. She ran a finger down his spine. 'You'd better stop that if you want breakfast any time soon,' he warned, pushing himself off the bed. 'I'm going to shower, then cook you the best breakfast you've ever eaten. I suggest you do the same. You've got some detective work to do.'

After showering, Fiona wrapped herself in Ru's dressing gown, breathing in his scent, then tidied the bedclothes and sat cross-legged on top, sipping a mug of hot chocolate.

They ate breakfast from trays, a light and frothy soufflé omelette, which Ru served with smoked salmon from a local smokehouse, along with Fiona's favourite cinnamon toast.

Fiona took a bite of omelette. It was so light it seemed to melt on her tongue. It might even be the best omelette she'd ever eaten . . . but then everything seemed better now. She was back with Ru, where she was meant to be. 'Can I ask you something?'

He laughed softly. 'Go on.'

'Did Ivy find you this flat to rent?'

He chuckled and the mirth rippled through her. She loved that sound. She'd missed it. 'What you're really asking is, did your aunt help me? And the answer is yes. She told me about the job, and she found me somewhere to rent. I wasn't sure it would work, but you'd blocked my number. I had to explain why I did what I did with the investors and show you how much I loved you. It wasn't easy though, especially when you kept disappearing for lessons with Josh.'

Fiona smiled; grateful that Ivy had intervened. Ivy had been at the heart of everything. She had orchestrated the reunion with Fiona's parents too.

'Tell me, why do you think Kim tried to frame me?'

He spoke gently. 'I think that was my fault.'

She frowned. 'How so?'

'Kim kept pestering me to take her out for a drink. I told her I was in love with someone else. I think she guessed it was you, and then set you up, because after you left, she cornered me and asked me to give her a chance. That's when I confessed that you and I had been a couple and that I was still in love with you.'

Fiona felt a rush of love for Ru, tinged with sympathy for her rival. Ru's admission that he was still in love with her must have been what she'd witnessed on the stairs the last time she'd been at the pub, after Fiona's unsuccessful attempt to make Rose listen to her side of the story. What must it have been like for Kim to hear those words from Ru? No wonder she'd lashed out. But that didn't explain why Kim had been so nasty to her for weeks. 'She's never liked me.'

'That's not true.'

Fiona thought back to all the incidents that Kim had orchestrated to catch Fiona out. 'Hmm.'

'She's afraid of you . . .'

Fiona's eyes popped wide. 'Why?'

'Josh told me about some pairing notes she dropped in the staffroom. I suspected she didn't know anything about wine when I asked her advice about what to add to enhance a new dish. When I challenged her, Kim told me why she keeps those notes. She's got. She's got no sense of smell or taste – tricky if you want to work in a fine dining restaurant.'

'And she wanted her parents to be proud of her, to prove to them that despite her anosmia, she could work in fine dining, which of course they've invested in?'

'Exactly. And you, my dear, as the sommelier, Rose's go-to, right-hand special agent, represented all she could never be. When Rose interviewed her about the missing wine, Kim thought the boss was going to discover her secret and fire her.'

'Wow. That explains a lot.' Like why Kim had been so defensive and prickly; she couldn't smell or taste the wines or dishes she was supposed to be recommending to customers. No wonder she carried those detailed, stilted notes everywhere and panicked when they were almost discovered. If Rose found out about her anosmia, Kim's career in fine dining would be over in a heartbeat.

'Kim expected suspicion to fall on her, so she set you up with the Krug.'

'But Kim knows nothing about wine; she's not the thief, and

she couldn't have pulled that stunt with the courier. That must be someone else, but who?' She dropped her fork, sighing, 'I don't know what to do!'

Picking up her fork, he fed her a mouthful of soufflé. 'Fortunately, I think I do. When you've finished, I think we should have a family confab.'

The autumnal sun streamed through the windows of Ivy's cottage, highlighting dust motes in the air. To Fiona the room felt smaller than usual, crammed not only with people but with tension. She was sitting in a worn, floral armchair, her chest tight with a mix of gratitude, anxiety and frustration. Ru sat beside her, his hand resting over hers.

Her parents normally concealed their emotions behind calm exteriors, but Fiona could see the strain on her mother's face.

Her aunt, sitting near the fireplace, had been unusually quiet. Fiona studied Ivy's face, noting the averted gaze. She was glad she wouldn't have to press Ivy to break her confidence. Kim had been downright nasty, and there was no excuse for her trying to frame Fiona with the Krug, but she wasn't the key to proving Fiona's innocence.

'Let's go over this again,' Ru said, breaking the tension as his eyes danced round the room, falling on each person in turn. 'Lots of expensive wine is missing, and somehow, *miraculously*, all the evidence points to Fi?'

'Yes,' Fiona replied, her voice strained. 'But I didn't do it.'

'Of course not,' her mother said. 'All the evidence has been planted; we just need to work out who did that.'

Ivy flinched, and Fiona's mother turned towards her sister, brows furrowing. 'Ivy, surely you don't believe this nonsense?' Her mother's words were as much an accusation as a question.

'Ivy, it's okay,' said Fiona, surprised she was taking the lead on this point, not Ru. Her mother was pursuing a dead end. Kim wasn't the thief. Fiona smiled at her aunt. 'We know about Kim; you don't need to protect her anymore'

Ivy glanced down, shifting uncomfortably. 'Ivy, what are you hiding?' demanded Fiona's mother.

'She's protecting the person who Ru and I think planted that bottle of Krug and then stuck the sticky note on it the next morning.' explained Fiona.

'Why would you do that Ivy?' asked Fiona's mother.

'I know nothing about the Krug,' said Ivy.

'But you know something . . . I know when my sister is hiding a secret. Are you protecting this Kim woman?'

'No. I am not protecting Kim.'

'Not . . . not . . .' stammered Fiona.

Fingering the cross round her neck, Ivy swallowed, then spoke slowly. 'It's not that simple. You don't understand.'

'Oh, I think we do,' Fiona's mother replied. 'What I don't understand is why you won't tell us who you think is behind this. Out with it!'

Fiona felt a prickle of resentment. She had always trusted Ivy, relied on her in ways she hadn't her own parents. Now, that trust felt tenuous, stretched thin by Ivy's choice to withhold a vital clue that might reveal the identity of the thief, when they might have only hours before the police came to arrest Fiona. Ivy's gaze darted Fiona's way. 'I . . . It's complicated.'

Fiona's mother folded her arms, her eyes narrowing further. 'Complicated or not, it's my daughter they're accusing. We need to get to the truth, and we need to get there soon, before this charade—'

Ru's hand tightened around Fiona's, his voice cutting her mother off. 'Something's been bothering me. Last night I was running through that suspect list again . . .'

The room quieted. Fiona looked at him gratefully, feeling a wave of reassurance.

Her mother reached over, touching Fiona's shoulder gently. 'Whatever it takes, we'll prove you're innocent. If they try and arrest you, we'll hire the best lawyer.'

Fiona swallowed, emotion clogging in her throat. She met her mother's gaze, sensing the support radiate from her.

Ru gave her hand a final, reassuring squeeze. Then he winked at her. 'Let's stop badgering Ivy. I think I know who took that wine and how we can prove it.'

'Who? How? Tell me!' Fiona cried.

'By stealing the evidence,' said Ru.

She recoiled, glancing at her parents to check their reaction. 'Stealing? What if we're caught?' asked Fiona.

'Hang on a minute,' said her father sitting bolt upright in his chair.

'Proving Fiona's innocence should not involve committing a crime,' said her mother.

'But if the evidence is hidden, what choice do we have?' asked Ru.

Fiona rose, nervous but smiling. 'Let's do this – sometimes you've gotta' take a gamble on life.' She wondered if she'd imitated an Aussie accent. If she had, Fiona hoped everyone would assume it was her parents she was mimicking.

'This isn't us,' her mother said, shaking her head. 'We don't break the law. But . . . you're innocent. We must find the real culprit, even if it means bending the rules.'

Ivy's brow furrowed. 'I don't like this. Theft is theft, no matter the reason. It's wrong.'

Ru rose, a grim look on his face. 'Either Ivy commits a sin and breaks her vow, or we commit a crime. I know which one I'm more comfortable with.'

Fiona's mother glared at her sister, then her father rose and spoke. 'We are law-abiding citizens. But we are also parents, and that comes first.'

'So, are we doing this?' Fiona asked, still stunned but determined.

Ru grimaced. 'Sorry, not *us* . . . just you.'

'What?'

He gave her a reassuring look. 'Everything's going to be fine,' he said, and for the first time in a while, Fiona truly believed it.

Ru's text arrived at 8 p.m. 'Coast's clear. You've got an hour. Good luck.' He signed it with a beating heart that made her own flutter. Wearing a black beanie hat pulled over her ears and one of Ru's jumpers, which reached her thighs, Fiona bolted out of his flat. Her father was right behind her, his long strides matching her pace despite his age. When a last minute attack of nerves had struck Fiona that afternoon and she asked him to help, he had smiled and replied, 'let's do this!'

Together they jogged down the hill, past the pub and onto the narrow path beneath the harbour wall. Fiona's breath came in quick clouds, the wind tugging at her clothes and pulling at her conscience. To clear her name, she was about to commit a crime. If caught, it would provide more evidence implicating her in the wine theft. It would also damage her father's reputation. That last thought made her heart clench.

Under the faint light of the moon, they moved swiftly, the stillness of the night broken only by the sound of their footsteps and the distant crash of dark waves against the harbour wall. Her father undid his thick woollen coat and pushed his glasses – which must have slipped down his nose while he was running – back into place, then scanned the surroundings with a professor's meticulous eye. It was tough to imagine her academic dad prowling around, but he had spent the afternoon playing the amateur detective, studying the building, noting every entry point and assessing every potential risk.

Her former employer's flat loomed above her, a shadow against the night sky. Ru believed it held the evidence they needed, but getting inside and back out again without being seen was a daunting prospect. Every step felt leaden, and although he wasn't admitting it, Fiona sensed her father's nervous energy. This was unfamiliar territory for them both.

'Keep an eye on that back door,' he murmured, his voice steady but low.

The pair crouched in the pub's car park, waiting for the signal Ru and her father had agreed. Suddenly, the back door opened. Fiona took a sharp breath but felt a steadying hand on her shoulder. 'Wait,' hissed her father.

Josh emerged, a crate of empty bottles rattling in his arms. Fiona exhaled slowly.

For what seemed like hours, she and her father stood hunched over in the shadows, listening to the waves rumble and roar around them. For a second time, the back door opened, letting out a triangle of light. This time, no one emerged. She started forward, only for her father's hand to catch her arm. 'Wait. Patience. Count to ten.'

She left the counting to her father – she lost track after reaching three. He released her arm, then whispered, 'Ready?'

Fiona nodded, her pulse quickening. Together, they moved forward silently, like shadows in the night.

Thirty-two

Noiselessly, Fiona tiptoed through the deserted reception, her heart thumping in her chest, then started up the stairs, grateful for the reassuring soft tread of her father's footsteps behind her.

The flat door hung ajar, as Ru had promised it would. The faintest sliver of light cut through the gap, inviting her in, yet filling her with dread. She puffed out a breath – Ru hadn't explained how he was going to achieve this, and she hadn't asked, but it must have involved pinching George's keys. She felt the invisible threads tying her to the two men she loved, a sense of safety enveloping her like a fortress built of soft pillows. Her hand hovered over the handle, but she realized she didn't need to touch it; Ru had purposely left it like this.

She nudged the door open, stepping inside silently, then paused, allowing her eyes to adjust to the dimness, cocking her ears to listen for sounds of the children despite Ru's reassurance that they were both away on a sleepover. Her father moved beside her, treading with the same stealthy care.

The air was thick with the musty scent of old wooden floorboards reminding Fiona of Ivy's sitting room, and for a second, Fiona wished she was there instead, but she crept forward.

'You're certain this is the right place?' whispered her father in a tone so low it almost merged with the silence.

Fiona met his eyes. 'Yes. I've been here lots of times,' she hissed back.

'Right. Let's be quick.'

Guided by the soft light from her phone's torch she inched towards George's desk, her breath sounding unnaturally loud in the silence. She pulled on the top flap, but it wouldn't budge. 'It's locked,' she whispered. *Where did he keep the key?*

'Try the drawers,' suggested her father, his voice clipped, as though his mind had already analysed the best course of action.

As she opened each drawer, the quiet sound of rasping wood seemed to echo through the space. Cold handles slid open one by one, revealing papers, old menus, clutter. No key.

A soft rustle broke the silence. Her father lay on the floor, peering under the desk. 'The drawer to the right. I think there's something wedged beneath it.'

Fiona's heart thudded. She crouched, carefully lifting out the drawer. A sliver of paper caught her attention. She fished it out, unfolding a betting slip. 'Ru was right,' she murmured, her voice tight with realization. Spurred on by her discovery, she dug inside that drawer a second time.

Then, as if by magic, her fingers brushed against something cool and metallic. She pulled a key out from beneath a pile of invoices, the weight seeming far too significant for such a small object.

Her father's eyes gleamed. 'Eureka.'

The key slid smoothly into the desk's lock, and with a soft click, she opened the flap. She dived in with gusto. Papers rustled under her fumbling fingertips as she discarded receipts, half torn menus, stray paperclips, dozens of biros – so that's where all Rose's pens had ended up! And then she saw it, between two old notebooks . . . a crumpled list in George's handwriting. Names of betting apps, odds calculations, all jotted down in a frenzy, as if scrambling to balance the books.

She recalled the many times she had seen George glued to his screen. Fiona had always assumed it was work related, never imagining the darker truth. As she stared at the list, a wave of empathy washed over her, and for a moment, the triumph of securing the evidence to prove her innocence faltered.

Yes, George had been wrong to frame her, just as Kim had been, but she couldn't ignore the sadness in her chest. He wasn't a villain; he was a man trapped in an addiction, and for all his faults, she couldn't help but feel sorry for him.

With the list safely in her pocket, they moved through the darkened flat heading for the door. But just as Fiona reached for the handle, the door opened a fraction. She froze.

'Not now,' she whispered, her pulse racing.

Clutching onto her father, images of an astonished Rose popping back to the flat flashing through her mind, Fiona watched the door, her eyes glued there like the last few stubborn leaves of autumn refusing to let go of a tree. The thought of explaining this break-in terrified her, as did the potential consequences for her father's career. She held her breath, straining her ears for sounds from outside, but she couldn't hear anything.

'I don't think it's a person,' whispered her father. He crept forward and nudged the door with his foot. It swung open, revealing an empty corridor, and she guessed a gust of air had been driven up the staircase by someone using the back door. But her father's analytical brain was one step ahead. 'Careful,' he warned. 'Whoever it was might be about to come back inside.'

Fiona crept down the stairs, then flattened herself against the wall, peeking round the corner to study their escape route.

At reception, Rose was chatting with a man in a suit. With her heart in her throat, Fiona listened to their muffled conversation, willing them both to hurry up and leave. Then she noticed a third person. Kim. Her would-be rival turned, her eyes meeting

Fiona's; she felt her mouth open into an astonished 'o' and had the sensation of falling into a deep pit. Kim would relish exposing her.

'All clear?' whispered her father.

Fiona closed her eyes and bit her lip, shaking her head. 'No,' she whispered. With every second that passed she expected Kim to reveal what she could see. Beside her, Fiona's father stiffened, then she felt a reassuring hand grip her arm. After what seemed an eternity (or perhaps less than sixty seconds), Fiona opened her eyes. Kim was still there, looking up at Fiona, but the other woman's eyes weren't blazing with the self-indignation of spotting a thief, they were calm, almost vulnerable, and this time she had a finger pressed against her lip, miming for Fiona to keep quiet.

Fiona exhaled as quietly as she could, watching as Kim and Rose ushered the man through reception. She seized the opportunity.

'Let's go,' she hissed, rushing forward, yanking open the door and slipping outside to the safety of the harbour wall. When her father joined her, she turned, a quiet urgency in her voice. 'You need to go back. Mum will be worried.' Her father hesitated, concern flickering in his eyes, but Fiona gave him a determined look. 'Ru will take over from here. It's time.'

Her father nodded and started back up the hill.

Fiona peeked in through the kitchen window. The bright lights assaulted her eyes, making her blink. From her vantage point, she could see George and Ru, but not Josh. George, his brow furrowed in concentration, was wiping down the counters. Ru, with an almost unsettling calmness, was chopping vegetables and adding them to a saucepan. She guessed he was preparing a bone broth to simmer overnight, finding an excuse to be there until Josh left, clearing the way for them to confront George. She heard someone whistling *Sweet Caroline* and assumed it was Josh loading a dishwasher out of sight.

Fiona slunk back down, pressing herself into the shadows beside the kitchen window, listening to the pub's weathered sign creaking in the night air. She hugged the woollen jumper tightly around her shoulders, feeling the coarse fibres oddly comforting against her skin – she must be alert for Josh leaving. Fiona edged back slightly, her fingers brushing against the cold, damp stone wall, listening to Josh whistling. It might be a long wait.

The back door swung open, letting out a shaft of light. Then Kim stepped outside, resplendent in a new navy wool coat. Her eyes darted toward the shadows.

'Fiona?' whispered Kim, her voice catching on the wind.

She emerged slowly, her movements deliberate but not threatening. 'I know what you did, Kim.'

Kim's composure cracked. A sob escaped her, raw and primeval. 'I'm so sorry.'

Fiona stepped forward and placed a hand on Kim's shoulder. The touch was light, almost tender. 'I also know *why* you did it. Don't dwell on this. I forgive you.'

Part of Fiona wanted to snatch back her words, to hold on to her anger and bitterness, but she suddenly felt lighter. Kim was a frightened woman. She hadn't set out to destroy Fiona's life – Fiona had nearly achieved that herself, months ago, when she'd rejected Ru's proposal.

The headlights of a car illuminated the empty terrace, curling round the carpark then stopping yards away from where the former rivals now stood.

'That's Daddy come to collect me.'

'Go on, get off home.' said Fiona.

Kim hesitated, 'Can I help? Is there anything I can do?'

'No. But thank you.' said Fiona. And she meant those words.

Kim climbed into the car, and Fiona watched it drive up the hill, before walking back to the wall to recommence her vigil.

Eventually the kitchen fell silent. Fiona peered in through the window, her heart pounding like a drum. George was rummaging through a cupboard, his back turned to her; Ru was cleaning a knife. There was no sign of Josh. The back door swung open, and she glimpsed the kitchen porter's silhouette. She heard a soft click, then saw the blue glow of his vape, a brief light in the darkness.

Watching Josh jog down to the street, she felt a mix of relief and trepidation. She tracked the light of his vape as he moved away before she ran up the back steps and strode through the deserted reception area. Her whole body was shaking, a combination of adrenaline and the anticipation of confrontation.

The only person in the kitchen was Ru.

'Where is he?' she whispered. Ru turned and winked at her, refreshing her confidence. He pointed at the storeroom, from which George was backing out. Her heart pounded. Frustration mixed with vindication as she glared at her near destroyer.

'A word please, George,' she said, battling to keep her voice calm.

He spun round, his eyes fiery. 'What the hell are you doing here?' he snapped.

'Not in here,' said Ru, shaking his head. He took off his hat and apron. 'George, can we have a moment in the staffroom, please.'

The room was quiet and cold despite the radiator ticking weakly in the corner. Fiona stood near the table, her eyes glued to a single hook along the row on the wall. It was empty now, but she could still see her lavender coat hanging there, feel the thump of the Krug heavy against her leg as she had pulled on her coat that night.

George was sitting by the radiator, his face weary, his hands fidgeting with a loose thread on his apron. Ru stood close beside her, his hand on her arm, a silent pillar of support. His expression was tense, his jaw set as he watched George. She looked at the hook once more, feeling the familiar burn of resentment.

When George spoke, he sounded almost fatherly. 'Look, Ruben, you've had a long day. Go home, put your feet up. I'll deal with Fiona.'

Ru crossed his arms and grinned. 'I'll hang around, thanks.'

Clearly unused to Ru standing his ground, George's eyes narrowed. Then he smiled awkwardly. 'Well, that doesn't change anything, does it? Fiona, you're not worming your way back into your job. No one's asking Ruben to work alongside a thief. You know me. I'm a decent bloke.'

A decent bloke? she thought, barely containing her frustration. She spoke in a tight, clipped voice, 'A decent bloke who plants evidence? You're not doing anyone any favours, George. Not me, not yourself. This . . . this *mess* of yours isn't just going to go away.'

'My *mess*? That's a bit rich,' blustered George. 'You think you can stroll back in and play the victim? Now please go home. I promise to speak to Rose, try and convince her not to call the police.'

Ru took a step closer to George. 'You seem awfully keen to bring this meeting to a close without even asking what we want to talk to you about. Almost like you've got something to hide.'

His voice shaking slightly, George said, 'I don't have to explain myself to either of you! I have a business to run.'

'George,' said Fiona, 'isn't it time to come clean?'

He looked away, seemingly unable to meet Fiona's eyes. 'Get out. Both of you.'

Fiona pulled out the sheet which she had taken from George's desk, laying it on the table, together with the gambling slip.

'What's that?' George asked, his voice cracking.

'It was you, wasn't it?' she said, her voice steady but cold. George had been prepared to see her branded a thief to protect his own reputation. This explained why he hadn't wanted his wife to investigate. At least he'd tried to protect the team – he knew they were all innocent – but when Rose wouldn't back off, he'd sacrificed Fiona to save his own skin. 'That is a list of some of your gambling debts.'

Beside her Ru was looking at George with barely contained rage. 'You allowed Fi to take the blame.'

George stared at the page, his eyes narrowing as if searching for a way out. He opened his mouth to speak, but Fiona cut him off. 'Don't bother,' she said, her voice sharper now. 'You sold the wine to fund your gambling.' She felt a strange mix of satisfaction and sorrow as she spoke, knowing George was a victim himself, a gambling addict who needed help.

'Those pouches weren't for herb rubs, it was wine. I know how those companies operate – they're the perfect channel for selling the odd bottle here and there without leaving too much of a mark. But your email traffic will prove I'm right. There will be stacks of emails chasing up their offers to buy whatever you offered them.'

In the silence that followed, George seemed to struggle for words. Then he put his head in his hands. 'I'm sorry! I thought I could stop . . .'

Fiona had a sudden thought. 'You've done this before, haven't you? In London, you were the thief there too. No wonder Rose never caught you – she would never suspect it was her own husband.'

He let out a long sigh, his lips vibrating. 'In London, she caught me gambling but never connected it with the missing booze. I promised her I'd quit when we moved here, turn over a new leaf. For I while I managed, but . . .'

'You need help, George,' said Ru. 'It's a disease.'

George blew out a breath, scraping the evidence into a pile. 'Are you going to tell Rose?' he asked.

'No,' said Ru emphatically. '*You* are.'

Fiona sent a text to Ivy:

> Mission accomplished. Staying at Ru's tonight. See you all tomorrow xxx.

Then she switched off her phone. She wanted nothing to disturb the rest of the evening. With his hand in hers, they headed back through Brambleton, the streetlamps shimmering above them. The sound of crunching leaves beneath their feet was oddly reassuring. Each step made a satisfying, crisp sound. Each leaf crushed was like an obstacle overcome. The steady rhythm of her footsteps was a reminder that, like one season changing to the next, Fiona was moving on, from struggling to stability.

The distant murmur of the sea softened as they climbed. Ru pulled her closer, but she shivered. He took off his jacket and scarf and draped both around her.

Outside Prosecco & Prose, Ru stopped. 'This café is a special place for me.'

'Why?'

'It's where I realized you still loved me''

She gasped. 'Did you?'

He squeezed her hand, sending a shiver of love through her body. 'Yes. But I also realized you didn't love yourself. I had to let you go, so that you could learn to love yourself, and just had to believe you would discover how loved you are, not just by me but by all your family too.' He shook his head, looking down at her with his dark eyes. 'Fi, you don't need that exam. I knew that. *Everyone who works with you* knows that. You just don't need to belong to the CMS. But *you* don't see that. I'm sorry that I wasn't more sensitive about it. By being cavalier about my own talent, I was making you feel inadequate about your own.'

She thought about his words. Ru was right. For years she'd hidden her insecurities behind a wall of certificates, but what really mattered, what made her the first-class sommelier she was, were her boundless enthusiasm for wine and her desire to share that love with others.

A streetlamp sputtered overhead, its dim glow pooling on the damp pavement. Oblivious, Ru knelt on one knee, then reached into his trouser pocket, pulling out a small blue velvet box. His gaze met hers, a mixture of love and nervous anticipation lighting up his eyes. His voice was steady. 'Will you please marry me?' he whispered. Silence wrapped around them, as if Brambleton was holding its breath.

Tears welled in her eyes as she looked down at him, the light casting a warm halo around his hopeful figure. She pictured him kneeling in the sand three months earlier and her heart swelled.

With a shaky breath, she smiled, her voice soft but full of certainty. 'Yes,' she said, knowing that she meant it. He stood and slipped the ring onto her finger.

'But let's not do the whole glitzy wedding thing,' she added. He laughed as he pulled her close and kissed her.

Warming to her theme, she pulled away, and the words tumbled out, 'Let's just elope, you and me, go somewhere special, and not tell anyone until we come home.'

'I promise, I hear what you're saying. I really am listening to you this time. But let's discuss it together properly, perhaps over Morning Prayers?'

'I'll bring an agenda,' she joked, and pulled him to her again, wrapping her arms around her fiancé, never wanting to let him go.

Thirty-three

Three months later

Nestled into the rolling Devon hillside, the small church stood resolute against the winter. A thin blanket of snow covered the ground, making everything seem hushed and still. Bare trees reached skeletal branches toward the grey sky, their dark silhouettes contrasting with the pale surroundings.

The church doors stood open showing the flickering candles warming the stone walls inside, casting shadows that danced in the stillness. The wooden pews, worn and weathered, were full of people, colourful outfits jostling for space. At each pew end, someone had tied bunches of variegated holly, their bright red berries like little beacons of encouragement.

The opening notes of Handel's *Arrival of the Queen of Sheba* shattered the stillness. In unison, the congregation swivelled, a sea of hats and cheerful faces beaming at her. She spotted Trish first, wearing a purple fascinator with a vivid pink ostrich feather, reminding Fiona of the pen that Ru gave Rose. This feather was so long that Fiona suspected it was tickling the nose of the man sitting behind Trish. In the pew in front, their faces scrubbed clean, stood Becky and Timmy – two little fizzing meteors of joy, who kept popping out into the aisle to wave at Fiona. In the same row sat Rose, beaming with pride as if she was the mother of the bride. Rose had responded to her wedding invitation with such an emotionally raw letter of acceptance that Fiona had teared up when reading it. How many times would she need to tell Rose that she was forgiven before the woman finally believed her? Fiona suspected Rose's lingering guilt stemmed partly from her initial suspicion George was the culprit; in her desperation to protect her husband, when evidence emerged linking Fiona to the wine thefts Rose had latched onto the alternative suspect. Fiona understood, but Rose's mistake still seemed to haunt her.

George sat beside his wife, then Josh, and next to him – in fact, extremely close to him – was Kim, in a clinging green dress that, Fiona noticed with a smile, was totally unsuitable for the cold weather.

The Smuggler's Inn was closed for the day; the wedding reception would be held there after the service – at no charge. It was George's present to the couple, by way of apology. That, and his regular attendance at a gambling awareness clinic. The clinic was Ivy's recommendation. Ivy knew all about George's gambling habits and had been urging him to seek professional help – that was the confidence she had vowed not to betray. Fiona was pleased she hadn't pressed her aunt to divulge her secret.

The wedding celebration would be a traditional breakfast, anchored by kedgeree made with haddock from the local smokehouse and eggs from the rescued battery hens at the farm on the edge of the village. Fiona had chosen South African wines for the occasion – a quiet tribute to her new in-laws. Ru had suggested that she wait until after the speeches to taste the wine. He wouldn't be making a speech himself. 'I want to hear what you have to say,' he'd told her with a smile.

It seemed fitting that their honeymoon would take them first to South Africa, then on to Melbourne, as if retracing the story of their union. On their return, the new London restaurant would be launching, with Ruben as the head chef, Fiona as the sommelier. She no longer cared that she wasn't an official partner in the business. She was a partner in Ru's eyes, and that was what mattered.

At her side, still looking a little jet-lagged, Fiona's father waited, his smile tender as he offered her his arm. She glanced up, seeing his eyes slightly misty behind his glasses, then down to the front pew at her mother, whose face glowed with pride.

Fiona took a deep breath and stepped forward, her father beside her. Ru had been right – the best way to cast off her memories of his first proposal was to say her vows now, before their friends and family. Not to elope and hide away, but to allow those who truly loved her to share this special day. She felt a happy calm settle over her, knowing this was exactly where she was meant to be.

As they moved down the aisle, she caught sight of Ru's parents. The statuesque woman and her even taller husband radiated warmth. Fiona smiled. She already felt a fondness for them and looked forward to growing closer.

At the far end of the aisle, a golden stole glowing around her like a beacon, stood Ivy. And just ahead, looking unbelievably attractive in a traditional morning coat, a spring of holly in his buttonhole, was the man Fiona would soon call her husband.

Dear Reader,

As you close the final page of this story, I want to take a moment to say thank you. Sharing these stories with you is a privilege, and knowing you've spent your time with my characters truly means the world to me.

At the heart of every story are people – flawed, wonderful, and utterly human. I love exploring relationships, whether romantic, familial, or friendship, and watching how they change under pressure. My hope is that these characters stay with you long after the story ends.

While I start these stories with a plan, I leave space for inspiration to strike. Often, the best twists and emotional moments come unexpectedly, and weaving them in keeps the story alive. I also enjoy adding little insights – quirky details, interesting facts, or a glimpse into an unusual job – that bring depth and texture to the world my characters inhabit.

Finally, can I ask a tiny favour? If you enjoyed *A Perfect Devon Pub*, would you mind leaving a quick review online? It doesn't have to be Shakespeare – just say how you feel. I read all my reviews and I am grateful for every single one (yes, even the bad ones!). Writing can sometimes feel solitary, but knowing you're out there connecting with these stories makes it the most rewarding thing I could ever do. You can also visit my website at www.debbiemorrison.co.uk. I love hearing directly from readers, and I often send out exclusive new stories through my newsletter.

Thank you for being part of this journey – I can't wait to share the next one with you.

With love,
Debbie x

Did you love A Perfect Devon Pub?

Welcome to Brambleton!

Nestled along North Devon's rugged coastline, Brambleton, although of course fictional, is everything you'd hope for in a village – picturesque cottages, winding lanes, and a community where everyone knows your name, even if they don't know your secrets. And trust me, there are plenty more of those hiding behind its pretty stone walls!

The Brambleton books aim to take you right into the heart of this little haven, where friendships are lifelong, love is full of twists and turns, and surprises have a habit of appearing as often as the wildflowers in the hedgerows. It's a place where life isn't always perfect, but it is always full of heart.

Each story brings a new cast of characters, from the hilariously endearing to the quietly courageous. While each book stands alone, you'll spot familiar faces and places as you explore Brambleton's nooks and crannies, making it feel like coming home to old friends.

So make yourself a cuppa, grab a blanket, and lose yourself in one of these feel-good, light-hearted tales. They're brimming with warmth, laughter, and the kind of moments that remind us that even when life feels a bit off the tracks, love and community can see us through.

The next book in the series is *A Perfect Devon Christmas*, starring Fiona's aunt Ivy, who took on a life of her own while I was writing *A Perfect Devon Pub*. I enjoyed writing her character so much, I knew I had to tell her story. It's set in the month leading up to Christmas, when Brambleton is all aglow with fairy lights and Christmas cheer. But as always in Brambleton, nothing is simple. And when a mysterious stranger arrives at Ivy's door, looking for shelter, it changes everything for the village.

Here's an exclusive extract to introduce you to *A Perfect Devon Christmas* . . .

I hope you enjoy it!

Love, Debbie x

One

Ivy tugged at a loose thread on her sleeve. It kept pulling, kept fraying. Just like her life, coming apart, stitch by stitch. Strange how the world she'd carefully knitted together – first around him, then deliberately without him – could unravel so quickly. Twice she'd woven her future with conviction, and twice reality had sliced through it, leaving her with nothing but threads slipping through her fingers.

The familiar scent of beeswax and old books wrapped around her like a well-worn cardigan, stirring memories of when this comfortable sitting room had belonged to her. She had moved out nearly two years ago, and she missed it. Not just its handsome proportions and cosy nooks and crannies, but the memories it held of a happy life, full of purpose. Still, this would have been a difficult place to train a wilful dog. She pictured her rented cottage, where her ten-week-old puppy was loose, no doubt scampering through her open-plan reception area, creating as much damage and destruction as Storm Edna had done in her garden. What if he found the magazine rack? Or the bin – oh lord, the food caddy. Could he open that? Could he reach the sofa? Puppies didn't eat cushions, did they? The article she skimmed didn't mention that.

A man's voice, clear and bright, cut through her musings. There was an energetic quality to the timbre, with a crispness in pronunciation; it sounded absurdly young for a vicar. 'Ivy, do you agree?'

She blinked and switched her attention to the speaker, perched awkwardly on the edge of her old fireside chair. The room's Victorian proportions seemed to emphasise Victor's tall skeletal body. The seat used to be a snug fit for Ivy's five-foot stout frame, but Victor's long limbs jutted out, making him look like a crane attempting to nest in a teacup. Why hadn't he rearranged the furniture, chosen a more suitable chair for himself, like the one Ivy was sitting in? Her feet dangled childlike a few inches off the floor.

'Oh! Yes, of course,' she said.

What was she agreeing to? Who cared? She gripped her notebook. She shouldn't have released the puppy. But he'd looked so *happy* running free. Probably still running. She peeked at her watch. If she was lucky, she'd be home before the afternoon post arrived, sparing any letters from his curious investigations. She swallowed hard, trying to recall if she'd put her slippers away. It didn't matter; she had nothing planned for the rest of the day. Plenty of time to clear up any mess.

Drizzle spattered against the tall sash windows, and the weak November light did little to warm the space. Ivy's fingers itched to reach for the poker and shift the fire six inches to the right, where the draw was better.

'I really must insist,' Margaret Pembroke's shrill voice cut through Ivy's thoughts, 'that we use the traditional red and gold baubles. Vicar, this suggestion of . . . of . . . sustainable decorations made from foodstuffs is not very Brambleton!'

'Well now, Margaret, we must move with the times,' huffed Mabel Cartwright, folding her stout arms over her thick practical jumper. 'A new Vicar brings new ideas. Sustainability is very fashionable these days. Dried oranges and cinnamon sticks would be charming!'

'I simply won't stand for it!' Margaret's voice was sharp enough to pierce through the thickest holly wreath. 'Brambleton's Christmas tradition is red and gold. It always has been. It always will be!'

Victor's Adam's apple bobbed. 'I thought we could . . . modernise?' he ventured weakly, pushing his wire-rimmed glasses up his nose.

With the speed of a seasoned hawk, Margaret turned on him. 'Modernise? Young man, Brambleton does not *modernise* Christmas! First, it's dried oranges, next thing you know, we'll be lighting the Advent candles with solar power!'

'And why not?' Mabel shot back, now sitting bolt upright in her chair. 'We should be leading by example! This is God's creation, and we must protect it. You, of all people, should understand that, Vicar.'

Ivy stifled a chuckle. Victor's mouth was flapping like a fish gasping for air. He had been in Brambleton for four months and still believed logic could win out over tradition. That might be true of the inner-city parish he'd come from, but not rural North Devon.

As if sensing weakness, Margaret pressed on. 'Brambleton's Christmas has been red and gold since my grandmother's day, and I'll not have it ruined by . . . by *fruit!*'

'Fruit is a gift from God, Margaret,' Mabel countered primly. 'Unlike that ghastly tinsel you insist on draping over every available surface.'

Ivy shifted in her seat, the words of diplomatic intervention rising automatically before she swallowed them back. She used to chair these meetings – but she bit her tongue. The church's guidelines prevented any official involvement for two years. It was kind of Victor to invite her at all. Perhaps someone suggested including her. She ran a hand through her silver hair, a habit she'd developed since . . . well, since everything had happened.

Across the room, her neighbour Fred gave her the ghost of a wink. It seemed he, too, was enjoying watching the sparks fly between Mabel and Margaret. Fred was in his early sixties, of medium height and with a surprisingly trim frame given his age – the result of countless hours tending to his beloved garden. Today, like every day, he wore a well-tailored suit with a white shirt which Ivy knew would be meticulously ironed – not just the front, but the sleeves and back too – complemented by a pristine navy-blue tie. As a friend and her neighbour for nearly two years now, Fred had been a steadfast support, never pushing when she deflected questions about her early retirement with jokes that sounded like she was trying too hard. Encouraged by his presence, Ivy straightened in her chair, letting her feet drop until her toes touched the floor. The solid contact grounded her, giving her a small surge of confidence as she prepared to speak.

'Maybe,' Ivy ventured cautiously, 'we could use both? The traditional baubles on the main tree, and Margaret, I think your grandchildren might enjoy helping Mabel and Victor make the orange decorations for the side altar?'

Victor seized on this suggestion like a vulture diving toward the last scrap in the desert. 'Yes! Excellent! Very . . . um, inclusive.'

Fred shot her an amused smile, before rising, reaching for the poker and shunting the fire to precisely the right spot in the grate, 'Vicar, it's a bit chilly, mind if I load some more wood on here?'

'Chilly,' trilled Margret, shivering theatrically, 'it's positively glacial.'

Victor flapped a hand at the wood basket. 'haven't got the knack of that fire yet.'

'Let me help,' suggested Fred, removing his suit jacket and confirming Ivy's thoughts about his ironing. He moved the fire six inches to the right, then sat down next to Ivy, muttering, 'well done, if we'd waited for Victor to resolve that spat it might have ended in knitting needles at dawn on the village green.'

Ivy smiled but it didn't reach her eyes. At least she was still good at something. She'd been fighting off despondency all day after receiving three rejection emails this morning. That made ten jobs this week alone. She squared her shoulders, refusing to let them slump. She wouldn't let this defeat her. God would guide her to the right employer – in His time not hers.

'You look troubled, Ivy,' murmured Fred. 'What's bothering you? Want me to raise it if you think it's too sensitive?'

What have I done? And where do I go from here? The questions gnawed at her. She plastered on a smile that used to come naturally. 'Oh, nothing a cup of tea won't fix,' she said, but the quaver in her voice betrayed her. She hated feeling so adrift. This wasn't the Ivy who could fix failing marriages; persuade recalcitrant teens to spend more time with their family; cheer up poorly grandfathers. The Ivy who was the centre of the village and had been at the forefront of last year's crucial planning battle. The Ivy who was famed for her relaxed attitude and easy smile. She hesitated, feeling she must say something, or Fred would think she'd gone dotty, leaned in and whispered, *'I'm a bit worried about people nicking from the collection box.'*

Fred's eyes widened. He stood up abruptly, steepling his hands.

'My friends,' he announced gravely, 'we must pause to pray for feeble victims of the erection pox.'

The room fell silent. Margaret Pembroke clutched her pearls. Victor's mouth opened and closed like a baby bird waiting for food.

Despite clamping her lips together, Ivy's natural jolly disposition bubbled up and a snort of laughter escaped. Fred insisted he didn't need hearing aids – Ivy begged to differ. Somehow, she found her voice. 'I think Fred means to say we should remember those in need,' she said, glancing at Fred's bewildered expression with the fond exasperation people reserve for old friends. Ivy pushed herself off the chair. 'Vicar, perhaps this would be a suitable moment for refreshments?'

'Not so fast,' Mabel said, raising a hand. 'Before we break, can I run through the Christmas schedule?' She flipped a page and continued. 'Wreath making is next week. We're selling them at the Christmas market on Saturday the 22nd of November. After that, we've got the Christmas pudding race – same as always, first of December, which falls on a Monday this year.' She paused, scanning down her list. 'The Christingle service is two weeks later, followed by the carol concert on the eighteenth – a Thursday,' she added, glancing up at Victor. 'And the nativity play is on Christmas Day itself.' She set her notes down with a small sigh. 'Phew. Christmas at Brambleton seems to get bigger every year.'

'Spot on,' said Ivy, but her heart warmed at the thought. She adored preparing for a Brambleton Christmas – the scent of cloves and citrus as she pierced oranges for the Christingle service, the streets transformed for the Christmas market with twinkling lights strung from every eave, and the sweet sound of carol singers drifting through the crisp evening air.

Brambleton came alive, dressed up in festive finery to charm winter tourists. Even the garish army of flashing plastic snowmen that one villager always crammed into their front garden – tacky, over-the-top, and utterly beloved by everyone.

'I'm terrifically excited,' said Victor, beaming round the room. 'My first rural Christmas, what fun!'

In the kitchen, Ivy watched Victor fumble with a jar of instant coffee, spilling granules across the counter.

'Ivy always served proper coffee not instant,' scolded Margret waspishly.

A plate of chocolate digestives teetered precariously as the vicar spun around, nearly knocking over the milk jug. 'I've got this under control,' he insisted, though watching him drop a third spoonful of coffee granules into the same mug Ivy thought otherwise.

She stepped forward, catching the plate of biscuits in freefall. 'Victor, I think you'll find, one heaped teaspoon per cup is plenty. Why don't you make the tea, Margaret can carry the tray for you, and I'll finish making the coffee.'

Victor smiled sheepishly 'Yes, yes good idea. I'm a tea man myself. I've no idea how to make proper coffee, is that really what I should serve?' he asked, raising his eyebrows quizzically.

'Instant coffee won't hurt anyone,' replied Ivy.

The meeting resumed. Ivy's phone buzzed in her pocket – probably another rejection. Let them say no – she only needed one yes. Somewhere out there was an employer who would value her skills.

The door burst open, and in rushed Rose, the landlady of the local pub, the Smugglers Inn. She was panting, and her cheeks were pink, suggesting she had run all the way from the pub.

'Sorry I'm a bit late,' puffed Rose. Ivy suppressed a laugh; *late!* They had only just moved past the first agenda item. A series of setbacks had delayed the start of the meeting. First, Fred had to embark on a full-scale manhunt to track down Victor, whom he eventually discovered mid-serenade in the shower, bellowing Jerusalem like a one-man choir. Then came the ten-minute search for the missing agendas, which they finally unearthed from beneath a pile of tea-stained minutes. And just when they thought they were ready, Victor had declared himself completely unfit to read anything without his glasses – which had been right there on the end of his nose all along.

Rose shrugged off her coat, releasing the smell of spilt beer and fried food. Ivy tried to recall the last time she had joined her friends at the Smugglers Inn on a Friday night. Weeks ago. When she was the vicar, she used to go all the time. 'But you'll never believe what kept me.' said Rose, her eyes widening. 'Something's been found on the beach.'

A ripple of anticipation shot through the room.

'An inflatable dinghy,' Rose said, drawing out the words for dramatic effect. 'An abandoned one.'

Silence settled for a beat as imaginations leapt ahead, then the whispers began.

'Migrants,' muttered Margaret, glancing nervously toward the darkening sky outside. 'It's happening all along the coast.'

'Don't be ridiculous,' scoffed Fred. 'This is North Devon, not Dover. It's a long way across the channel to Brambleton.'

'But no one's looking for them here, are they?' said Margaret, wagging a warning finger at Fred. 'That's the point. It'll be the sort who stand no chance of being granted asylum. The desperate ones.'

Mabel's voice dropped to a conspiratorial whisper. 'The dangerous sort. My sister had asylum seekers moved near her, do you know what happened? Break-ins started the very next day.'

Ivy shot a look at Victor, but when he didn't intervene, she did. 'Mabel, your sister lives in Hackney. It's not the safest part of London, is it?'

Fred shifted awkwardly in his seat. 'Could just be kids messing about. Tourists bringing their teenagers down for the weekend.'

'I wish. Not many tourists in November, Fred,' quipped Rose.

'Or smugglers,' Mabel added, eyes widening. 'People still run booze, you know. Drugs too. I read about it in the Mail.'

Victor cleared his throat. 'Um, perhaps we could . . . turn our attention to item two? The roof fund?' he ventured, his voice cracking.

Undeterred, Rose crossed her arms, surveying her audience. 'No footprints in the sand, no sign of anyone. Whoever arrived in that boat they've covered their tracks well.'

'What if they're still here?' Mabel asked, her voice slightly wavering.

'Watching us right now,' Margaret nodded. 'Planning God knows what.'

'Margaret, please,' intervened Victor.

Fred rolled his eyes. 'Next you'll be telling me they're hiding in your garden shed.'

'Don't joke about such things,' hissed Mabel.

More whispers spread through the room. Someone muttered about needing to mount a search party, another suggested a night patrol. A nervous energy crackled in the air. In the silence that followed, Ivy could hear nothing but rapid breathing, as if each person was visualising the threat. A sudden crash from outside made them all jump.

Victor seized his moment, speaking with forced brightness, 'Why don't we form a neighbourhood welcoming committee? I've some lovely pamphlets about cultural sensitivity from the diocese . . .'

His words trailed off as several pairs of eyes fixed on him with identical stares of incredulous horror.

Ivy agreed with Victor – they should welcome refugees, not turn them away – but again she bit her tongue. She folded her hands together, a habit from years at the pulpit. She thought about the empty dinghy, the absence of footprints on the shore. Perhaps the rain had simply washed all the footprints away? From across the room, Victor's eyes met hers, his expression grave. He seemed to be the only other person concerned about the passengers' fate. Rain tapped gently against the window-panes. Questions stirred in her mind. *Where had those passengers come from? What were they fleeing? Where were they now?*

Join Ivy and Fred for a countryside Christmas that will warm your heart.

Will this Christmas bring love and hope to Brambleton?
Or does destiny have another festive twist in store?

Preorder now

Acknowledgments

Writing *A Perfect Devon Pub* has been every bit as joyful (and occasionally chaotic) as the first book in the Brambleton series. This time, though, every time I wandered into a pub, lingered a little too long in a café, or asked a bewildered bartender how to perfectly pour a pint, I got to call it "research". All in the name of authenticity, of course.

Truthfully, this book was inspired by the hospitality heroes who keep the heart of British communities beating – especially those brave souls running independent pubs, gastro gems, and the kind of cafés where your flat white comes with a book recommendation and a biscuit. Places like the (fictional, but only just) Smugglers Inn and Prosecco & Prose make life richer, warmer, and a bit more delicious. What you do matters, and this is a love letter to you. A special thank you to our local Tapas restauranteur Dawn Mullen, for explaining the different types of professional kitchens and putting me to rights on the crucial role of the kitchen porter.

With *A Perfect Devon Pub*, Brambleton continues to grow; its tangled friendships, unexpected romances and questionable bake-offs are all still going strong. Each book stands alone, but you'll notice familiar faces popping up (some with opinions, some with cake), because life in a village like this doesn't pause between stories.

To my publishing team: where would I be without you? Laura Palmer, you are the compass and the cheerleader, the one who brings boundless enthusiasm *and* brilliant editorial wisdom to the table (usually at the same time). You've made this process feel like a glass-more-than-half-full adventure, even when the deadline clock was ticking.

Hannah George—how do you keep creating covers that look like you've been living in my head? Your illustrations capture Brambleton so perfectly, I'm starting to wonder if you've been secretly visiting. And to Cherie Chapman—thank you for turning those illustrations into something beautifully crisp and utterly shelf-worthy.

To Jessie Sullivan, my social media lifesaver—thank you for making this digital dinosaur feel at home online. Your creative spark, savvy strategies, and good humour have brought this book to life in ways I could never have managed alone.

And to the brilliant Gale Winskill—thank you for wielding your editorial pen with equal parts precision and kindness. You always know when to gently rein me in (usually when I've gone rogue with a side character and three subplots).

Finally, and most importantly, to *you*. Yes, you, reading this. I'm so grateful for your messages, reviews, and the little notes you send, especially on Facebook, where I can actually see the face behind the words. It's like writing to a friend, not a void, and that's a rare and lovely thing.

Thank you for visiting Brambleton. I hope you'll come back soon; there's always another story brewing.

Love

Debbie x

The Brambleton Series

Have you read them all?

A Perfect Devon Farmhouse
A Perfect Devon Pub
A Perfect Devon Christmas
A Perfect Devon Manor

About the Author

Debbie Morrison was always meant to write, but real life held her back. She studied law, then qualified as an accountant, and went on to work for twenty years in the City. Now, finally freed from the shackles of the day job, she has moved from London to rural Devon to pursue her childhood passion and become an author, writing the kind of books she loves to read: fast-paced, escapist and visual with credible and relatable characters.

When Debbie is not writing, she can be found playing tennis (badly), bridge (a little better), walking her dogs, or tending to her garden. She also loves cooking her own home-grown produce for friends and family. She lives on the edge of Exmoor with her husband, miniature bull terriers and small flock of free-range hens.

Visit debbiemorrison.co.uk to find out more.